W9-CRU-803

Susan Flynn

"HERE, MR. SPLITFOOT"

ALSO BY ROBERT SOMERLOTT

THE FLAMINGOS

THE INQUISITOR'S HOUSE

"Here, Mr. Splitfoot"

AN INFORMAL EXPLORATION
INTO MODERN OCCULTISM

Robert Somerlott

NEW YORK | THE VIKING PRESS

Copyright © 1971 by Robert Somerlott
All rights reserved

First published in 1971 by The Viking Press, Inc.
625 Madison Avenue, New York, N.Y. 10022

Published simultaneously in Canada by
The Macmillan Company of Canada Limited

SBN 670-36876-8

Library of Congress catalog card number: 75-132185

Printed in U.S.A. by Vail-Ballou Press, Inc.

A portion of Chapter II originally appeared in
somewhat different form in *American Heritage*.

Contents

Illustrations

"HERE, MR. SPLITFOOT"

I

The Day of the Occult

In 1968 a discovery was made in the United States: ouija boards were outselling Monopoly games by a substantial margin. This had been the case for more than a year, but no one had bothered to report the fact, which seemed rather less than earth-shaking. The announcement, although several magazine writers would later remember it, stirred hardly a ripple in the newspapers.

Monopoly had been firmly entrenched in America's living rooms, game rooms, play rooms, and "rec-rooms" for decades, and, until elbowed aside by the ouija board, was always the sturdy best seller on department-store game counters. Much of Monopoly's unchallenged success came because it offers wish-fulfillment of a classic American Dream: owning four hotels on the Boardwalk and cornering the market on practically everything. The players handle vast amounts of cash, they speculate, they acquire real-estate developments. Monopoly, the reflection of a dream and an ideal, is perfectly designed to provide vicarious thrills in a capitalist, materialist society.

The ouija, if not Monopoly's opposite, is certainly altogether different. It suggests communication with a nonmaterial world, a world of ghosts and disembodied thought waves. As Monopoly reflects a hunger for riches, the ouija reveals a yearning toward contact with unknown powers, a seeking for what has been called the Unexplained. A "player" may not take the ouija seriously, but that is beside the point. A desire for nonmaterialist contact and at least a suspicion that it can be achieved must be present or the "game" would not be played at all.

It should be added that although the ouija is a very primitive and uncertain device in parapsychology, it has played a role in some astonishing cases. For example, a parlor-game encounter with a ouija board triggered the Patience Worth affair in St. Louis, and produced a classic mystery which remains fascinating and unsolved. The ouija has not always behaved like a toy and its effect upon the user can be unpredictable. Francisco I. Madero, who launched Mexico's major revolution of 1910 and was briefly the country's president until his assassination, had been told by the planchette that he would attain the nation's highest office— an achievement possible only through revolution. Madero subsequently led a revolt and the Díaz dictatorship was overthrown. "Patriotic" biographers have minimized the Mexican president's belief in the occult, which was obviously great.

The ouija's outstripping of Monopoly was only one small indication of a trend in the United States. A parlor game based on ESP has sold at the rate of a million sets per year despite a stiff price of seven dollars.

This upsurge of interest in mystic arts and psychic matters has been so obvious that there is little need to document it here. Suffice it to say that Hollywood astrologer Carroll Righter appeared on the cover of *Time;* a book about the prophecies of Edgar Cayce enjoyed twenty weeks on the best-seller lists in 1967 and 1968; and the mediums Arthur Ford and the late Eileen Garrett have become nearly as well known as many film stars.

Mystery cults such as the Rosicrucians of San Jose, California, have greatly increased their advertising—a sure indication of expanding membership. (The Scribe of the Rosicrucians will reveal no figures. This is characteristic of such organizations. From the smallest to the largest, they all seem to follow Mary Baker Eddy's injunction against numbering the faithful.)

Even witchcraft has come back into its own, with an official witch in Los Angeles County and unofficial witches clamoring for attention everywhere. Covens of witches and warlocks have been established in major American cities. At first there were no sensational exposés of them and one gathers that these covens were less sexual than their historic predecessors. But soon a transformation took place: the witches threw off their gentleness along with their modesty and unwashed clothes. This development drew the attention of the alert editors of *Esquire*, who published a long report indicating that witchcraft and satanism, two beliefs almost identical if considered primarily from the Christian viewpoint, have poured in a torrent, perhaps from some hidden spring in California's San Andreas fault. The Golden State, not surprisingly, is the new holy land of satanism, and its occult flood has divided itself into two main streams, two types of witches—the drugged and the drugless.

The more or less drugless witches seek excitement in the established rituals of satanism, studying the ancient descriptions of classical satanic worship and the more modern works of Eliphas Lévi. They are typified by Samson De Brier, a wispy, rather effete warlock reputed to have extensive, if vague, power. De Brier haunts a Hollywood residence-temple that is replete with death masks, moldering draperies, and fading photographs. Most of his efforts are directed toward combating the evil forces now being released by other, less admirable warlocks. Another benefactor

5

of humanity is artist Neke Carson, whose Hollywood Hills studio is the source of all manner of works of art and inventions designed to thwart such menaces as vampire-devils. One notable achievement is a cross-shaped bed inflated with water and rigged with vibrators. (This invention seems to echo the Scottish magnetist Graham, who contrived the famous nineteenth-century magnetic bed. It was saturated with Oriental perfumes, and magnetic streams flowed through it, conveyed by glass tubes and cylinders. It was not, however, cross-shaped. Graham, unlike Carson, was unaware of the possibility of "devilmen" lurking below the springs. The twentieth century obviously is more sensitive to mystical dangers.) Since vampires are attracted to blood but destroyed by a crucifix, Carson has designed a blood-filled plastic cross, thus setting a neat trap.

Most of the new witches and warlocks combine their satanism with drugs, and LSD serves as wine and wafers for their Black Mass. One of the high priestesses ferreted out for *Esquire* by Tom Burke, Princess Leda Amun Ra, says, "I give acid to persons who have never dropped it without telling them. I think of this as the administering of Holy Communion." One of the princess's haunts is a private night club on Hollywood's La Cienega Boulevard where devil-worshipers gather in front of a huge Satan's mask. Late at night she is reputed to preside at bizarre rituals in her temple, a Moorish castle in the Hollywood Hills.

Although California's satanic cults are usually private, Americans had a startling glimpse into one when the home life of the Manson Family was revealed by Linda Kasabian's story of the Sharon Tate murders. The Manson Family, while not a publicly proclaimed coven, reveled in all the forms of witchcraft: a high priest had visions, there was fanatical belief in his magic powers, and with the common confusion of theology that surrounds witchcraft, Manson was variously referred to as "God," "Jesus," and "Satan." There were tales of his being physically and magically transported from one end of the Spahn ranch to the other.

6

Group sexual experience, the usual diversion of covens, was frequent.

The Manson Family is exceptional only in its ability to make headlines and, it now appears, in its indulgence in mass murder. "The Family" was otherwise typical of numberless cults and communes. The public became aware of the Ordi Templar Orientalis when the United Press carried a story about eleven of the cult's members who were brought to trial in Indio, California, after they had chained a six-year-old boy in a sweltering box for fifty-six days. We have received reports from other California cities which show the existence of three satanist groups in Berkeley, two of them communes, one in the Big Sur, one in Venice, five in San Francisco, two just north of there, and one in San Diego. The number of satanist-witchcraft circles gathering in Los Angeles County is indeterminate but large.

Members of the covens tell of enjoying all the sensations which have been common to such groups since medieval times: out-of-body travel, illusions of flight, supreme sexual force, and the gift of magical power to destroy one's enemies. Female members have had hallucinatory sexual relations with Satan, a phenomenon notorious throughout the ages. This delusion once sprang from the hysteria of worshiping the Prince of Darkness, but it seems probable that its current vogue is due to a combination of drugs and an emulation of the ecstasy in the novel and film *Rosemary's Baby*.

These witches and warlocks, mostly youthful, defiantly announce their rejection of the past while they readopt one of mankind's oldest traditions. A Papal Bull, issued by Pope Innocent VIII in 1488, is surprisingly modern. The Pope outlined the practices then current—devil worship, sexual intercourse with "infernal fiends" by members of both sexes, the desecration of holy symbols such as wearing a crucifix upside down—now a common practice in the "tomorrow" communes in California. The witches of 1488 were also charged with economic crimes: "They blast the corn on the ground, the grapes of the vineyard, the fruits on the trees, the herbs of the fields." Their twentieth-century successors believe they possess similar powers, as when Princess Leda Amun Ra proclaims that she will crush white Anglo-Saxon Christians with Mind Power. (She envisions herself at the head of an army of flower children, a whip in one hand, a cross in the other. For a woman in her position, her knowledge of the dark arts seems vague, or perhaps it is only a careless manner of expressing herself. She should have specified that the cross would be held in the *left* hand, the whip in the right. All authorities agree that this is the only proper position.)

The Papal Bull of 1488 on satanism led to the establishment of the Inquisition. So far the governor of California has not issued a similar Bull against the covens in his domain, but doubtless such a proclamation will be forthcoming—once the stars are right.

Some Americans traveling abroad have taken their satanism with them. In March 1970, scientists from all over the world gathered on Mexico's Isthmus of Tehuantepec better to view a total solar eclipse. Unexpected entertainment was provided when a cult of expatriate Americans appeared naked in public, their nudity marred only by love beads and mystic signs painted on their jaundiced skins. During the eclipse they danced and capered around a pregnant member of their party, saluting the sun, the powers of darkness, and the gods of fertility. The Mexican government took a dim view of the performance, calling it scandalous and immoral. The authorities did not add that importing witchcraft into Mexico is more wretchedly excessive than taking coal to Newcastle.

Everyone recognizes the popularity of things mystic or psychic. A cartoonist draws a sketch of a distraught hostess checking seating arrangements for a dinner party. "Oh, dear!" the lady exclaims. "I *can't* put a Virgo next to a Taurus!" Ten years ago the joke would have been pointless. Today it recognizes that astrology is on the ascendant, a booming belief and business, and all the planets seem to favor its success.

Less than a decade ago when a writer wrote the letters ESP, he felt called upon to explain that they meant Extra-Sensory-Perception. Today it is taken for granted that the average reader is familiar with the term.

What has been true in the United States has been true in Canada, and the editors of *Maclean's* who devoted most of an issue to psychic studies, summed up the new trend bluntly: "The Western world plainly wants to believe in magic."

To believe in magic. Conservative souls should take warning. A very strong case can be made that forsaking one's Monopoly set for a ouija board is a highly un-American activity, a threat to the entire social system. The history of belief in the occult shows a pattern: faith flourishes in societies that are crumbling, endangered, or in the throes of radical change. Charles Mackay, the nineteenth-century authority on mass hysteria, made the famous observation that "credulity is always greatest in times of calamity." This is true in individual cases but in the long run it appears that forthcoming change, not necessarily calamitous, is often the force that raises an occult tide.

Oriental mystery cults took root in Greece as the classic civilization, wrenched apart, evolved into the Hellenistic. One of the hallmarks of that era is the turning away from logic, the rejection of the rational. It was an age of invention and discovery —developments which are always upsetting—and for the first time education was supported by public funds. Hand in hand with these innovations came the occult. James Henry Breasted wrote, "Oriental beliefs and oriental symbols were everywhere. Men . . . no longer looked askance at strange usages in religion."

Other groups of mystics, including Christians, plagued the Roman state at the beginning of its decline. Christianity and Zoroastrianism arrived almost as portents of upheaval and the former harped on the coming disintegration of the Roman state. Both cults took hold in times of uncertainty when the old Roman customs were giving way. The necessity for such decrees as the

9

Sumptuary Laws and the later limitation of the freeing of slaves show the alteration of traditional life. The new era was not calamitous; it was merely unfamiliar, and the occult thrived despite all efforts of the authorities to stamp out one superstition after another. Christianity eventually conquered Zoroastrianism, and it waxed as the stability of the Roman world waned.

Since the Middle Ages were more static and life was more fixed than in the times preceding and following them, we have a decline in occult activity. There were many outbursts, of course, for men's love of the weird and unusual never dies, only fades from public view. During this long period Mackay's observation about calamities is most valid. The great crowds and the hordes of pilgrims who streamed toward Jerusalem in A.D. 999 and 1000 were terrified by the end of the world as prophesied in the Apocalypse. However, the so-called Dark Ages and the medieval period were less rife with occultism than is commonly believed.

The Renaissance was an era of progress, but since it was a time when traditions were shattered, mystic arts and practices enjoyed renewed popularity. Catherine de Médicis, for example, was a skilled astrologer, and the age which produced Sir Francis Bacon and Galileo in science also gave birth to Paracelsus and John Dee in the occult. The latter pair in their own day attracted as much attention as the former and were more widely believed in. The alchemist is usually thought of as a medieval figure, but alchemy did not reach its height until the changing society of the Renaissance spurred mystic studies.

Comparative quiet followed the Renaissance outburst. Alchemy all but disappeared; astrology became unfashionable, and no new movements replaced them. The single exception is the seventeenth-century hysteria over witchcraft, which arrived in force much later in England and America than on the continent. But the actual prevalence of antique witches, unlike modern ones, is difficult to determine. It is highly probable that the reputed

10

"epidemics of devil worshipers" were really created by the authorities who were cleansing witches from their covens for God and profit. Modern "witch hunts" for Reds and suspected subversives provide an inexact but illuminating parallel to the seventeenth-century witchcraft furor. During the reign of terror of Senator Joseph McCarthy in the United States there seemed on the surface to be more Communist agents in America than ever before or since. In fact, there was only greater publicity, more spurious investigation. This could well be true of witchcraft and little is certain about how extensive its practice was at any time except the present.

The beginnings of the Industrial Revolution and the new thinking of the eighteenth-century Enlightenment disturbed society and there was a prompt flurry on the occult front. Mesmerism developed and enjoyed immense popularity and every form of mysticism spread from country to country. Lewis Spence, author of *An Encyclopaedia of Occultism,* has described this period as a time "when Europe was credulous about nothing except magic."

Industrialization accelerated, ways of living were altered, and advancing science assaulted established religion. When the full weight of change was felt, the time was ripe and the predictable happened: modern spiritualism erupted from Hydesville, New York, in 1848.

The new belief in the wonderful workings of spirits was an American export to England, where it progressed slowly, at first, in the more stable English environment; table-turning had been a delightful fad for an evening's entertainment but serious speculation about the occult did not run rampant in England until the last half of the Victorian era, a time of rapid change, scientific discovery, and social unrest.

It is significant that Robert Owen, the industrial-reformer and pioneer of the cooperative movement, was spiritualism's earliest champion in England. Owen, far in advance of his own day, put into practice such revolutionary notions as nonprofit stores and model industrial communities. His success as a manufacturer did not blind him to the suffering that the new factory life inflicted upon the working class. He wanted to create an instant Utopia. Here we have another link, this time a personal one, between social change and the acceptance of occult belief.

Anyone who repeats the cliché that history repeats itself is standing on doubtful ground. But in studying the ebb and flow of faith in things that lie outside the bounds of established science and religion, one is drawn strongly to the conclusion that change, or the demand for it, is a powerful factor in persuading men to believe in the Unaccepted. Often a threatened Establishment retreats to seek solace in mysticism, but sometimes the opposite is true—it is the rebels who embrace the occult. Perhaps it depends upon which side feels the more threatened.

The city of Berkeley, California, is a prime example. Berkeley was for generations a conservative community, orthodox in both science and religion. During the 1960s its campus was the most strife-torn of any in the United States. The rebellion overflowed the university, and, spreading to the city's streets, culminated in violence involving the "People's Park." There have been many reports about Berkeley's political radicals, but another facet of the student revolt has been ignored—the sudden upsurge of occultism in the area. Astrology, a study scorned by earlier generations of students, has been eagerly adopted—at least a half dozen organized groups were meeting in early 1970. Zen Buddhism flourishes, as would be expected, and a large "Meditation Society" has moved into the foreground. Meditation societies have sprung up at one university after another and there now are more than thirty such organizations actively meditating—not communicating or relating, just meditating. It is interesting to note that the recruits to mysticism come largely from the ranks of the political activist students—in other words, the rebels who want to change society radically.

Some Royal Scandals

Since crowned heads rest uneasily and are often subject to sudden removal, it is hardly surprising that they are also frequently filled with occult belief.

Elizabeth I of England, especially during her younger, less secure years, was fascinated by the astrology, alchemy, and dark arts practiced by Dr. John Dee. We do not know the depth of her belief but it stopped short of her financing Dee's more expensive experiments. With typical shrewdness, Elizabeth was not willing to bankrupt the kingdom in a futile search for the elusive philosopher's stone. However, she dallied with the idea and did give Dee considerable support—a great compliment from a lady so tight-fisted with her treasury.

Another Elizabeth, the Empress of Austria, Queen of Hungary, and consort to Emperor Franz Josef, caused tongues to wag by her carryings-on with at least one ghost and most likely others. Elizabeth, who lived from 1837 until 1898, endured an unhappy and uncertain existence. Her only son, Archduke Rudolf, died mysteriously with his mistress, Baroness Maria Vetsera, shot in such a manner that a double suicide seemed likely. Elizabeth's empire suffered military defeat, riots, and threatened revolutions. It was indeed beginning to crumble. Her Majesty sought and apparently found some consolation in an unusual way. She believed herself seduced by the ghost of the poet Heinrich Heine, whose spectral caresses she enjoyed at Godollo, her estate in Hungary. It is odd that she should have chosen Heine's ghost as a partner in this spiritistic, morganatic adultery. In life the poet had been a radical who fled Germany because of his revolutionary sympathies. Perhaps Her Majesty had no choice and accepted the ghost that came. Elizabeth's earthly anxieties proved to be well founded. She met death at the hands of an anarchist assassin in Geneva.

No crowns were ever more uncertain than those worn by
that glamorous couple, Emperor Maximilian of Mexico, who was
Elizabeth's brother-in-law, and his wife, Empress Carlota. Placed
arbitrarily on the throne of a hostile land and propped up by
nothing except French bayonets, the Empress and her glittering
but doomed court naturally sought refuge and assurance in the
occult. In 1864, Chapultepec Castle became the haunt of soothsayers and diviners. There were crystal-gazers and sand-readers;
with royal sponsorship, table-turning and séances fascinated the
spurious Mexican nobility. The Empress herself received mystic
premonitions and warnings. She would have done well to have
persuaded her husband to take these warnings seriously. When
the short-lived empire collapsed and Maximilian fell before a
firing squad, Carlota was luckily in France, pleading with Napoleon III for more troops. She was unsuccessful, and although
she survived her handsome husband by sixty years, became a
pitiable figure. The mystic voices in her mind grew louder and
drowned out all other sounds, and she ended her days in madness.

The royal court to which Carlota appealed, that of Napoleon
III, Emperor of the French, was a veritable menagerie of spirits.
The Empress, Eugénie, fell under the spell of several mediums,
but the outstanding one was the Scotsman D. D. Home, a talented
gentleman we shall meet later. Eugénie entertained enough ghosts
to fill a ballroom at the Tuileries. Among her spectral guests
were Rousseau, Pascal, Solon, and Saint Louis. Not omitting
members of her own family, she received and conversed with the
shades of Napoleon I and her late mother-in-law, Queen Hortense. Eugénie's only disappointment and social setback was the
refusal of Marie Antoinette to join the party. The beheaded
queen's ghost ignored all communications and absolutely declined to speak or materialize. Eugénie had to console herself
with furniture that walked about as though alive, musical instruments that played by themselves, raps, bellringing, and the
ghostly hands that touched the living. She could also enjoy the

presence of Home, one of the handsomest mediums who ever practiced, youthful, charming, his red hair vivid against his extraordinary pallor.

It is understandable that Marie Antoinette's ghost shunned these entertainments, for she had undoubtedly had her fill of such things in life. Paris, on the eve of the revolution and blood bath of 1789, was the world capital of occult activity. Both the ruling class and the future rebels participated. Every type of magician and fortuneteller was welcomed at the court of Louis XVI, but one figure towers above all others—Count Cagliostro. The notorious "count" (his title was bogus) has captured the attention, and sometimes the imaginations, of writers for a dozen generations. He served as inspiration for Goethe's *The Grand Cophte,* and Dumas based an important character in *Memoirs of a Physician* on the magician. Thomas Carlyle wrote a prejudiced and unreliable biography of him, and long afterward W. R. Trowbridge demolished most of Carlyle's work and restored at least a few shreds of Cagliostro's reputation.

Cagliostro presented himself as a man of many talents—necromancer, alchemist, physician, mesmerist, a chemist of miraculous potions and philters, discoverer of the philosopher's stone, etc., etc. He also claimed to be immortal, but this claim was disproved when he died in 1795 after years of tortured confinement in a papal dungeon that was little more than a cistern. His chief object was the founding, which he called the "revival," of a mystery cult known as Egyptian Freemasonry, and he, as its Grand Copt, established many lodges in several countries. Cagliostro was charming, bold, and wealthy—an ideal ornament for the world of Louis XVI. One of his most impressive feats was making phantoms appear in mirrors, and a number of French nobles recognized the faces of their departed relatives.

Cagliostro's talents as a showman and psychologist were superb, and a brilliant example of his ability is the initiation rites he devised for thirty-six aristocratic women who became converts to Egyptian Freemasonry. The ceremony took place at night, of course, and the ladies were clad in flowing veils and girdles, and after long preliminaries which included binding and lifting their robes to the thigh, a startling thing happened, according to the French writer Guillaume Figuier.

> The vaulted roof opened suddenly, and, on a vast sphere of gold, there descended a man, naked as the unfallen Adam, holding a serpent in his hand, and having a burning star upon his head. The Grand Mistress announced that this was the genius of Truth, the immortal, the divine Cagliostro. . . . The Grand Copt thereupon commanded them to dispense with the profanity of clothing, for if they would receive truth they must be as naked as itself. The sovereign priestess setting the example unbound her girdle and permitted her drapery to fall to the ground, and the fair initiates following her example exposed themselves in all the nudity of their charms to the magnetic glances of the celestial genius, who then commenced his revelations. . . .

This sounds, of course, like the promise of an orgy. Cagliostro was too shrewd for that. After revealing various secrets to the initiates, he mounted the golden sphere and departed through the ceiling.

We will not here go into the celebrated Diamond Necklace affair, in which Cagliostro and Marie Antoinette were both involved, except to comment that it added fuel to the revolutionary fires and resulted in the magician's banishment. From England he wrote a remarkably prophetic letter to the French, foretelling the storming of the Bastille, the revolt, and the destruction of the old regime.

During those troubled years in France, the mystery cults were by no means confined to the aristocrats. A secret sect of rebels met and held rites to encourage the materialization of Saint John the Baptist, who would set the day and hour for the future revolution. The saint did not appear, but the believers, who included some members of holy orders as well as mesmerists, managed to pass the time in orgy and debauch. It is a pity the two sides

could not have joined forces—in the matter of occultism they
had much in common.

There have been many attempts to link England's staid Queen
Victoria with arcane beliefs and diversions, and the rumors per-
sist, although they seem to be without foundation. One unlikely
story has her summoning a medium, Robert James Lees, for a
séance at Windsor. Lees was so successful in contacting the late
Prince Albert that the grateful widow wanted to appoint him
resident medium. Prince Albert's ghost objected that Lees had
other work to perform and suggested the faithful ghillie of Bal-
moral, John Brown, as a substitute. After that, Lees and Brown
alternated as medium, but at the final meeting before Victoria's
death the Queen expressed her boundless gratitude to Lees and
kissed his hand.

Victoria's most recent biographer, Elizabeth Longford, says,
"From what is known of the Queen's last years, she would have
been more likely to arrive for the Opening of Parliament
on a tricycle than to kiss a subject's hand." She then demolishes
Lees's story with a formidable array of facts.

Until 1963 the College of Psychic Science in London displayed
a gold watch, supposedly awarded by Victoria to the mediums
Georgiana Eagle and Etta Wreidt for "Meritorious & Extraordinary Clairvoyance." The watch was commonly called "Vicky's
Ticker." The story connected with it has been proved false, and
the thief who eventually made off with "Vicky's Ticker" did
not acquire a memento from the Queen.

There are only two actual instances that connect Victoria with
the occult. In 1853, when table-turning was the craze of London,
she and Prince Albert were staying at Osborne and one balmy
evening decided to give the table a try. They were instantly
successful, and Lady Ely, who was present, had only to touch
the table to make it spin at a great rate. Apparently the Queen
did not take the demonstration very seriously. Later in life,
Napoleon III aroused her curiosity with tales about the wonders

performed at Eugénie's séances by D. D. Home. She was curious but not sufficiently interested to pursue the matter.

The single psychic experience of her life impressed her deeply. She described it in a letter to the Princess Royal: "I too wanted once to put an end to my life *here,* but a *Voice* told me for *His* sake—no, 'Still Endure.'" So profoundly was she moved by the *Voice* that she made the words her motto: "Still Endure."

The major twentieth-century scandal involving royalty and unorthodox beliefs is too familiar to relate here. It is, of course, the story of Rasputin, who dominated Nicholas and Alexandra of Russia. Historians and biographers disagree about the significance of the affair in Russian history. Some hold that the Czarina's bondage to the "mad monk" greatly hastened the revolution and sealed the fate of the Romanovs. Others dismiss the matter as just one more outrage, one more scandal among many —a less romantic view better suited to the evidence. At least in the other cases examined the monarchies were doomed long before an excess of occultism surfaced. Their leaders' turning toward the mystic, cavorting with ghosts and demons, was a symptom and warning of a deeper malaise, but not the cause of their downfall.

In Cloud-Cuckoo Land

Royalty has suffered much and it is unfair to add to these sufferings by comparing Adolf Hitler and his hangman lieutenants to a king and his court, but the comparison is irresistible. The historian H. Trevor-Roper was so struck by the resemblance that he entitled the first chapter of his book about the dictator's death "Hitler and His Court." There were dukes, earls, an heir apparent, and even a royal wizard—Heinrich Himmler, who not only played the role of Merlin but was also in charge of His Majesty's spies, dungeons, and torture chambers.

If the Nazi leaders were kingly in no other way, many of them certainly reacted to the threatened loss of their power in the tradition of most royal figures of the past. As destruction became imminent, they sought reassurance in prophecy, the prophecies being founded on a form of astrology as quack as the world has yet seen. Astrology is the oldest, most thoroughly explored, and currently far and away the most popular of all arcane studies. Although it dates from the earliest civilizations, its present form was developed in the middle ages, and it traveled both east and west following the trail of Moslem conquests, then continued on its own. Leaving aside the question of whether astrology has any over-all validity or not, one can state definitely that there are differences of quality among astrologers, the first consideration being sincerity. In many parts of the Orient, especially on the Indian subcontinent, astrology is closely bound to religion and there can be little doubt that its practitioners, mistaken or not, are without hypocrisy. The same can be said for many western astrologers: they are conscientious, not deliberately fraudulent.

But in the world that has been so well described by H. Trevor-Roper as the "Nazi cloud-cuckoo land" the motto in all things seemed to be, "Never take the best when the worst is available." This held true in medicine, art, genetics, and apparently everything else except warfare and physical comfort. It is hardly surprising that the Nazis, for all their interest and belief, contributed absolutely nothing to our understanding of occult phenomena.

So far no one has undertaken a complete study of the influence of mystic arts, sciences, and faiths in the Third Reich, but it is abundantly clear that such influence was enormous. From the beginning the whole Nazi system was overlaid with mysticism and mythology, and when the tide of war turned against Germany, the esoteric beliefs of its leaders became ever more apparent. Diaries, captured documents, and the transcript of the Nuremberg trials abound with references to peculiar creeds and

19

techniques; yet we are now seeing only the top of the iceberg, and we can only guess the magnitude of what lay below the surface.

Heinrich Himmler, head of the S.S. and Grand Inquisitor of the Germans, not only swallowed the entire Nazi mythology as absolute truth but was ravenous to find still more myths and superstitions. At the height of the war, when the shortage of money and manpower was acute, Himmler had thousands of men engaged in such projects as researching the mystical aspects of Freemasonry and Rosicrucianism, the significance of the Ulster Harp, the magical aspects of Gothic towers and Eton headgear. Himmler, and countless others from the top to the bottom of the system, constantly used such words as "soul," "spirit," "fate," and "destiny" in extraordinary ways. The Nazi anti-miscegenation laws were enacted not merely to prevent the birth of children of mixed ancestry but also to prevent a foreign "spirit" from taking permanent possession of an Aryan's body. "The Jews," said Nazi spokesman Julius Streicher, "have long known this racial secret."

There is ample evidence that many Nazis were terrified of Jewish magic. Hitler, in *Mein Kampf*, described the first time he saw an Orthodox Jew in Vienna. "I suddenly encountered an apparition in a black caftan and black sidelocks. Is this a Jew? was my first thought. For to be sure they had not looked like that in Linz. I observed the man furtively and cautiously. . . ." Writers and psychologists have often attributed the Fuehrer's frenzied anti-Semitism to sexual envy, and although this is undoubtedly true, another factor was also playing upon his emotions: a superstitious conviction about "blood" and "spirit." It is no accident that Hitler used the word "apparition." He was frightened.

Himmler shared this fright, these superstitions, and added a good many of his own. Runes, which formed the ancient alphabet of Northern Europe, were especially fascinating to him, and he was confident that they were laden with esoteric information, strange Nordic secrets which when deciphered would reveal wondrous things, including the "fact" that the Japanese and Germans were closely connected racially. So fanatical was Himmler on this subject that near the end of the war, when he was in a desperate, last-minute conference with the Swedish diplomat Count Bernadotte, he digressed from the talk of a possible armistice to lecture the startled Swede for an hour on this pet theory.

At least one of Himmler's subordinates knew how to capitalize on his chief's gullibility. General Walter Schellenberg, an unsavory character who for his own advancement sought to seduce "the faithful Heinrich" into treachery against Hitler, used tricked-up astrology as a lure. The following is from the transcript taken at the Nuremberg trials:

> COLONEL BROOKHART (*American interrogator*): You made reference to your astrological influence with Himmler. Will you tell us what you meant by that?
>
> SCHELLENBERG: . . . Kersten [Himmler's masseur] prepared the way with Himmler in that direction and reported to him that he knew an astrologer who would be able to clear up the future of Germany. . . . We had progressed so far in our common effort that toward the end of 1943 Himmler declared he was ready to receive the astrologer Wulf from Hamburg. I myself made the acquaintance of Wulf early in 1943 through Kersten. . . . I gave him the instructions to first of all point out the untenable situation of the Reich and to influence Himmler in favor of taking matters into his own hands. . . . Wulf also read Hitler's horoscope. . . . The influence of the horoscope and the doubts planted in Himmler's mind were very great. . . .

The astrologer, aside from his rigging horoscopes to serve immediate ends, was a better historian than prophet. He was invariably right after an event, always wrong before.

Mysticism and high finance are seldom thought to go hand in hand, but they did in the case of a group Himmler called his

"Circle of Friends." To join this elect group, a businessman had to contribute a huge amount of money to an esoteric project—such as sending a mission to Tibet to find ancient Nordic mysteries concealed in the Himalayas. The financier Wilhelm Keppler headed this peculiar club and he, along with others, believed that Hitler had direct, literal communication with God; he once startled an international economic conference by declaring this in public. (Keppler described Hitler as equipped with an "antenna.")

With or without an antenna, Adolf Hitler cannot be described as an occultist in the strict sense of the word, for the term implies study as well as belief. He was far more a fanatic given to many ill-assorted superstitions which he did not trouble to investigate or verify. To him the Aryan mystique was a political tool, not a personal religion, and this made him less a crank than Himmler. Yet he was impressed by somnambulistic utterances and accepted fortunetelling uncritically, as long as the forecast brought him good news.

One of the first things he did after being named Chancellor of Germany was to have his horoscope cast, and a copy of it was given to Himmler, who served as Keeper of the Sacred Archives. This was but the first of many star-readings. That they gave him contradictory information did not disturb him.

(Hitler was less demanding than the Roman Emperor Tiberius. Before attaining the throne, Tiberius was exiled for a time on the island of Rhodes. He would stroll along the cliff-tops on starry evenings accompanied by an astrologer and a stalwart slave. Tiberius asked questions, and if correct answers were not given, the slave tossed the mistaken soothsayer over a precipice. We do not know how many promising astrological careers were cut short this way, but the fortuneteller Thrasylus must have heard about Tiberius's unpleasant test, or else he was an excellent prophet. On the night he first strolled with Tiberius, he suddenly interrupted the questioning by crying out in terror that his own life was in peril at that very hour. This accurate pronouncement so impressed the future emperor that he never lost faith in Thrasylus.)

When the Russian armies approached Berlin and the end was near, the horoscope made at the time of Hitler's accession to power provided the basis for a lunatic scene enacted in the famous bunker fifty feet under the Chancellery. The Fuehrer had taken refuge there with a few intimates such as Goebbels, who one night read aloud from Carlyle's *History of Frederick the Great.* He came to a pertinent passage wherein Frederick, on the verge of losing the Seven Years' War, declared that if his condition did not improve by February 16, he would swallow poison. Carlyle and Goebbels then reached lyric heights: " 'Brave King! Wait yet a little while, and the days of your suffering will be over. Already the sun of your good fortune stands behind the clouds and soon will rise upon you.' On February 12, the Czarina died, the Miracle of the House of Brandenburg had come to pass. . . .''

Hitler, moved to tears by these comforting words, sent for his own horoscope and another star-reading, anonymous, cast on November 19, 1918, the day the Weimar Republic came into being. The documents were compared, and Goebbels told the Nazi diarist Count Lutz Schwerin von Krosigk that "an amazing fact has become evident, both horoscopes predicting the outbreak of war in 1939, the victories until 1941, and the subsequent series of reversals. . . . There would be stagnation until August and peace that same month. For the following three years Germany would have a hard time, but starting in 1948 she would rise again." At least that is what Hitler and Goebbels saw in the readings. Krosigk himself, when he examined the horoscopes, could not "fathom everything in them." But a newly typed reinterpretation attached to the originals made it all clear.

Several days later, Goebbels was still harping on horoscopes, destiny, fate, and the miracle of the House of Brandenburg, when an officer inquired skeptically, "What Czarina will die this time?"

Goebbels could offer no name, but the answer was fast in coming. News of Roosevelt's sudden death, not mentioned in the horoscopes, reached Berlin that night and the apparent fulfillment of the prophecy was celebrated with the best remaining champagne. "My Fuehrer, I congratulate you!" cried the excited Goebbels. "Roosevelt is dead! It is written in the stars that the second half of April will be the turning point for us. This is Friday, April the thirteenth. It is the turning point!"

Even the diarist Krosigk, a bit dubious earlier, was now convinced. "This was the Angel of History! We felt its wings flutter through the room. . . ." Presumably this fluttering was not literal, but in cloud-cuckoo land one cannot be sure. (In justice to Carlyle, it should be added that either Goebbels or Krosigk misquoted him.)

Some authorities have argued that Goebbels himself had too practical a mind to believe all this—that he was trying to comfort his beloved master and keep morale high. But at this point in his career the Propaganda Minister could well have been as deluded and irrational as all those around him. At any rate, Carlyle and the stars inspired him to make a rousing broadcast to beleaguered German troops, and he spoke murkily of "destiny" and the fact that Hitler now knew the "very hour" of an upturn in fortune.

The whole mad affair of the horoscopes was the wildest grasping for straws; the Nazis and their system were inescapably doomed. Meanwhile, there had been other occult straw-graspers in the land. Certain anti-Nazis were busily consulting the heavens for ways to overthrow Hitler. Trevor-Roper comments drily, "It is a pity that the science of astrology should have failed *all* its devotees."

Considering the vast, monstrous tragedy the Nazis inflicted upon the world, it seems niggling to complain that they also wasted money. But Hitler's Germany remains the only nation in modern times that has invested large sums for research into unconventional science and belief. A fraction of the amount, used sensibly, could have advanced parapsychology a century. Like the odious medical experiments, the Nazi occult studies were not designed to find truth, but to bolster a mythology. The opportunity was lost, the time and work wasted, and after it was all over the Unexplained remained as much a mystery as ever.

"Something in It after All"

We have taken so far the rather bleak view that today's heightened interest in things supernatural has its roots in a troubled, changing society—that history is repeating itself, in effect.

But another opinion is tenable. It can be argued that for the first time at least some of the belief and activity springs from rational convictions and honest curiosity. For nearly a hundred years psychical research groups in various countries have hammered the public with the sensible idea that because a matter does not fall within the neat framework of traditional science, it is not therefore to be dismissed out of hand as "nonsense." Has this message at last reached a large number of people? It is quite possible—there are indications that it has.

The experiments of Dr. J. B. Rhine at Duke University are widely known even if they are not widely understood. The New School of Social Research offers a credit course in parapsychology and for a time the Massachusetts Institute of Technology sponsored a psychical research group. Dr. Charles Tart of the University of California in Sacramento has conducted serious experiments that would have been scoffed out of the laboratory a generation ago. Additional research has been done at McGill, the University of California at Los Angeles, and other universities. For scientists it is still risky to become involved too deeply in any work that smacks of the occult. "Many scientists are more interested in the paranormal than they are prepared to admit because it's still not scientifically respectable," says Professor Henry Margenau of Yale. But he goes on to add that "the old distinction between the natural and the supernatural has become spurious."

But though scientists may still encounter prejudice, the average man realizes that his interest in the Unexplained will no longer mark him as a crank or idiot. If he joins a witches' coven and capers naked in the woods decked in goat horns, he will certainly be thought eccentric, but in less excessive ways he is quite free to express his beliefs.

And he has such beliefs. Despite the harangues of scientists and orthodox preachers, most men have always cherished at least a small amount of faith in the occult—a faith that is often summed up in the cautious remark, "I may be crazy, but I think there's something in it after all." Today he knows that that mysterious "something" is receiving the attention of science.

For those who doubt the prevalence of occult belief outside areas already known for peculiarity, we would like to draw on personal experience: when it became known that the author was engaged in writing a book about the paranormal, he was instantly deluged with unsolicited case histories both written and oral. They came from unlikely quarters—from doctors, attorneys, and businessmen, most of whom had no broad belief in supernatural occurrences but were eager to report psychic events of their own lives. These stories were unsupported by outside evidence, but this made no difference to the people who experienced them. They were unfamiliar with parapsychology, but they *knew* what they *knew*.

Parapsychology has had great publicity in recent years, but most people are still confused about its terms and history and vague about what has been established and what remains without foundation. Even the so-called classic cases of earlier days are little known except to students and avid fans of the occult. Modern writers are wary of mentioning the past, and such once-famous names as D. D. Home and Eusapia Palladino are anathema to contemporary researchers. Their colorful stories are, in fact, in danger of being lost to a new generation.

It is understandable that the past should be an embarrassment, since the entire field has been rife with frauds, mistakes, and exaggerations. The new tendency is to wipe the slate clean and start afresh.

But whether one takes the reports of older generations as fact or fiction, they cannot be dismissed. They are stories of the weird, the strange, and the wonderful. Looking backward, even with a skeptical eye, one is compelled to say that "there were giants in the earth in those days. . . ."

II

Occult Stars:
Some Remarkable
Ladies

Mediums are the stars of the preternatural theater, and the practitioners of the other unexplained arts pale beside them. It is the medium who purports to bridge the gulf between the living and the dead, the here and the hereafter; she links the physical world with the unknown, raising ghosts, conjuring with spirits, providing the fleshly instrument through which phantoms reveal themselves by speech, sound, writing, and—sometimes violently—by direct action.

One tends to think of a medium as "she," and almost all mediums who appear in fiction and drama are women. The spirits themselves, however, seem to have no special preference for the female sex. The most famous modern medium is a man, the Reverend Arthur Ford. There is also the Reverend George Daisley of Santa Barbara, who, in the summer of 1967, assisted the late Right Reverend James A. Pike in establishing occult contact with Bishop Pike's son, James, Jr., who had killed himself a year before. (Arthur Ford also figured prominently in the Pike case.) Daisley, a conservative practitioner, stresses the religious aspects of spiritualism and is hardly to be compared with the flamboyant male mediums of earlier generations. Today's spiritualists seem pallid when one thinks of their predecessors.

At present there is no one in the field half so colorful and puzzling as the Reverend William Stainton Moses, for example. Moses, born in Lincolnshire in 1839, seemed to live two disparate lives which are almost impossible to reconcile. As an Episcopal clergyman and schoolmaster he attracted little attention except the favorable comments of his associates, who praised his dedication, quiet efficiency, and high intelligence. The first thirty-three prosaic years of his life gave no hint of what was to follow. Then, after reading a book on the occult and attending a series of séances, this self-effacing man of the cloth blossomed into mediumship of the most extravagant variety. Such minor miracles as spirit rappings and the levitation of furniture were child's play to the Reverend Moses, and soon he himself began to float about the séance room. Mysterious lights appeared and, although one skeptic insisted that they must be bottles of phosphorus, a number of seemingly reliable witnesses were deeply impressed. This strange double life continued for years; during the day Mr. Moses remained a conscientious teacher and orthodox clergyman, but his evenings—when his frail health permitted—were devoted to bizarre rites accompanied by the twanging of mandolins and guitars plucked by ghostly fingers.

Many of the Moses séances were observed by Dr. and Mrs. Stanhope Spear, and Dr. Spear reported some unusual evenings in his own home and at the clergyman's house on the Isle of Man. Unseen hands carried dozens of objects about, especially toilet articles, and once made an artistic arrangement of these things in the middle of the Reverend Moses' bed. The Spears saw a large cross topped by a clerical collar to represent a halo. Even more remarkable was the night when, in the presence of Dr. and Mrs. Spear, a ghost named Dicky brought pieces of an ivory puzzle from the drawing room. The Reverend Moses seems to have been somewhat disturbed on that occasion, for he writes (and the italics are his): "I felt something crawling over my right hand—which Mrs. Spear held—and could not make out what it was. When a light was struck we found it to be a marker from Mrs. Spear's bedroom. It had *crawled* over my hand, and was placed directly in front of her, with the legend, 'God is our refuge and strength' right before her eyes."

Stainton Moses was not unique among his contemporaries. There were many like him, and no figure of modern spiritualism is as dramatic as Andrew Jackson Davis, the "Poughkeepsie Seer," who summoned the phantoms of Galen and Swedenborg. Davis, whom we shall meet later at a haunted Presbyterian manse in Stratford, Connecticut, gave several remarkable demonstrations of occult power but was inclined to involve himself in the ridiculous. One of his forays into the absurd concerned "The New Motor," a marvelous machine devised by John Murray Spear (not connected to Dr. Stanhope Spear, above), a prominent American social reformer of the 1850s, who, except for such lapses as "The New Motor," was regarded by his contemporaries as not only sane but intelligent. Spear, now acting under the orders of a band of spirits who called themselves the "Association of Electricizers," constructed a device that was to draw power from "nature's warehouse of infinite magnetic force." A cult sprang up immediately, hailing the gadget as the "Physical Savior of the race," and "The New Motor" quickly became the "New Messiah." The craze was not without its sexual aspects. A lady of Lynn, Massachusetts, obeyed a vision which ordered her to the machine's presence at the High Rock, and there endured pains similar to those of childbirth as part of her soul was wrenched from her body to give life to the machine. Her sufferings were not in vain, for the contraption immediately began to vibrate—or at least the witnesses thought so. Andrew Jackson Davis thereupon announced that "The New Motor," although devoid of practical value, was certainly the creation of spirits with a bent for engineering. Unfortunately, "The New Motor" was removed from the safety of Lynn to the more excitable town of Randolph, New York, where it was smashed by a mob of outraged Christians.

Although Davis suffered a loss of reputation in this scandal (and inventor Spear suffered a loss of some two thousand dollars), he continued for many years as one of America's foremost mediums.

Davis and even the Reverend Moses were secondary lights compared to the brilliance of Daniel Dunglas Home, most celebrated of all male mediums and certainly the most astonishing. Home, who floated in and out of second-story windows with the ease of a zephyr, has received a good deal of attention in print and merits a good deal more. He can be compared with the greatest women in the field, a worthy rival to Eusapia Palladino, and if he was not Mrs. Piper's equal this should not detract from his fame. Mrs. Piper had no equals, as we shall see shortly.

Regardless of male achievements, people continue to think of mediums as female. In the Western World at least, women have always dominated all occult arts except faith healing and magicianship. Astrology is another exception, although the greatest modern astrologer was a woman, Evangeline Adams. There is a clear sexual division of labor shown by this pattern: men, according to traditional prejudice, are more logical and scientific, more adept at alchemy and occult medicine. Women are more sensitive, intuitive, and spiritual, better practitioners of mediumship, witchcraft, and instinctive fortunetelling. There was no Greek or Roman god so eerie as the goddess Hecate, patroness of dark arts, and no man in the Homeric epics has the mysterious powers of Circe and Cassandra. The witch Medea lacks a male counterpart in Greek drama. Shakespeare makes his alchemist-magician Prospero a man, but all his witches are female. "Witch" is a common word in the English language, but "warlock" is rare.

For whatever causes, mediumship from earliest times to the present day has been connected, in popular belief, with a strange female mystique. And over the centuries a large number of women have fully justified the notion that females have a special talent for trafficking with devils and ghosts.

Since the desire to communicate with the dead and with other unknown powers is basic to man's nature, the medium's profession dates back to prehistory. The famed Greek oracle at Delphi, often carelessly called a soothsayer, was actually a medium, for she did not prophesy through her own power or through a gift of "second sight" but supposedly foretold the future when her body was possessed by a god; in other words, she was a "medium" of communication between the spirit and the listener.

The earliest detailed record of a séance appears in the Bible in the first book of Samuel, where we are given a graphic description of King Saul's visit to the Witch of Endor. Although it is a good story and well told, the tale has been an embarrassment to Christian theologians, for it lends scriptural aid and comfort to all sorts of anathematized cults. Clearly the ancient Hebrews believed in mediumship, and the woman of Endor—"witch" is later, Christian terminology—materialized no insignificant ghost but the shade of the patriarch Samuel. It is notable that the best Catholic study of mediumship, *Spiritism and Religion* by Baron Johan Liljencrants, omits the Endor séance, although necromancy in Chaldea, Egypt, and Greece is discussed. As Holy Writ, the Endor story is not easily explained away.

> Then said Saul unto his servants, Seek me a woman that hath a familiar spirit that I may go to her and enquire of her. And his servants said to him, Behold, there is a woman that hath a familiar spirit at Endor.
> And Saul disguised himself and put on other raiment, and he

went, and two men with him, and they came to the woman by night: and he said, I pray thee, divine unto me by the familiar spirit and bring him up whom I shall name unto thee.

And the woman said unto him, Behold, thou knowest what Saul hath done, how he hath cut off those that have familiar spirits and the wizards out of the land: wherefore then layest thou a snare for my life to cause me to die?

And Saul sware to her by the Lord, saying, As the Lord liveth there shall be no punishment happen to thee for this thing.

Then said the woman, Whom shall I bring up unto thee? And he said, Bring me up Samuel.

And when the woman saw Samuel, she cried with a loud voice: and the woman spake to Saul saying, Why has thou deceived me? For thou art Saul.

And the king said unto her, Be not afraid: for what sawest thou? And the woman said unto Saul, I saw gods ascending out of the earth.

And he said unto her, What form is he of? And she said, An old man cometh up; and he is covered with a mantle. And Saul perceived that it was Samuel, and he stooped with his face to the ground and bowed himself.

This ancient account is surprisingly modern. The woman's "familiar spirit" would now be called a Control, the contemporary term for a spirit, usually friendly, who *controls* the medium physically during her trance and who serves as a guide, courier, and general go-between with phantoms on the "Other Side."

Saul's attending the séance incognito is also modern behavior. Practicing mediums affirm that new clients often give aliases because of guilt or embarrassment, as in Saul's case. Frequently the anonymous or pseudonymous client is planted as a method of testing the medium's power and leading her into blunders. We shall see this form of entrapment tried repeatedly with Mrs. Piper, and it produced some startling results.

The Witch of Endor at first denied possession of an occult talent, and this is typical of many a medium today when confronted with a stranger who may be an undercover policeman assigned to the Bunco Squad. In many communities a medium may operate only under the guise of religion. She will remain unmolested as long as she summons only law-abiding ghosts: ghosts who do little more than reminisce about their past lives or discuss the weather on the Other Side. But the unlucky medium who contacts a prophesying spirit runs a grave risk of being clapped into jail for illegal fortunetelling.

It will be noted that Saul, who in happier and more stable times had launched a persecution of witches and wizards, turned to the occult when he found his kingdom breaking up and his own person attacked on every side. Surrounded by turmoil and rebellion, he appealed to the witch—just as Adolf Hitler in his beleaguered capital in 1945 clung desperately to the astrological forecasts of the charlatan Wulf, and, indeed, as Americans today, surrounded by an unstable society and facing an uncertain future, consult the occult in ever-increasing numbers.

The finest demonstrations of mediumship, whether sincere or bogus, are by necessity shown to a limited audience and, despite their influence in history, mediums achieve little publicity compared to other psychics. Seers and soothsayers, clairvoyants, astrologers, faith healers, mind readers, telepathists, and even water dowsers attract broader attention. Some, such as Edgar Cayce, the "Sleeping Prophet" of Virginia Beach, acquire international fame. Cults flourish around them. Books by or about mystics climb best-seller lists and remain there week after week; astrologers enrich themselves by advising millions through magazine and newspaper columns.

When a police department in any country appeals for help to the Dutch clairvoyant Peter Hurkos, an otherwise routine murder or robbery becomes a headline event. Will the amazing Dutchman, who has a world-wide reputation as a psychic ferret, sniff out the criminal by some extra-olfactory sense? For although Hurkos does not have the success record of a Sherlock Holmes, he has made a number of accurate hits and a few of them have been uncanny. Whether or not the guilty party is tracked down by psychic means, we are treated to a good show, as when Hurkos apparently read the mind and recounted the recent kitchen-table sexual adventures of a Massachusetts state trooper during an unsuccessful foray into the Boston Strangler case.

But despite the publicity lavished on psychics and soothsayers, a medium of enormous gifts—a Eusapia or a Mrs. Piper—occupies the position among occultists that a Galli-Curci held among singers. Real genius has the ultimate rank, the ultimate glamour. The medium is mistress of the séance, and it is in the séance that occult experience reaches its height.

The séance grips the imagination, lays hold of emotions, causes blood to tingle and hair to rise. The lowered lights, the hushed assemblage, the slowly intensified trance, the medium's assumption of an alien personality, the real or fancied presence of the ghostly Control—all these combine to play upon our sensibilities, creating an effect which no utterance of prophecy, no reading of minds, stars, crystal balls, or tea leaves, can produce. The séance is immediate, it is *now*, and the tension is overpowering— almost unbearable. It offers the most daring of all occult endeavor: the attempting to convoke spirits through the agency of the medium. The spirits may be presented as ghosts, the voices of the human dead echoing from another universe, as Mrs. Piper believed; or the congregated spirits may not be phantoms at all, but bodiless forces, physical extensions of the medium's mind: thought becoming force to produce the feats of Eusapia Palladino.

And, of course, there are those who will insist that the spirits are always our own imaginings or the medium's trickery coupled with the longing of the believer, who often has not just a will but a desperate passion to believe and so deludes himself into hailing a cheesecloth ghost as a departed loved one, finding a fool's consolation in the shimmery glow of a phosphorescent trumpet—a stage property obtained from a supply house in Chicago which specializes in creating very material and very tawdry phantoms for the spiritist market.

Whatever the truth, and the truth appears not to be the same in all cases, the séance remains the most dramatic of demonstrations. We are surrounded. We are in the presence of our own beliefs or doubts and we sit wary and watchful, always in anticipation. If our medium is another Eusapia, we shall not have to wait: *something* is bound to happen and more likely than not it will be an apparent miracle. For Eusapia, along with Mrs. Piper and a very few others, seemed to achieve the impossible not once but many times.

Yet these talented ladies, as different from each other as they were from the rest of the world, have become almost forgotten women during the half century which has passed since they ceased to amaze believers and confound skeptics. Their names are unknown to the general public; encyclopedias omit them or give them short shrift. Students of the occult and devotees of psychic matters are, of course, familiar with the stories of both women, for to omit them from any broad study of the occult would be like ignoring Duse or Bernhardt in a history of the theater. But only in the narrow field of mystic literature are Palladino and Piper dominant names. Biographers have lost interest —an undeserved neglect, since the careers of both were extraordinary, to say the least, and Mrs. Piper deserves a place not just in the annals of psychic research but in general history.

These two women confound us. If only a fraction of their purported power was genuine, all thinking about the way the world operates and how the human mind works must be revised. Mrs. Piper, in her unassuming way, is perhaps the most disturbing figure a materialist can encounter. Eusapia, far more open to doubt, must be proclaimed a great artist in one field or another. She remains a tantalizing riddle that suggests disconcerting possibilities.

The words "disconcerting possibilities" may explain why great mediums seldom gain the tolerance and quasi-acceptance that the public readily grants fortunetellers and clairvoyants. Seers and astrologers provide entertainment without causing a disturbance. Even a "scientific" man can afford to have a little faith in astrology without doing violence to his other convictions. He can follow his daily horoscope in safety, perhaps chuckling to himself. Mind-reading, telepathy, and other aspects of clairvoyance are now lumped in the scientific-sounding term Extra-Sensory Perception, and many experiments, especially those of Dr. J. B. Rhine at Duke University, have given ESP a new respectability. One is permitted to say that "there is something in it" without being called a crank or an idiot. ESP challenges neither the scientific nor the religious establishment. It can be incorporated into the rational order of things.

Other occult phenomena may appear foolish but are harmless. The diagnoses of Edgar Cayce, involving both telepathy and the trance, in no way threaten the tenets of medical science. Cayce can be dismissed by physicians as a quack who made some lucky guesses and his long-distance cures can be explained by the probability that the patients' ills were psychosomatic to begin with. No harm was done, except perhaps to those who followed his nostrums and deferred real treatment until too late, and there is a general feeling that victims of faith healers have none but themselves to blame. Cayce's story is not alarming: he can coexist in the public's mind along with more reasonable beliefs.

All forms of fortunetelling share this quality of harmlessness. A dozen American states and hundreds of communities have passed laws to banish card-readers and crystal-gazers, but they reappear instantly under such euphemisms as "Spiritual Adviser" and "Reader and Counselor." Their practices flourish. No skeptic and no priest is really outraged when a fortuneteller makes a series of correct predictions. As with astrology, we are permitted to have "a little faith" in the tea-room gypsy.

But mediumship as demonstrated by Mrs. Piper and Eusapia is quite another matter. Here we do not have the ambiguous star-readings of Hollywood's Carroll Righter or the vague, unverifiable *Search for Bridey Murphy*. Piper and Palladino cannot be ignored, and perhaps this is why they *have* been ignored. They remain two thorns in the materialist flesh, impossible for most people to accept, impossible to explain, and to have "a little faith" in either is like having a little leprosy—the consequences are major.

These two women appear to overthrow the beliefs of rational man. They strike at our innermost convictions, they repeal the "laws of science." Eusapia was marvelous but vulnerable; Mrs. Piper was marvelous and practically unassailable. Anyone who wishes to have his convictions or prejudices undisturbed would do well to avoid these ladies and that is exactly what the world has done. But their stories, after half a century, remain to confound us and to lead us to questions that are as yet unanswered.

Neapolitan Virago

Eusapia Palladino charges into the spiritist arena, head lowered, nostrils distended, peculiar cold winds emanating from her knee and temple as she challenges all comers—the Amazon of the occult. She is no materializer of frail, insubstantial ghosts who sigh in passages or flit through the darkness of haunted libraries. The spirits she invokes are like herself, as robust as a gang of stevedores. They hurl furniture across the room, they lift weights and overturn cabinets. Being Neapolitan, the phantoms are noisy: bells ring, horns blow, there are thumps and raps which build to crashes. An accordion, touched by a heavy but invisible hand, squeals and wheezes. A cupboard takes legs and darts across the chamber while poltergeists hammer to be released from an apparently empty chest. This is Eusapia at her greatest, or perhaps merely at her trickiest. But even the latter is no small achievement.

Learned men, the gray-bearded fathers of the Society for Psychical Research, seek out this peasant woman and peer at her as an entymologist peers at an exotic insect. Solemnly they stuff gags into her mouth, they bind her wrists and hang onto her ankles. Still the séance table tilts sharply and the spirits descend with a clatter and a bang and a thumping.

The drama of Eusapia versus the scientists does not lack comedy: an elderly gentleman hides himself beneath a table, crouching for hours under its long cloth. In the midst of the séance, he springs from ambush shouting, "Her foot! Her foot! She's wiggling it!" The medium shrieks, flails her arms, writhes in a fit, and another scientific gathering ends in tumult.

Eusapia's birthplace is uncertain. One account makes her a native of a village somewhere called La Pouille, born on January 21, 1854. Another authority has her coming from Minervo Murge near Bari and gives her birthdate as unknown. According to her own account, her mother died during her infancy and her father placed her in the unloving hands of a peasant family who neglected her and, through carelessness, allowed her to have a serious accident to which she later attributed the origin of her mediumship. At the age of one year, or perhaps two or three, she fell, striking her head on the wheel of a cart. The resultant scar, sometimes described as a cranial opening, became the source of a mysterious "cold breeze," a peculiar exhaling of chilly air that several investigators swore they felt issuing from her after séances. A lock of snow-white hair grew above the scar, partially concealing it and accenting the swarthiness of her face.

From the beginning Eusapia's life was melodrama. When she was either eight or twelve—again authorities disagree—her father was murdered by brigands. A Neapolitan friend then took the child to the city and turned her over to a pair of foreign ladies eager to adopt an orphan. A year of misery followed: she was compelled to bathe daily, to endure piano lessons, and to suffer other instruction, to which she proved impervious. Eusapia remained illiterate to the end of her days. Unable to bear further civilizing, she fled to the family of her Neapolitan friend, and it was in their house that she first learned about séances and the practice of table-turning. Although her occult gifts were quickly revealed, Eusapia found séances boring and soon gave up spiritism for more congenial work as a laundress.

She must have been an unusual washerwoman, for within a year or two she made the acquaintance of M. Damiani, an Italian medium of considerable prominence who rekindled her interest in matters psychic. The social and financial disparity between the two was vast and, as usual, we have conflicting explanations of Damiani's sponsorship of young Eusapia. Her defenders say he recognized a great artist; her enemies, with raised eyebrows, say, "Sex."

Sexuality is so often mentioned or implied in writings about Eusapia that we must conclude her aura was not entirely spiritual. Mostly we see Eusapia through the eyes of Victorian Englishmen and their even more prudish American contemporaries. It is hardly an unprejudiced view. Still, there must have been *something*—something that aroused pure outrage in the breast of a Mrs. Finch, once editor of the *Annals of Psychical Science*. In a 1909 editorial, Mrs. Finch excoriated Eusapia as a monster of "erotic tendencies" and charged that her sitters, presumably male, were deluded and "glamoured," spellbound by the very fact that she was a woman. The fact that Eusapia was Italian by birth and a witch by profession did not improve her reputation. To the Anglo-Saxon mind this implied eroticism doubly damned.

Her sexual charms, however, seem to have existed in the eye of the beholder. Professor Camille Flammarion, who met her in 1897, was hardly enchanted. He described her as a "woman of very ordinary appearance . . . rather stout." Mme. Paola Carrara, who wrote the first biographical sketch of the medium, felt she was "not ugly, but her face is wasted by the suffering and the fatigue of her séances. She has magnificent black eyes, mobile and even diabolical in expression."

Under Damiani's influence Eusapia soon relinquished the washtubs for the séance table, and before long she developed an abiding friendship with a new acquaintance, a ghost named John

King. King, who became her Control, was a colorful and ubiqui-
tous spirit, a sort of phantom-about-town, a frequent caller at
séances in both Europe and America. In life he had been a buccaneer, a sea hawk of the Spanish Main and, speaking from the
Other Side, he recounted his adventures not only through the
mouths of various mediums, but also via the ouija board and in
automatic writing. The pirate's roughness was softened by the
presence of his sister, Katie King, a gentle ghost who provided
much consolation to the bereaved. (Confusion exists about the
relationship between the two; some mediums insisted that Katie
was John's daughter. As we shall see, the King clan was so numerous that it is quite possible that there were two Katies, one
a daughter who was the namesake of her aunt.)

John King was international and polyglot. Long before appearing in Naples he was an habitué of a raucous salon presided over
by Jonathan Koons, a farmer-medium of Athens County, Ohio.
Koons, inspired by a prophecy that he and all eight of his children would attain mediumship, built a log séance room on his
farm in 1852, a building ample to accommodate a crowd of spectators and an infinite number of spirits. The spectral carryings-on
that took place there were surely the rowdiest in the history of
spiritism. One night, for example, the spirits staged a full-scale
concert, ". . . the fiddle, drums, guitar, banjo, accordion, French
harp, the horn, tea bell, triangle etc. playing their parts." Ghosts,
their voices hollow and amplified as they spoke through horns
and trumpets, chatted with the audience. Furniture was jolted
and tossed great distances. Not only did the phantom of John
King manifest himself, but no fewer than sixty-five other King
spirits appeared, all claiming to be the pirate's lineal ancestors.
But this was merely the beginning of the Kings' ghostly descent
on Ohio: one hundred additional shades arrived using King as
a generic name, since they were the pre-Adamite forebears of
John and Katie, beings who existed before the creation of the
earth.

Spirit messages poured into the Koonses' log temple, some scribbled on paper placed under the séance table, others chalked on closed slates or the arms and foreheads of sitters. Witnesses shuddered as bodiless hands darted blindly around the room seeking pencils with which they wrote notes complete with signature. John and Katie King were frequent signers. Meanwhile, a Mrs. Draper of Rochester had got in touch with the shade of Benjamin Franklin and from that scientific phantom learned the art of spirit-telepathy, communication by raps and clicks that resembled the chattering of a Morse key. The whole band of King spirits adopted this novel form of expression, adding yet another noise to the psychic uproar on the Koonses' farm. The Methodist residents of the nearby village were at first awed, but later became articulate about their shock and disapproval.

This record of excesses did not deter Eusapia from adopting King as her Control. In fact, the idea of excess seems to have been unknown to her, and perhaps she found the ghost of a buccaneer an ideal companion. However, King did not dominate Eusapia as he and his relatives had dominated the Koons ménage thirty years earlier. It is most unlikely that Eusapia had ever heard of Jonathan Koons or of the remarkable activities on his farm; the pirate became her Control because he was a celebrity, popular with mediums and clients in a dozen countries. She attributed many of her achievements to his intercession, and at times she delivered vague messages purporting to come from King, but Eusapia seldom conveyed any word from the Other Side. She was primarily a *physical* not a *trance* medium. Since Eusapia went into trances, this appears to be a paradox, so we must here clarify some of the confusing terms of psychical research.

A *physical medium* such as Eusapia produces physical manifestations—table-rapping and -tilting, bell-ringing, the levitation of objects and their unexplained transportation. Eusapia was the outstanding female practitioner in this field, as Daniel Dunglas Home was the outstanding male. The fact that Eusapia performed her work while in an apparently hypnotic trance does not change her category, for classification of mediums depends on the results, not the methods used.

A *trance medium*—Mrs. Piper, for example—materializes no trumpets, summons no visible specters. Her work is mental, she hears "voices" with an inner ear, translates thought waves for which she has a special sensitivity. Because of this talent, trance mediums are often called *sensitives*, a better term which the public shows no sign of adopting. (The very word "medium" is unfortunate, since it assumes a force outside the *sensitive*'s own mind. Researchers are galled by the term, as we shall see in the case of Mrs. Piper.)

Using John King as a contact with the Other Side, Eusapia began her public career in Naples. At about the same time she married Raphael Delgaiz, the owner of a small shop and an amateur theatrical performer. It has been charged that Delgaiz coached Eusapia in the arts of stage conjuring, prestidigitation, and sleight of hand. There have even been suggestions that he played Svengali to his wife's Trilby. Actually, Delgaiz was only a theatrical dabbler of no special skill or talent and had no gift whatever except good looks. Observers who met the couple went out of their way to mention the husband's handsomeness and they noted rather slyly that he appeared much younger than Eusapia. Thoughts of what Mrs. Finch called "erotic tendencies" seem to have lurked behind the comments.

Eusapia and her new husband began a life which was hardly extraordinary yet not quite conventional. She gave séances and "readings" for small groups of paying clients, she helped out in the store, she did her housework. Before long she had become a neighborhood *strega*, a family witch and psychic adviser, a common type which Neapolitans consulted more regularly and more casually than they consulted the family physician. Curious reports about this new medium reached the ears of Professor Cesare Lombroso, a distinguished savant and a member of an informal group of scholars who were then opening the field of psychical research in Italy. Lombroso journeyed from Milan to

Naples, where he attended a séance. A skeptic by nature, he expected little, but he emerged from his first session with Eusapia baffled, shaken, hardly able to believe the evidence of his own eyes. It is small wonder that Lombroso's reaction to the séance caused a stir among his colleagues. The professor was one of Italy's outstanding men, a celebrated anthropologist and a pioneer in the field of psychology. His contributions to the study of sexual psychology are noted by Krafft-Ebing in *Psychopathia Sexualis*. Perhaps more important in the case of Eusapia, Lombroso was recognized as the country's leading criminologist, a detector of fraud, a man not easily fooled. His theories about criminal types once dominated criminology in most countries.

As a result of Lombroso's report, Eusapia was summoned in 1892 to preside at a series of controlled séances in Milan, where she would be scrutinized by half a dozen trained and skeptical observers. They were indeed prominent men, these first investigators of Eusapia Palladino: Lombroso, Professors Brofferio, Geroso, Schiaparelli, Richet—all lions of the academic world— and Alexandre Aksakof, former Councillor of State to the Russian Emperor. It is ironic that, with the exceptions of Lombroso and Richet, little record remains of these distinguished men beyond their connection with an illiterate medium.

In Milan Eusapia faced the first major test of her power in front of an audience that was not merely suspicious but decidedly hostile. Although the gatherings were held in darkness or dimness, the medium's hands and feet were restrained. Under these controlled circumstances, no ordinary fraud seemed possible, and even Lombroso doubted that anything extraordinary would happen. But suddenly there came mysterious raps and thuds, the heavy table developed a will of its own, tilting crazily and refusing to stay upright while other objects were levitated into the air at a distance of more than a yard from the medium's body. The astonished scientists found themselves witnessing what appeared to be telekinesis, the ability to move matter by mental power. It was as though Eusapia had repealed the known laws

44

of physics. But was this mental or something more ghostly? Both then and later the watchers saw impressions of insubstantial hands; diaphanous faces hovered in the dimness of the séance chamber.

Since measuring and weighing are tools of science, the medium was placed on a huge balance. (And here one pauses to look at the picture of Eusapia entranced, her chair poised on one end of a great teeter-totter while the professors solemnly add counterweights to the opposite side, their notebooks open to record the specific gravity of a poltergeist. The scene is somehow monkish and medieval, the corpse being weighed before and after the instant of dying to determine the poundage of the soul.) One would expect little from such a procedure; but Eusapia was anything but predictable. As her trance deepened, the balance began to fluctuate, counterweights were added and removed. Readings during the séance showed a variation of seventeen pounds! It was preposterous, yet it happened. And the witnesses were neither Eusapia's superstitious Neapolitan neighbors nor the yokels who sought signs and wonders on the Koonses' farm. They were six distinguished and reliable men—not even impartial, since their natural inclinations were to disbelieve the medium.

Unfortunately, Eusapia's Milan sittings were a qualified triumph, and the worst facet of the medium's character was revealed. Whenever Control was lax and whenever too little seemed to be happening, she would resort to quite obvious fraud and trickery to produce an effect. Her Neapolitan clients demanded miracles on a heroic scale, and Eusapia was not one to disappoint them. Mme. Carrara described her character as "a mixture of silliness and maliciousness, of intelligence and ignorance, of strange conditions of existence . . . her appearance and words seem to be quite genuine and sincere. She has not the manner of one who either poses or tricks or deceives others. . . ." Perhaps this was true of her as a woman, but as a medium she was a good deal less than honest. Since this is plain fact, many critics have dismissed Eusapia as an utter charlatan. But to do this lightly is to resort to the patent illogicality of "once a thief, always a thief." The Italian professors took her attempts at fraud into account and were well aware of the type of character they dealt with. Nevertheless they were disturbed by the things they had seen, phenomena beyond explanation that could certainly not be charged off to the rather simple tricks of which Eusapia was quite capable.

Before concluding their study of Eusapia, the investigators observed her at seventeen different sittings. Telekinesis was reported many times, once in full light. While the medium's hands were tied to the hands of controllers, levitations occurred. Fingerprints appeared on smoked paper placed at a distance from her, apparitions formed, there was contact with unknown human faces and always the mysterious movements of the table when—at least to the satisfaction of the professors—Eusapia had no possible physical contact with it.

The document which summed up the Milan study is one of the greatest tributes ever paid to a physical medium. Although baffled by the nature of Eusapia's power, the savants had no doubt of its existence. It took a good deal of courage for eminent men of science to announce that they had secured "a large number of facts apparently or really important and marvelous." To indicate the least belief in a physical medium is to open oneself to instant attack. This was as true then as it is now.

The investigators expressed disappointment that

in the greatest number of cases we were not able to apply the rules of experimental science . . . [but] we do not believe we have the right to explain these things by the aid of insulting assumptions, which many still find to be the simplest explanation. . . . We think, on the contrary, that these experiments are concerned with phenomena of an unknown nature, and we confess we do not know what the conditions are that are necessary to produce them. To desire to fix these conditions in our own right and out of our own head would be as extravagant as to presume to make the experiment of Torricelli's barometer with a tube closed at the bottom. . . .

The Italians realized that pure "laboratory conditions" may be impossible in testing occult phenomena: the very methods of testing may, for all anyone knows, inhibit the forces being investigated. One cannot disprove electricity by cutting some wires, then noting that a lamp gives no light. The fact that Eusapia could not always and under all conditions produce amazing results is hardly surprising.

What are the proper methods for determining the truth or falsity of a psychic demonstration? The answer is not so simple as many investigators have assumed. For example, the ESP experiments at Duke University have involved identifying cards which the subject cannot see. On the surface, this seems a fair enough test. Yet, since no one had the remotest idea of how ESP operates, conclusions drawn from this experiment are open to serious questions. Perhaps telepathy requires an emotional stimulus not present in a laboratory test. Perhaps the subject's struggle to guess correctly inhibits a natural power. Perhaps the physical conditions of the testing are not conducive to ESP. In other words, only the *positive* scores obtained at Duke show anything conclusive. We have entered a world so unknown that familiar scientific methods may be worthless.

The report of Eusapia's Milan sittings takes this unknown factor into account, and in this regard it makes much more sense than later evaluations of the medium. Other investigators, mostly English and American, held a simpler, more mechanistic view, insisting that if Eusapia could produce an apparent miracle in dimness, then she should be able to do the same thing in broad daylight, perhaps in the middle of a public square. Further, they claimed that straps, ropes, gags, and other physical restraints would have no debilitating effect on her power. They felt Eusapia should be undisturbed by the presence of observers beneath the table where she sat. However, the medium *was* disturbed and expressed her displeasure with Neapolitan bluntness.

The success of the Milan séances encouraged Professor Richet to arrange a second series at his home in 1894, this time with a different group of observers, the most distinguished of whom were the English physicist Sir Oliver Lodge and Professor Henry Sidgwick, first president of the Society for Psychical Research. Again Eusapia triumphed. Sir Oliver could find no explanation for what he saw except "the working of some external agency." Since Eusapia always fared better with gentlemen than with ladies, it is hardly surprising that the one doubting voice is that of Professor Sidgwick's wife, who alleged that all that took place could have been engineered by the medium herself if "she had had the use of her hands and feet."

But Sir Oliver and Richet are emphatic that Eusapia's limbs were restrained at all times. As in earlier séances, the table was levitated high off the floor in full light, but this time Eusapia had new marvels—or tricks?—to astonish the observers. A music box was hung from the ceiling by a string. Suddenly it wound itself, played a tune, then after a series of jerks and jiggles it fell to the floor, the string broken. A key in a door seven feet from the medium turned in the lock, seemed to take wings, and flew to the séance table, then was whisked back to the door, where it reinserted itself in its proper hole. This was not a trick worked from the outside, for Dr. Ochorowicz, stationed as a guard in the hall, heard the key turn and swore that no one approached the door.

Sir Oliver Lodge was not a credulous man. He attained knighthood because of major contributions to science and was an international authority on wireless telegraphy, electrons, lightning, and the atmosphere. Deeply shaken by his experience with Eusapia, he wrote:

> However the facts are to be explained, the possibility of the facts
> I am constrained to admit. There is no further room in my mind
> for doubt. Any person without prejudice who had had had the same

experience would have come to the same broad conclusion, *viz:* The things hitherto held impossible to do actually occur. . . . I concentrated my attention mainly on what seemed to be the most simple and definite thing, *viz:* The movement of an untouched object in sufficient light for no doubt of its motion to exist. This I have now witnessed several times; the fact of movement being vouched for by both sight and hearing. . . . The result of my experience is to convince me that certain phenomena usually considered abnormal do belong to the order of nature. . . .

Eusapia's fame spread quickly through international circles of psychical research and she became a celebrity. Even the general public became aware of her existence, mostly through attacks upon her written by "men of science" who had never observed the medium but were convinced that her reported achievements were absurd and impossible. As is usual in occult cases, the prejudices of both scientists and believers were monumental and unshakable.

In America members of the Lily Dale spiritualist colony, an occult Chautauqua which flourishes in upstate New York, spoke of her in awed tones as "the Divine Eusapia." (It is easy to guess the origin of the title: Sarah Bernhardt was then at the height of her fame in the United States.) Lily Dale cultists talked longingly of making pilgrimages to Naples, and doubtless a good many of them did. Eusapia was turning the Italian city into a spiritualist mecca.

By now the medium had acquired a reputation which seemed impregnable. But disaster lay just ahead in the form of Dr. Richard Hodgson, the doughty secretary of the American Society for Psychical Research. He was a man who prided himself on his ability to expose bogus mediums and had enjoyed great success in detecting fraud at séances in the United States. After studying Oliver Lodge's report on Eusapia, he took up the case as a personal challenge, writing a lengthy reply to Lodge in which he attempted to show how all the reported phenomena could **have** been produced by various tricks. Lodge was unimpressed and continued to insist that he had seen what he had seen.

When Hodgson persisted, arrangements were made for him and Eusapia to meet in England in 1895 for a series of séances at the home of Mr. F. W. H. Myers in Cambridge. Among other distinguished observers was John Nevil Maskelyne, the celebrated stage illusionist whose specialty was feats of levitation. No doubt Maskelyne was especially curious about a performance Eusapia had given in Milan in 1892. On that particular evening, while Professors Lombroso and Richet were restraining Eusapia's hands, the medium complained of mysterious and painful pressure under her arms. Suddenly her familiar spirit, John King, spoke through her lips, saying, "Now I will bring my medium upon the table." Richet and Lombroso gasped to see the chair with Eusapia seated in it rise gently into the air, place itself atop the table, then descend to its former position. Lombroso might not have believed his own eyes had not the same thing happened again a few evenings later!

(It might be noted here that the ghosts of John and Katie King far outdid John Nevil Maskelyne in the field of levitation if we can believe an account printed in *Echo* magazine, June 8, 1871. The writer is anonymous and unfortunately we have only the *Echo*'s editor to vouch for his veracity. The story concerns a certain Mrs. Guppy, a lady who was levitated several times despite her great obesity. One night the author attended a séance and among other phantoms contacted were the famed John and Katie King. The sitters were not only skeptics, but were in a "merry mood," and one of them jokingly requested the Kings to bring stout Mrs. Guppy to the séance room, hardly a serious suggestion since at the moment Mrs. Guppy was known to be at her home three miles away. "While the company were laughing at the absurdity of the idea, there was a loud bump followed by shrieks and exclamations. A match was struck and there in the center of the table stood Mrs. Guppy, an account-book in one hand, a pen in the other, and apparently in a state of trance."

The lady's distrait condition is not to be wondered at, since she had been transported through the air at a speed of a hundred and twenty miles per hour. "The idea of her being concealed in the room is as absurd as the idea of her acting in collusion with the media.")

If John Nevil Maskelyne hoped to observe such wonders at Eusapia's séances in Cambridge, he was doomed to disappointment. The sittings proved to be a fiasco. At first nothing at all happened and then the medium, according to observers, was repeatedly detected in fraud. In every case the trickery involved Eusapia's freeing a hand or foot which was supposedly under firm control and using it to perform what Myers described as "marvelous feats of prestidigitation which could only have been learned through years of systematic trickery." There were, however, a few cases where phenomena occurred while restraint of her limbs was absolute. "She must have used her head," the experimenters declared, somewhat vaguely—and the double meaning of their remark is unintentional.

Dr. Hodgson was gleeful over his victory, and his report has an "I-told-you-so" tone that is annoying after the passage of seventy-five years. Although fraud should certainly be exposed, it is a pity that Eusapia came to grief at the hands of such a man as Hodgson. His writings reveal him as an unlikable smart aleck, waspish and pompous.

It would seem that such an exposure would spell the end of Eusapia's career, would discredit her utterly. But a talented medium is usually able to survive one and even several convictions for trickery; the faith of the faithful remains unshaken. Perhaps this is not as illogical as it first appears. Eusapia's defenders, and they were many and prominent, pointed out that the Cambridge observers found exactly what they were determined to find. Hodgson, for one, had staked his reputation on exposing the medium, and exposure, not truth, was the object of the experiment. F. W. H. Myers, the host for the séances, wrote in the *Journal* of the Society for Psychical Research that "in several cases the impression first made on [our] minds was distinctly favorable," and goes on to say that fraud became apparent only after the investigators insisted upon changing the conditions of the demonstration.

This immediately raises the question of how far conditions can be set by investigators without affecting the medium's power. It had been known for years that Eusapia would resort to fraud when nothing was happening and a séance became dull. The "Divine Eusapia" was determined never to give a bad performance. She may well have been a "mixture of silliness and maliciousness," but a broad streak of vanity ran through her character, too.

She would also try trickery when control was lax, and her defenders pointed out that this condition existed at Cambridge. Sir Oliver Lodge and the score of Continental investigators who had studied Eusapia remained steadfast in their belief in her power, even though Professor Sidgwick, President of the Society for Psychical Research, now reversed his position to fire a blast at Eusapia in the *Journal*, ending his remarks on a haughty note: "Inasmuch as trickery has been systematically practiced, apparently, by Eusapia Palladino for years, I propose to ignore her performances in the future as those of other persons engaged in the same mischievous trade are to be ignored."

But although Sidgwick might ignore the Neapolitan marvel, others would not. Far too much remained unexplained. The Cambridge exposure in no way accounted for such things as the medium's rising in her chair to the tabletop and down again. Certainly the freeing of a hand or foot would not accomplish such a feat. The story is hard to accept; it is even more difficult to believe that both Lombroso and Richet were lying or hysterical. The same is true of the key episode witnessed by Lodge and others. And these two incidents almost sum up the mystery of Eusapia; we are confronted with a dilemma, and one hesitates to impale oneself on either horn.

During the next twelve years at least a dozen tests and investigations were made in France and Italy, and among the many impressed observers were Nobel laureates Pierre and Marie Curie. Records are incomplete, and a few accounts seem positively lunatic. There are mad descriptions in which tables and chairs dance about the room, a vase speaks, furniture laughs, objects of all kinds whirl, wobble, and bounce.

Since experiments with electricity were much in vogue at the time, three Italian doctors arranged tests of Eusapia's power using a cardiograph, a Morse apparatus, wires, and rubber tubes. This bizarre demonstration, which also involved the use of a cabinet and the smoked surface of a *tambourine Marey* with an automatic pen, defies clarity in description and suffice it to say that the gentlemen were convinced that their instruments had registered "an unknown force."

In Paris, the Institut Générale Psychologique studied Eusapia for four years, reporting forty-three sittings, and at last came to the conclusion that although Eusapia was known to practice fraud, still they were unable to say that trickery was the extent of her power. They were puzzled, they could not explain her, they simply did not know.

It was not until the following year, 1908, that the medium met her greatest champion and publicist, psychical investigator Hereward Carrington.

Carrington, who was born in 1880 on the Isle of Jersey but spent most of his life in the United States, is an interesting figure, a type frequently found in occult research, a man who was not a pseudoscientist but an almost-scientist. He was a doctor of philosophy, a well-known lecturer, and the author of several popular books which today molder unread on library shelves—a pity since he was not only a keen observer, but a lively reporter of matters strange and curious. Psychical research has been called "the Dreyfus Case of science," and Carrington became a self-appointed Émile Zola, desperate to bring respectability to the occult. He devoted most of his life, and a great amount of money, to tracking down reports of odd phenomena. No journey was too long when his curiosity was whetted and there can be no question of his dedication to his cause.

Carrington's writings reveal intelligence and broad knowledge but, like many dedicated men, he was often carried away by his own zeal, thus creating the suspicion that he was something of a crackpot. For example, he became fascinated by a story that a certain herd of trained horses could talk and solve mathematical problems. Months of investigation followed, bringing him to the conclusion that although the story was greatly exaggerated, there is far more in the equine mind than is generally detected.

A well-brought-up, properly educated gentleman of conservative background, he nevertheless harbored a streak of eccentricity which prompted him to dart off onto tangents: far-fetched explanations of comets and meteorites, original but preposterous theories about the source of human life, and diatribes against Sigmund Freud which are almost incoherent with outraged sensibility. (Later he modified his view of psychoanalysis.) Carrington was devoted to the outlandish, and relished tales of psychological peculiarity. An example of this fascination is his report on "sympathetic manias."

> In the fifteenth century in a German nunnery a nun fell to biting her companions. In the course of a short time, all the nuns of this convent were biting each other. The news of this infatuation among the nuns soon spread, and it passed from convent to convent through the greater part of Germany, principally Saxony and Brandenburg. It afterwards visited the nunneries of Holland and at last the nuns had the biting mania even as far as Rome.

In 1908 the British Society for Psychical Research, after several angry debates, decided to launch yet another investigation of Eusapia, determined this time to establish the truth once and for all. A committee of three of its "most skeptical investigators" was sent to Italy, and Hereward Carrington was named one of the trio. His credentials as a skeptic were not, perhaps, first rate;

nevertheless, he was an expert on the tricks used by bogus mediums, and, being knowledgeable, he was hard to dupe. His companions were the Hon. Everard Feilding and Mr. W. W. Baggally, an amateur conjurer versed in the skills of stage illusion.

Feilding, the senior member of the committee, was for many years secretary of the Society for Psychical Research and brought a great deal of social prestige to that office, since he was the son of Lord Denbigh and brother of the Earl of Denbigh. He had an adventurous career in exposing charlatans of the occult and two of his cases (not exposures) are well worth brief mention. In 1911, Feilding investigated the case of Abbé Vachère, a French priest who owned a picture upon which fresh blood repeatedly and mysteriously appeared. This gory puzzle continued year after year, and when Feilding had the liquid analyzed his worst suspicions were confirmed. It was not only blood, but human. No explanation was ever found. During the course of another investigation, in Transylvania in 1914, Feilding became the victim of a jinn who was haunting the house of an attorney. Once a four-foot pole hurled itself at him from the corner of a room, a glass fell at his feet, and a rusty knife was hurled into a room where he was writing. By hypnotizing the attorney's wife, Feilding discovered that this lady was somehow involved in these goings-on. Then World War I cut short his stay in Transylvania, and the story of the jinn was left without a proper ending.

Feilding and Carrington arrived in Naples on a rainy day in 1908, armed with letters of introduction (which Eusapia could not read) from the staff of the Paris Institut Générale Psychologique. The two gentlemen (Mr. Baggally was delayed several days) found their way through a labyrinth of streets, alleys, and piazzas to the medium's house, a small apartment up three flights of rickety stairs. The visitors were greeted by Eusapia's husband, whom Carrington describes as "young and handsome" (Eusapia would have been in her mid-fifties then) and while awaiting the medium they inspected an impressive collection of autographed photos of celebrities, Eusapia's clients and admirers. Then the lady herself entered:

> Her charm and magnetism were truly extraordinary. Though unlettered, she possessed a keenness of mind, an alertness, a scintillation, a personal charm and magnetism quite unique and unrivalled. Whenever Eusapia entered a room she was sure to be the centre of attraction and interest. Her bright, flashing eyes seemed to emit streams of living fire; her whole form radiated magnetism; her conversation was so witty and so pungent that it often required an intellect of no mean order to keep up with it. . . . Arrangements were soon completed for a series of sittings to be held in our rooms at the Hotel Victoria, and we left. . . .
>
> How different a picture was presented to us by this same Eusapia at the conclusion of our first séance: weak, drawn, ill, nauseated, hysterical, deeply lined about the face, physically and mentally ill . . . such was the wreck of her former self which we perceived. . . . Hardly able to walk, she leaned heavily on us for support. All her energy had vanished; her memory was gone, likewise her interest in everything, her magnetism, her vitality. She seemed to have actually lost weight during the proceedings (experiments subsequently proved that she actually did so at times). . . . We saw her drive off, a broken, shrivelled old woman. . . .
>
> Yet the next day, when we again called upon her, she was practically as vivacious and lively as ever: a night's rest seemed to have restored her completely. We learned that Eusapia's powers, vital in character, seemed to accumulate as the days passed . . . and particularly at night . . . and were expended during a séance with prodigious rapidity and extraordinary force.

What did Carrington observe during the séances that impressed him so profoundly? Telekinesis (or the presence of poltergeists?) was dramatically demonstrated. The table rose in the air, cold breezes swept the room while the sitters heard raps and the ghostly playing of musical instruments. There were eerie materializations, half-formed faces and bodies shimmering in the dimness. Modeling clay was placed some distance from the medium and impressions of hands and facial features appeared upon it.

The small table, which had been placed inside the cabinet, climbed up of its own accord on to the séance table. . . . It came up at an angle of about forty-five degrees and, while it was endeavoring to clamber up on the séance table by a series of jerks, I placed my hand upon its surface and pressed downward in an attempt to force it to the floor. I experienced a peculiar elastic resistance, however, as though the table were strung on rubber bands and was unable to force it downward. I continued this struggle for several seconds, then yielded and allowed the table to clamber on to our séance table which it almost succeeded in doing. While this was happening, we verified, several times, that our control of head, hands, elbows, feet and knees was secure.

Carrington, on the lookout for fraud, was surprised that the most striking demonstrations took place when the medium was absolutely immobile.

When she was fidgety the phenomena were weaker. . . . When the head of the medium was resting on my shoulder and every part of her body was passive and adequately controlled, the most startling occurrences were witnessed, sometimes at great distance from her; where she could not possibly have reached even were her hands and feet freed; and when there was a clearly lighted space between her body and the objects . . . in which everybody could see that nothing visible existed.

These tests, like the Milan sittings, suggest some undignified pictures, and it is clear that Eusapia endured much for her art: "When [her power] was strong, the phenomena would begin at once and nothing we could do would prevent them. We might tie her with ropes, encase the legs in wooden cones, etc. . . . nothing mattered."

One example of Eusapia's performance will show why Carrington became a convert whose faith never diminished. At the end of the second séance, a curtained cabinet with a mandolin inside it was placed in the room at the Victoria Hotel. The medium stood a foot or so from the cabinet, its closed curtains behind her. As an added barrier, a small table was turned on its side and put between the mandolin and the curtains. While Carrington and Feilding watched, and there was ample light, Eusapia began to wiggle her fingers. Suddenly the mandolin began to play, its strings twanged in exact synchronization with Eusapia's "plucking." Carrington and Feilding searched the floor for hidden wires, they passed their hands between the medium and the cabinet, and they detected nothing. Eusapia, perhaps bored by their efforts, took one of Carrington's hands and holding it palm upward "picked" on it; to Carrington's astonishment (and one suspects to his delight) a mandolin string responded instantly each time she touched him. Although they were in their own hotel room, the two men opened the cabinet and closet, looking for a possible intruder. They found no one.

This demonstration, although impressive to witnesses, was not typical. Eusapia's familiar spirits were frequently neither musical nor gentle. On one occasion, when Eusapia was securely held hand and foot, Carrington attempted to crawl into the cabinet and did seize the small table which was resting therein. He instantly found himself in a wrestling match with an invisible roughneck of a poltergeist which, after a brief but fierce struggle, hurled both the table and the astounded investigator out of the cabinet—no mean feat, since Carrington writes with pardonable pride that he "had always been considered quite athletic and done much boxing, etc. in my younger days." Later he could console himself that he was not the only one worsted by Eusapia's muscular phantoms. When the medium visited New York Mr. S. S. McClure, the renowned editor and publisher of *McClure's* magazine, attempted to approach the cabinet and was violently ejected by what he described as "two hands placed on my chest." The unfortunate publisher was knocked halfway across the room in the presence of several witnesses, and Eusapia herself can hardly be charged with the assault since there was a brightly lighted space nearly two yards wide between her and Mr. McClure. Carrington and McClure, however, got off lightly compared to one victim of the pugnacious Palladino ghosts: Professor Flammarion reports that during one Paris séance an intrepid observer opproached the "spirit cabinet" and attempted to present it with a music box. His generosity was rewarded by having the box snatched from his hand and hurled back at him, wounding his cheek beneath the left eye. (If this was the ghost of John King, we must conclude that the old buccaneer was unregenerate even on the Other Side.)

Eusapia's phantoms were not always so belligerent. When in good humor they could be delightful and entertaining. Professor Flammarion's wife, a lady skeptical of all psychic phenomena, attended a test séance with her friend, Madame Brisson. Both ladies were rather bored until

> . . . all of a sudden the curtain behind Eusapia began to shake and move gracefully back as if lifted by an invisible curtain band . . . and what do I see? The little table on three feet, and leaping, apparently in high spirits, over the floor at the height of about eight inches, while the guilded [*sic*] tambourine is in its turn leaping gaily at the same height above the table, and noisily tinkling its bells.
>
> Stupefied with wonder, quick as I can pull Madame Brisson to my side, and, pointing with my finger at what is taking place, 'Look!' said I.
>
> And then the table and the tambourine began their carpet-dance again in perfect unison, one of them falling forcibly upon the floor and the other upon the table. Madame Brisson and I could not help bursting out into laughter; for, indeed, it was too funny!

Although Carrington was no physical match for the spirits Eusapia conjured, he did not lack courage. During one séance, while Baggally and Feilding restrained Eusapia, he climbed atop the séance table—a risky venture since the table often leaped into the air and moved as far as eight feet across the room before hitting the floor with a bang. Poised atop it, Carrington held one end of an accordion and, stretching as far as he could, he pressed the other end of the instrument against the cabinet curtains behind Eusapia. A mysterious "hand" seized it and began to play a sort of duet with the investigator, this concert taking place about five feet above the medium's head. Had an undetected confederate, perhaps a black-clad midget, somehow crept into the cabinet? The room was locked and searched thoroughly both before and after the séance. Furthermore, this feat was not performed in Eusapia's house, where there might have been a sliding panel, a trap door, or another secret device. The demonstration, like all others in this series, took place at the Victoria Hotel, where there was no chance of Eusapia's smuggling in an accomplice or setting up some mechanical means to trick the observers.

During these sessions, the three investigators were fascinated by the "cold breeze," a strong emission of chilly air seeming to come from the childhood scar above the medium's left temple. At times it also issued from her kneecap, but the prudery of the age prevented Carrington from studying Eusapia's knee as thoroughly as he may have wished. The breeze from her temple was noted by a dozen witnesses in several countries, and whatever its true source, it clearly had existence outside the imaginations of the witnesses. Professor Münsterberg, who did not believe in Eusapia's powers, was sure the breeze had reality but suggested it was produced by some gadget concealed in Eusapia's clothing; such a device was never discovered. Others asserted that the medium subtly puckered her lips and blew, a sort of respiratory ventriloquism. However, one investigator clapped his hand over Eusapia's mouth and at the same time pinched her nostrils, and despite this suffocation of the medium the breeze blew unabated.

Not only did winds seem to emanate from her body, but gales billowed curtains in the séance rooms and sudden icy draughts chilled the spectators. To spiritists, Spiritualists, and some Theosophists this would suggest the presence of *Elementals*, occult beings who traditionally take the form of a cold wind. *Elemental* is a shorter term for Elementary Spirit. They are not ghosts, having been born disembodied and remaining in that state forever. (Many Theosophists disagree, identifying Elementals with *Shells*, the "astral remains" of corrupt humans who linger at the scenes of their evil pleasures long after earthly death. They haunt ancient castles where murders were perpetrated; the *Shells* of highwaymen lurk on certain deserted roads at night. They are especially prevalent during the dark of the moon.) The majority of occultists give Elementals a rather low social rating, relegating them to a ghetto existence in the spirit world. They rank far below angels, considerably below human souls, and are only a little superior to demons and imps, if, indeed, they are not actually members of the diabolic family. Although many people have written extensively about Elementals, no one seems to have had a genuine interview with one, and so the whole classification is scholastic and arbitrary.

Eusapia cast no light on the question of Elementals, for she would not identify the mysterious winds. Curtains fluttered, doors banged, and sitters shivered, but as far as the medium was concerned the forces were simply there; she could offer no explanation.

Hereward Carrington, the "skeptical investigator," was so overwhelmed by what he saw in Naples that he soon became Eusapia's defender and publicist, proclaiming her miraculous powers in a series of magazine articles, lectures, and eventually in a book. He was convinced that after years of searching he had at last found in Eusapia the proof incarnate of true mediumship, and in 1909 conceived the idea of bringing her to the United States where doubting Yankees could see this marvel for themselves. The trip was planned solely in the interest of science; there was no attempt to exploit Eusapia for profit and undoubtedly the visit cost Carrington a large amount of money.

By now Eusapia was certainly no stranger to testing. She had been a subject of scrutiny for twenty years, submitting to investigations which ranged from the sensible to the outlandish in Italy, England, France, Germany, Russia, and "other European countries" whose reports have apparently been lost. Carrington now arranged a series of sittings with members of the American Society for Psychical Research and, as a climax, séances for a group of professors at Columbia University.

Carrington had no premonition of what was soon to happen to Eusapia, but he might have reconsidered the American expedition if he had had as much faith in other mediums as he had in his Italian star. Not long before he announced his plan, a certain Mrs. Holland, who was a trance medium of some repute, warned the spiritualist world against Eusapia, declaring that the cause of spiritualism would soon receive a tremendous setback because of Eusapia's chicanery.

Mrs. Holland received inside information about the Italian woman's duplicity in a most unusual way. F. W. H. Myers, who had been host at Eusapia's unsuccessful Cambridge séances, had since died and Passed to the Other Side. Apparently not content with the scathing attack he had once made on Eusapia in the *Journal*, his ghost contacted Mrs. Holland while the lady was entranced, and said, "Palladia . . . Mrs. Eustace Lucas . . . Annie Bird . . . Euphronia . . . Katie King . . . Eustonia . . . Pallonia . . ."

Although reception was not at its best, it is clear enough that the phantom was speaking of Eusapia Palladino. "I am anxious. From an apparent trifle may rise the ruin of all we have been working for so long. . . . Materializing flowers we know all that of course, but it seems new to him [Carrington?] and he has a strange gift of credulity. . . . There may be raps genuine enough of their kind. . . . I concede the raps. . . . Poltergeist merely . . . but the luminous appearances, the sounds of a semi-musical nature . . . the flower falling on the table . . . trickery . . . trickery!"

The following is from Mrs. Holland's journal, written just after Myers' ghost again communicated with her at midnight on December 5. Eusapia was again the subject.

MYERS: She is no fool, far from it, but she has the power of be-fooling. . . . Wilson knows about it. Miss J. will be the best help in this case. . . . E.P. willing not to sit near her, but that can be easily overborne. . . . The trance condition is partially genuine, the manifestations are simply fraudulent. . . .

Ask her to allow you to secure each foot in a slight cardboard box. . . . She will refuse for the instep does most of the phenomena of raps and movement. . . .

Two nights later, on December 7, the ghost of the psychical researcher again communicated with Mrs. Holland in regard to his fear that Eusapia would give the entire occult movement a bad name. He reached her at eleven-thirty p.m.

MYERS: The lights are turned out and a screen is drawn before the fire. . . . E.P. does not care for the environment it is not sufficiently simpatica for her. If she wore soft felt shoes, there would be fewer imposing raps and cracks. The toes can do it inside the boot. . . .

Pockets . . . inner pockets will hold a surprising amount. . . . Surely lazy tongs have been superseded by something a little more modern.

Carrington undoubtedly read the Myers admonitions as reported by Mrs. Holland, since they were published in the *Proceedings* of the Society for Psychical Research. But heedless of the warning, or perhaps of the omen, he brought Eusapia to New York in December 1909.

Among those present at the first sitting were Professor Hugo Münsterberg, Professor Trowbridge of Princeton, and G. P. Dorr, a psychical researcher. All three gentlemen agreed that the two initial evenings were moderately successful. The table levitated in good light, then performed antics and gyrations which were impressive, although "less dramatic than the observers had hoped." (And at this point one wonders exactly *what* they hoped for.) Sensing the disappointment of her audience, Eusapia requested that the lights be lowered, and once this was done objects from the séance cabinet moved about, the curtains billowed, and some unearthly being apparently entered the room, for the observers were tweaked, pinched, and patted in a playful manner. However the dimness of the chamber made the performance "less than satisfactory."

On the third night a trap was laid for the medium. Professor Münsterberg was seated at Eusapia's left, controlling one hand and a foot. Meanwhile, a young man, an agent of the professor, crawled silently across the floor into the nearby cabinet. He crouched in the near-darkness for some time, then was astonished to discover Eusapia's left foot "fishing about for objects." When he seized her by the ankle, the medium let out an enraged bellow and, kicking wildly, upset the table.

The séance ended in consternation. Eusapia flew into a hysterical rage, and it is a pity that we have no verbatim record of the Italian imprecations she hurled at the observers. Given her character and background, they must have been expressive. Professor Münsterberg's confusion was almost as great as the medium's. He was positive he had constantly felt the pressure of Eusapia's left foot against his right. Later he declared in print that the medium must have freed her foot from its shoe and, strangely unnoticed, lifted her leg almost three feet in the air to ransack the cabinet while the weight of her empty shoe gave him the illusion of being in control. But the young man who grasped the offending foot was convinced it was shod. Although no explanation could be given for Münsterberg's illusion, Eusapia had suffered a major reverse.

Hereward Carrington, undaunted, soon arranged several informal sessions which attracted wide attention and did much to rehabilitate the medium's reputation. She was at her best. The phenomena were spectacular: winds, luminous mists, bobbing furniture, mysterious handprints in wax and clay. It was during this time that the outmatched Mr. S. S. McClure lost his wrestling bout with the spirit in the cabinet, but, apart from that assault, the phantoms were in an affectionate mood. Sitters felt themselves kissed and caressed, a courtship they seem to have

64

found startling but not unpleasant. Those who enjoyed, or at least sampled, this unearthly titillation reported their experience, arousing the dudgeon of Mrs. Finch and other puritan spiritualists. Eusapia was promptly denounced as a monster of vice; there were hints of orgies, although what actually took place during the séances seems less erotic than a grammar school hay ride. Apparently the medium had weathered the storm of publicity.

Then, in April 1910, Eusapia's American farewell performance brought another disaster. The scene was the home of Professor Lord of Columbia University, a wily savant who was determined to unmask Eusapia. Unknown to her, he planted two spies beneath the séance table, where they were hidden by its long cloth. Lurking there, surrounded by a forest of human legs, they waited for the medium to make a false move. (Their subsequent report, published in *Collier's Weekly*, does not dwell on what they endured for the sake of science that night, but the gentlemen, crouched together in the heat and darkness under a small table, can hardly have been comfortable.) For a long time nothing happened, then the unsuspecting Eusapia managed to free a bound foot and used it to agitate the table. At this point the gathering, like its December predecessor, broke up in a tumult of accusations, wails, and curses that would have shocked a Neapolitan longshoreman. The press made much of the medium's exposure; the scoffers appeared to have won the field, and one has the feeling that Professors Lord and Münsterberg took pride in the fact that a simple Yankee ruse had revealed what the best investigators of France and Italy had failed to uncover in nearly twenty years of observation. Eusapia, who appears to have made no printable comment, sailed for Naples, her reputation shattered. The Myers-Holland prophecies seemed fulfilled.

Few people at the time gave any serious attention to Hereward Carrington, who was saying, in effect, "So what's new?" Eusapia's willingness to resort to fraud had been common knowledge for years. As early as the Milan sittings, observers noted that she was a slippery character and, given a chance, would happily practice a little manual or pedal conjuring. Although hailed on two continents as "The Great Palladino" and "The Divine Eusapia," she remained at heart a neighborhood witch. When nothing occurred, she always attempted to impress her clients with manufactured "spirits." Failure was unthinkable. "Here lay her streak of vanity," says Carrington. "Herein lay her undoing."

The European investigators, notably Professors Lombroso and Flammarion, were well aware of her duplicity, and so was Sir Oliver Lodge. Still they found it impossible to believe that what they witnessed could have been produced by the medium herself, no matter how great her dexterity. They *saw* distant objects rise and float, they *felt* cold winds, they *heard* unearthly sounds with their own ears, and were convinced that "some unknown force was working." They were more impressed by Eusapia than by the Yankee ruse, and they remained so.

Although Eusapia lived another eight years, dying in 1918, the American trip was really the end of her career. She continued to give séances, was visited by roving reporters, and was often consulted by titled ladies who wrote descriptions of the experience. But the international testing was over, the scientific furor ended, and no doubt there were many sighs of relief: it was more comfortable to brush her aside than to examine her phenomena carefully.

Today her name is known only to occultists and to a few collectors of bizarre stories. Modern psychic research is almost entirely devoted to various facets of ESP, and those seeking to prove telepathy or any other psychic phenomena have a difficult enough task without the added embarrassment of any physical medium, least of all Eusapia. Despite the vast increase of interest in the occult, belief in physical mediumship is at a low ebb. Table-tipping, levitation, apports, the banging of doors, and the whipping of curtains are dismissed as childish tricks, unworthy of scientific attention. The few modern writers who mention Eusapia at all comment that she was "discredited in Cambridge and later in New York" and then ignore her altogether.

But was she totally discredited? Certainly she was disgraced. Yet when one examines her entire history, a gnawing doubt remains. William James says in *Memories and Studies:*

> *Falsus in uno, falsus in omnibus*, once a cheat always a cheat; such has been the motto of the English psychical researchers in dealing with mediums. I am disposed to think that, as a matter of policy, it has been wise. . . . But however wise as a policy, the Society for Psychical Research's motto may have been, as a test of truth I believe it to be almost irrelevant. . . . Man's character is too sophistically mixed for the alternative of "honest or dishonest" to be to be a sharp one.

Hereward Carrington put the matter more specifically:

> To attribute all she did (over more than eighteen years) to the few simple and clumsy tricks which were discovered here and which had been discovered years before in Europe is merely an insult to the intelligence and good sense of those eminent men of science who have worked over her case in Europe.

The most remarkable thing about Eusapia's story is how it strains our credulity in one direction or another. If we accept any of her apparent miracles, any of the unexplained manifestations of the séances, as genuine, all our rational ideas about the world are upset. Yet when we reject her totally, as most people will, a new set of problems arises.

If she was merely an illusionist, then she was among the world's greatest, certainly surpassing such artists as Harry Houdini and John Nevil Maskelyne, gentlemen who needed equipment and a barrier of space between themselves and an audience. Eusapia worked with sharp-eyed observers hanging onto her— or at least they thought they were hanging onto her. If she had any mechanical aids or devices they were minimal. One English witness claimed he saw a piece of thread between her teeth on occasion, and that is the extent of the evidence in that area.

Many of the "tricks" seem far too elaborate to be performed by the use of one foot, unless we grant the human foot abilities never demonstrated before or since. In trying to account for Eusapia in a rational way, we are reduced to saying that most of the witnesses were fools, liars, or both. And plainly they were not. This position is as untenable as any other.

The question comes back: "How did she do it?" And there is no answer.

Mrs. Piper

Unlike Eusapia Palladino, who charged headlong onto the scene, Leonora Piper makes such a quiet entrance that she is almost unnoticeable: a shy, self-effacing woman as wary of publicity as any other prim Bostonian. Spiritualists—and others —hailed her as proof of the soul's survival of physical death; skeptics found it safer to ignore her than to attack her. Attempts to expose her as a fraud ended in failure, and efforts to explain her peculiar power ended in confusion. Now, sixty years after her final séance, the least that can be said about Leonora Piper is that her case offers the most convincing and dramatic evidence for ESP ever recorded. And that is the *very* least. She was truly amazing.

The public's impression that mediums are colorful people is founded on fact. If occult practitioners share one common quality it is a flair for showmanship. A doubter might say that personal flamboyance is the stock in trade of charlatans; a true believer could retort that such vividness is actually inner power surging to the surface. Eusapia was perfectly cast for the medium's role: the dark, expressive features, the white forelock, the inborn sense of the dramatic. Daniel Dunglas Home was her male counterpart. His gaunt body appeared quite capable of miraculous elongation, and when one examines Home's portrait, it is easy to imagine that the Scottish medium's eyes, deep-set in hollow sockets, were just the eyes to see demons and poltergeists. As in the case of Palladino, observers found their glance "hypnotic," and the eyes of both mediums seemed to "flash fire."

Palladino, Home, and most of their rivals strike us as romantic figures. The Reverend Stainton Moses, if not romantic, was at least eccentric in manner and appearance. Even Mrs. Guppy, whom we last saw standing astonished in the middle of a séance table with her account book in hand, was impressive by sheer bulk and apparently had a redoubtable personality as well.

But Mrs. Piper, who outshone them all, was outwardly the world's most ordinary woman. One pictures her crossing the Boston Common, where she suddenly pauses to catch her breath; she was plagued by a dozen minor ailments, and shortness of breath was chronic with her. She carries her inevitable black umbrella in one hand and a shabby needlepoint bag in the other. Inside the bag are pill boxes, patent medicines, smelling salts to counter the "vapors," and very little money, for the world's greatest psychic medium did not profit by her talent. Her black shoes are sturdy, sensible, and high-buttoned. (We need not suggest that she wear felt slippers during séances. At sittings with Mrs. Piper we shall hear no "spirit raps" or other ghostly tappings. Indeed, we shall hear nothing except the scratch of her quill pen and, perhaps, the voices of the dead.) Her features are plain, her complexion ashen. Socially and educationally, she is above the local mill women, but it would be too flattering to call her middle class. The brown skirt and unadorned bonnet she wears give the impression of an underpaid schoolmarm. If we try to sum her up in a metaphor, she becomes a drab house sparrow slightly grayed by the factory smoke of Boston.

There is nothing extraordinary about our picture. But lurking in the background, just out of sight, there may be a pair of inconspicuous gentlemen, private detectives hired to shadow this harmless-looking woman. Mrs. Piper was frequently under surveillance. Her comings and goings were noted, her contacts observed, her mail scrutinized. No foreign spy was ever trailed more closely than Leonora Piper. At one period in her life she was a virtual prisoner of the Society for Psychical Research, led about without being told where she was and kept completely in the dark about her next destination.

THE NEW SPIRITUALISM

To understand Mrs. Piper's remarkable career it is necessary to see her against the background of the modern spiritualist movement. Spiritualism, as Leonora Piper came to understand it, is a serious religion with its prophets, philosophers, creeds, and articles of faith. It is splintered into so many sects and cults that generalizations about its tenets are risky, but usually spiritualism is overlaid with a veneer of Christianity. A spiritualist can attend a Methodist service on Sunday morning and a séance on Sunday night with no conflict of beliefs. Spiritualism, as the word suggests, concerns itself not only with invisible spirits (ghosts) but also with matters and values that are "spiritual" in the Christian sense of that term.

On the other hand, what is often called "spiritism" emphasizes the physical manifestations of occult forces: levitations, table-tappings, floating trumpets, and mysterious transportation. It is in no sense a religion. (The term also refers to a particular French cult of spiritualism, but that meaning is not used in these pages.) Spiritualism seeks to establish the survival of the soul and to communicate with the Other Side. Spiritism is more related to witchcraft and magic. Obviously, the two overlap at times, and the choice of term depends on which aspect of occult practice is emphasized.

Although spiritualism in various forms is an ancient faith, the modern movement is American in origin and dates back only to the mid-nineteenth century. Despite countless examples of fraud, excess, and at times sheer lunacy, to its followers it remains a matter of deepest conviction. Unhappily for these believers and most unfortunately for psychical research, the movement's genesis is traced back to three women who were tricksters of the cheapest variety.

Since the United States is so often called a materialistic society, it is odd that the four comparatively large and enduring religions the United States has contributed to the world are among the most mystical of all faiths. Christian Science, Mormonism, spiritualism, and Adventism (Seventh Day and otherwise) are diverse creeds, but all four stress the individual's direct contact with a greater power; three of them have no clergy in the usual sense, and all involve matters which, except to their followers, are decidedly miraculous. All four claim to be restatements of primitive Christianity by divine revelations, but all are quite untraditional, especially in the realm of mystical experience.

It is also odd that all four sprang up in the same corner of the United States, and three of them were extremely close neighbors both geographically and chronologically: Mormonism, Adventism, and spiritualism were founded within a fifteen-year period and within a few miles of each other.

The coming of the industrial revolution to America in the early nineteenth century brought—or coincided with—an era of unrest and agitation. As pioneers poured westward there was a general dislocation of family life and tradition. At the same time the sons and daughters of farmers were moving to new factory towns, finding there a different and far less settled way of life. Families were separated, a series of financial panics endangered or destroyed old fortunes, and—as in our own time—traditional values were questioned and upset. This restlessness and change was reflected politically in the election of Andrew Jackson to the presidency and the famous, rowdy invasion of the White House by "common men." The burgeoning Abolitionist movement excited radicals and alarmed conservatives.

In religion, this breaking up of the old society produced a wave of zeal and mystical fervor unknown in America for a century and a half. The age of Jackson was also the age of the great camp-meeting revivals, gatherings whose hysteria is described by Mrs. Trollope in her *Domestic Manners of the Americans*.

Nowhere was this fervor more prevalent than in an area of rural New York around the city of Rochester. At nearby Palmyra Joseph Smith claimed to have unearthed the famous golden plates of the new Mormon revelation in 1827, and three years later, after translating the plates with the aid of miraculous spectacles, he founded the Church of Jesus Christ of the Latter-Day Saints there. It is not surprising that Smith encountered extremes of acceptance and hostility among his neighbors, for the whole region was in religious ferment.

Less than a year after Smith established his church, William Miller, another rural New Yorker, uttered prophecies of the second coming of Christ and the consumption of the universe, prophecies which started the Millerite craze. The world was to end in 1843, and on the appointed night Miller's disciples gathered on a hilltop to welcome their arriving Lord with hymns and rejoicing, and, incidentally, to observe from afar the utter destruction of everyone outside their sect. At dawn they straggled back to their homes to face the ridicule of their neighbors. Their bitter disappointment was soon relieved by Miller, who recalculated, uncovered an error in his arithmetic, and now proclaimed the apocalypse for the following year. So convincing was the prophet that when the dread date arrived a good many people who did not fully expect the millennium nevertheless retreated to their cellars to spend the night in prayerful watching. When the world in all its wickedness survived, the Millerites were inconsolable, especially those who had given away their earthly goods in anticipation of wings and harps. Although the world did not end, neither did the Millerite movement. It flourished, giving birth to the Seventh Day Adventist Church and various Churches of God, most of which still retain practices usually associated with the occult—miraculous healings, prophecy, and physical possession by the Holy Ghost. The more radical and primitive cults of this order sometimes make headlines when their members are discovered passing venomous snakes from hand to hand in an Appalachian shanty. Modern snake-handlers do not call themselves Millerites and know nothing about the origin of their beliefs. But most of these sects, including the less extreme Remnant of the True Church of God, are theologically rooted in Miller's teachings, and some are direct offshoots of the fervid religious movement he created in the early 1840s.

During this same period, ghostly events at Watervliet, New York, foreshadowed the coming of spiritualism. A colony of Shakers, properly called the United Society of Believers in Christ's Second Coming, had been established there since 1776. For sixty years they lived their industrious lives in comparative quiet, practicing primitive communism and absolutely not practicing sexual relations, since reproduction was contrary to their belief. Then, in 1837, mysterious rappings of no discernible origin startled the Believers. They soon attributed these knocks and thumps to the spirit of their founder, the prophetess Ann Lee, who had died in 1784, and the colony decided that Mother Ann was attempting ghostly communication with her disciples.

The happenings at Watervliet are a perfect illustration of conditions that usually lead to outbreaks of occultism. In the early days, when the Shaker colony was thriving and making converts, the Believers showed no tendency toward spiritism. But when hard times came and the sect, unreplenished by the birth of children, showed signs of dying out, its members sought occult miracles.

The spectral communiqués from Mother Ann were repeated frequently during the next seven years and might have resulted in the earlier founding of spiritualism had the Shakers been less clannish and less isolated by their communistic mode of living and prohibition of sex. Nevertheless, Mother Ann's rappings did receive some publicity, and perhaps this is why modern spiritualism sprang up—or, more accurately, erupted—from this mystically fertile New York soil.

In December 1847, John D. Fox, his wife Margarete, and their two youngest children, Margaretta and Katie, took up residence in a modest frame house in the village of Hydesville. They were an undistinguished family, and John Fox, a Methodist farmer, attracted no special attention. Fox was not bothered by certain dark rumors concerning their new dwelling. For several years there had been reports of nocturnal disturbances there, and the neighbors harbored a vague misgiving that the place was haunted. During the first months, the Fox family slept soundly, although a few peculiar noises were heard at night. Then, in February, the sounds became distinct and sometimes alarming. On Friday evening, March 31, 1848, the tenants went to bed early. The familiar raps and thumps began almost at once, louder than ever, and Katie Fox, then age twelve, suddenly called out the words that were to mark the beginning of spiritualism: "Here, Mr. Splitfoot, do as I do!"

The phantom obligingly coordinated its rappings with the child's movements, and counted her silent motions by knocks. She summoned her mother, crying, "Look! It can see as well as hear!" Mrs. Fox, with great presence of mind, asked the invisible rapper if it knew the ages of her children, and a reply came promptly: fifteen raps for Margaretta, twelve for Katie.

The Fox family slept little that night. The neighbors were invited in to take part in a fascinating investigation, and very quickly a communication system was established: rapping for yes, silence for no. This method soon evolved into an alphabet system, and it was ascertained that the mysterious presence was the ghost of a peddler named Charles Rosna, who, for the sake of his meager possessions, had been murdered on the premises by a previous tenant.

Later on, when the Foxes dug up the cellar, they disinterred such grim relics as hair, teeth, and bones. No proper examination of these objects was made, and there was no real evidence that a murder had taken place. This did not matter. Spiritualism was exactly what the world craved at the moment, and the raps heard

74

in Hydesville were soon reproduced in a dozen countries. The local impact was tremendous. Mrs. Fox and her daughters became instant celebrities. Soon afterward, young Margaretta went to visit her married sister, Mrs. Fish, in Rochester, and apparently the ghost followed her, for rappings immediately began in the home of Mrs. Fish, attracting so much attention that the crossroads village of Hydesville was robbed of its rightful place in history: modern spiritualism is attributed to the "Rochester rappings," not the Hydesville ghost.

Meanwhile, Katie Fox visited Auburn, New York, and there, too, the spirits were promptly aroused. Counting off the alphabet in response to spectral signals became a craze in the town.

Mrs. Fox, Katie, and Margaretta turned professional on the spot. So did Mrs. Fish, who claimed mediumship by heredity and demonstration. In fact, Mrs. Fish, who was the last of the Fox sisters to enter upon this career, was also the last to leave it. She maintained a profitable circle after the rest of the family had retired, and her successive marriages to a Mr. Brown and then a Mr. Underhill did not conflict with her career.

Although the Fox women had broken the ground, they were not left alone in the field. Two ladies who heard the Auburn tappings went into the séance business, and many mediums, both male and female, announced themselves in Rochester. Spiritualism reached epidemic proportions. Within three years after the Hydesville sensation there were more than a hundred mediums in New York City and between fifty and sixty séance groups assembling regularly in Philadelphia.

The Fox sisters were venerated and, despite stiff competition, they reaped the most in honor and profit, even though their first exposure as fakes came as early as 1851 at the hands of three doctors who observed public séances in Buffalo. The doctors denounced the rappings as fraud executed by cracking the knee joints, and not long afterward the girls themselves admitted this was so. Furthermore, they explained something the investigators had overlooked. Margaretta and Katie had also developed the art of "toe-cracking." The girls were self-confessed tricksters and, worse, they were instructors of fakery who gladly taught their youthful friends the skills of charlatanism.

One might forgive the girls' duplicity and wish them nothing worse than a sound spanking had they stuck to such romantic and harmless adventures as communicating with the ghost of a murdered peddler. But they were not merely self-dramatizing juveniles. The Fox sisters were greedy little creatures, utterly heartless and amoral, who sought profit by giving false consolation to the bereaved. They capitalized on the grief of widows and mothers who had lost their children. They were the first American mediums-of-prey; unfortunately they were not the last.

The complete exposure of the Fox sisters had little effect on the growing spiritualist movement. Unlike some other religions, spiritualism was not dependent on a single miracle or prophet. The Hydesville ghost was merely the match that lit the wildfire. Unformed beliefs and impulses toward spiritualism had been smoldering for a long time. Many intellectuals, especially in America, were spiritually homeless. They found the eighteenth-century apostles of reason, such as Voltaire and Thomas Paine, to be sterile. The Religion of Democracy, promised by the French Revolution and implied by what patriotic orators called "America's Great Democratic Experiment," was mocked by the rise of an industrial society. These intellectuals abhorred Catholicism and found no outlet for their religious yearnings in the crude Bible-thumpings of contemporary Protestant preachers. The ignorant circuit-riders and shouting revivalists who baptized thousands of hysterical converts in the shallows of rivers and lakes were repulsive to sophisticated minds.

It is small wonder that spiritualism found such prominent followers as Horace Greeley, William Lloyd Garrison, and the social reformer John Murray Spear, who was the leading Universalist minister of his area; among the converts were John W. Edmunds, a Supreme Court justice and former governor of New

York; Wisconsin's governor, N. P. Talmadge; and many other political figures, novelists, clergymen, and men of letters. Similar lists can be compiled for England and Europe. Elizabeth Barrett Browning and Victor Hugo used spiritualist automatic writing and indulged in such spiritist practices as table-turning and planchette experiments. (The planchette, from which the modern ouija board evolved, was named after the Frenchman who invented it in 1853. A small, triangular piece of wood was mounted on tiny casters with a pencil attached, point downward. When human hands were placed on the wood, spirits were supposed to produce automatic writing. The modern ouija board, with its semicircle of letters, produces messages far easier to decipher than the scrawls of the planchette.)

Percy Bysshe Shelley seems to have anticipated the invention of the planchette: in the 1820s he tried automatic writing and not long before his death in 1828 he claimed to have seen his own wraith. So did Goethe in Germany, although the extent of the poet's belief is not known.

Spiritualism offered the appealing promise of direct communication with departed loved ones. This remains its most powerful attraction but does not entirely account for its instant popularity and rapid spread across the world. In its early days, it was decked with the trappings of mesmerism and electricity, two fascinating "scientific" phenomena about which little was known. Electricity appeared to have infinite potentialities; mesmerism suggested unknown corridors of the mind, and when combined in an "Electrical Mesmeric Trance" they were irresistible.

The first few years of the movement produced no great mediums. Daniel Dunglas Home was the earliest, and his amazing demonstrations of levitation, physical elongation, and fire-ordeal did not reach their height until 1860. Nor was there a Mrs. Piper to give the new faith an evidential basis. But there were multitudes of practitioners, such as farmer Jonathan Koons with his menagerie of Ohio ghosts. Borrowing a bit of drama from Pentecostal Protestantism, in 1854 two mediums of Keokuk, Iowa, began to utter in "tongues," speaking Latin which could be verified, Indian speech which no one knew, and a German jargon surprisingly identified by the mediums themselves as "Swiss."

American spiritualism quickly developed theology, philosophy, technique, science, and an historical heritage. The Shawnee Prophet, a brother of Chief Tecumseh, who lived from 1768 until 1837, was rediscovered and became America's legendary seer. The "far-seeing warrior" was said to have received messages directly from the spirit world without the aid of a Control, and while entranced he predicted the solar eclipse of 1806. His powers, whatever they may have been, derived from his tribal religion and had no connection with spiritualism; nevertheless, the new believers claimed him as their own. The immense popularity of the Shawnee Prophet may explain why Indian maidens, warriors, chiefs, and medicine men appear so frequently as Controls. Indeed, there are enough Indian ghosts in occult history to overcrowd a large reservation.

To provide a Biblical basis for their beliefs, early spiritualists cited the Witch of Endor, the appearance of Gabriel to the prophet Daniel in a vision, and Joseph's interpretation of dreams. Some claimed that Jesus practiced automatic writing, pointing to John 8:6: "But Jesus stooped down, and with his finger wrote on the ground, as though he heard them not."

Andrew Jackson Davis, the "Poughkeepsie Seer" whom we encountered in connection with the New Motor, was not only the Thomas Aquinas of modern spiritualism but also its John the Baptist. His volume *The Principles of Nature, Her Divine Revelations, and a Voice to Mankind*, a collection of trance discourses published in 1847, was written before the Rochester rappings were heard, and thus he is the forerunner of the Fox sisters and helped pave the way for their success. His complete works run to no less than twenty-six volumes.

Although the spiritualist movement continued strong, the initial rage soon abated. There was far too much revealed fraud and too little hard evidence. Crudities easily swallowed by the natives of Hydesville could not withstand the least scrutiny. Sharper intellects and keener investigators entered psychical research, and although they discovered many unexplained events and phenomena, the excess of trickery and foolishness was so great that truth-seeking investigators had almost concluded that to scratch a medium was to find a charlatan.

Daniel Dunglas Home was the only prominent practitioner never detected in trickery up to this time. Home's achievements were astounding—perhaps *too* astounding. There is something preposterous about a man who hovers outside windows in mid-air, who handles fire unsinged. Marvel though he was, Home's case lacked the elements needed to give respectability and seriousness to spiritualism.

Such was the state of affairs when, in 1884, Leonora E. Piper, plagued by ailments including the aftereffects of an accident, decided to consult a psychic healer in Boston.

MRS. PIPER BECOMES ENTRANCED

Leonora Piper's first venture into the occult was neither satisfying nor successful. The professional clairvoyant whom she consulted gave her little relief from her aches and pains. Yet she felt some power, a disturbing but attractive force, beckoning her and she returned to the psychic gentleman a second time. While seated with other clients, she suddenly felt herself drawn into a state of suspended animation. The furniture appeared to whirl around her, her mind reeled, and, collapsing on the table, she fell into a deep trance, apparently hypnotic. Her body convulsed, she groaned, mumbled, then began to speak—but not with her own voice.

An alien being had seized the lady, blotting out her personality, and although the mouth was Mrs. Piper's, the words and inflections were those of another presence, a dead girl with the surprising name Chlorine who, less surprisingly, proved to have Indian ancestry. (Since Mrs. Piper was a genius, it is a pity that her first Control should turn out to be Chlorine. Of all trance personalities none are quite such clichés as Indian maidens.) This first trance was primitive compared to Mrs. Piper's later work, and Chlorine, though less taciturn than many of her race, proved rather unresponsive. Still, it was an impressive demonstration, and Mrs. Piper, to her own complete astonishment, attained full-fledged mediumship by one initial plunge into the occult void. Hereafter, she was able to invoke the entranced state by her own will, a trance so deep that every trace of the everyday Mrs. Piper vanished. She was unaware of events that happened while she remained in this state and had no memory of them afterward. She was examined repeatedly by physicians, psychologists, and even vaudeville mesmerists, and their verdict was unanimous: Leonora Piper, as her conscious self, became utterly submerged.

Chlorine was soon ousted as a Control, and during the next four years a number of spirits possessed Mrs. Piper, vying to hold their positions, as though a ghostly struggle were being waged on the Other Side. They were spirits of prominent people, among them the actress Mrs. Siddons, Henry Wadsworth Longfellow, and Johann Sebastian Bach. Some observers believed that the sharp physical pain and the racking of body that Mrs. Piper suffered while sinking into a trance was caused by conflicting spirits crowding upon her in a battle for possession. Eventually the more celebrated ghosts were overcome by the persistent shade of a Frenchman named Dr. Phinuit. Phinuit was to remain with her a long time.

In early séances, Mrs. Piper gave a number of remarkable demonstrations of "psychic knowledge," but records were poorly kept and the investigations superficial. At this period she was dealing mostly with believers who were easily satisfied. But this situation changed in 1885, when she became a subject for study by the philosopher-psychologist William James of Harvard. James, favorably impressed by his first findings, introduced Mrs. Piper to Dr. Richard Hodgson of the American Society for Psychical Research in 1887, and from then until 1911 examination of

Mrs. Piper was unceasing. Paid detectives often trailed her, volunteers watched her, her utterances were checked and double-checked, and every facet of her private life was scrutinized for evidence of fraud. No fraud was discovered; Mrs. Piper was integrity itself.

William James began his study with an impartial attitude, even though his patience had been sorely tried in the past by fakers and zanies. Dr. Hodgson, on the other hand, was an out-and-out skeptic. He had exposed one humbug after another and although he had not yet become the bane of Eusapia Palladino's career, the doctor was already known as the curmudgeon of spiritism. His doubts about *all* mediums, nurtured by experience, went beyond suspicion.

One can appreciate Hodgson's point of view. The techniques of fraud in séances had developed far beyond the toe-cracking and knee-cracking of the Fox sisters. Such fakes as the Davenport brothers had been able to impress the public for years. The two Davenports, Ira and William, staged their spurious séances in theaters or large halls and the presentation resembled a vaudeville act. They sat face to face in a wooden cabinet resembling a topless wardrobe chest and invited any two men of the audience to bind them securely. Musical instruments were then placed in the cabinet, half-doors were closed, and the lights were dimmed. Soon would come the tones of trumpets and banjos while glimmering hands waved at the spectators. The trickery of the Davenports was easily duplicated by a number of stage performers and the pair came to real grief when, in Liverpool, they were tied with a special "Tom Fool's knot" which foiled the spirits completely. The audience rose up in a mob and the tricksters had a narrow escape. Their act would have been harmless enough had it not been decked out in the guise of religion. (When the Davenports made their English tour, they took along a chaplain, the Reverend J. B. Ferguson, whose task was to dispel doubt and inspire confidence.)

The Brothers Davenport were by no means the worst of the

frauds rampant in both England and America at the time when Mrs. Piper entered spiritualism. One of the most slippery mediums was William Eglinton, whose demonstrations of spiritwriting on slates baffled experts for years, although early in his career he suffered an enormous mortification when a sudden search of his portmanteau uncovered false whiskers, hair, and strips of muslin identical with those clipped from a supposedly materialized spirit.

It is no wonder that when James and Hodgson began their study of Leonora Piper they were a pair of skeptical gentlemen. But as time went by they were astonished to realize that here, at last, was not only an honest woman but a talented one.

They first turned their attention to Dr. Phinuit, the Control, and the Hodgson-James reports reveal the strangeness of Mrs. Piper's trance personality. Phinuit, unlike the spirits who invested Mrs. Piper later, communicated orally, employing the medium's mouth but using a French manner of speaking English and his own masculine voice. Whether Phinuit was a spirit or an emergence of Leonora Piper's subliminal self, he appeared to have an independent existence within the trance and a vivid, definite personality. Sitters were disconcerted by his presence. They felt an uncanny sense of Phinuit's Frenchness, individualism, and above all his masculinity, although the medium herself was the epitome of the feminine.

The James-Hodgson method of investigation seems foolproof. They would assemble a group of sitters who were unknown to the medium and were never introduced to her by their real names. No indication of their background was given. The séance then consisted of conversations between Phinuit and the anonymous sitters, the spectral doctor chatting about members of a visitor's family, often reciting full details of name, relationship, character, occupation, dress, and appearance. There was no distinction between the living and the dead. The personal details about deceased relatives were reported with accuracy equal to Phinuit's revelations about the sitters themselves.

The doctor liked to hold the floor and was intensely jealous of his post as Mrs. Piper's Control. Usually he insisted upon being sole narrator; rarely, he permitted another spirit to speak directly through his medium. Phinuit was at times inclined to be rude. He interrupted often and spoke with a Gallic directness and bluntness which were utterly foreign to Mrs. Piper's natural personality.

A striking aspect of the trances was the relationship between Mrs. Piper's clairvoyance (or telepathy) and physical objects. If something belonging to a person being discussed—a letter, pin, or brooch for example—was pressed against the medium's forehead ("offered to Phinuit"), communication was greatly strengthened. The doctor then spoke rapidly, releasing a flood of copious detail. At times the Control would become confused, would ask questions, and go off onto "fishing expeditions," seeking to make a correct hit when the facts eluded him.

Strangely, there was often uncanny accuracy in the midst of a major mistake. At one séance Phinuit gave a graphic description of a sitter's father, but the name he attributed to the subject was not the name of the father but the name of the sitter himself, who had been introduced to Mrs. Piper under an alias.

After two years of intensive study, verification and checking, Hodgson and James recommended that the British Society for Psychical Research invite the medium to England. Since she had never been abroad, her ignorance of the country and the people she would meet was assured and this made testing conditions ideal. She traveled there in 1889, was kept secluded on shipboard to prevent her making any contacts, and what happened upon her arrival sounds more like a kidnaping than a welcome. Oliver Lodge, then Professor of Physics at Liverpool and head of the committee to test Mrs. Piper, awaited her on the dock. He permitted her to talk to no one, but whisked her away by closed carriage to his own home, where every possible precaution had been taken. Photographs, letters, and personal papers had been locked away, no callers could get past the guarded doors, and even the servants were temporary replacements for the usual staff, since Lodge feared that a household worker might accidentally let slip some information to Mrs. Piper.

The lady was searched, both her luggage and her person. Then a group of absolute strangers was presented to her under assumed names. As soon as Mrs. Piper was entranced, Phinuit began to identify them one by one, revealing incidents, details, and occupations. The sitters were astounded. One correct hit after another piled up. Phinuit made a few mistakes and a few near-misses, but the over-all impression was amazing; he described homes and rooms, mentioned names of children, and even diagnosed ailments in the light of the subjects' past medical histories—histories Mrs. Piper could not possibly know.

Where could such information come from? Lodge, determined to find out, devised a test which has now become a classic case. He had twin uncles, Robert and Jerry, and the latter had died two decades earlier. Uncle Robert had been requested (by mail) to send Lodge some possession of the deceased Jerry and at the next séance a gold watch was "offered to Phinuit." The doctor spoke at once. "It belonged to your uncle." Then followed hesitations, false starts, then: "Uncle Jerry."

With Phinuit acting as interlocutor between Lodge and the uncle's ghost, Jerry cheerfully reminisced about boyhood events, mentioned a skin he once owned which he believed to be a snakeskin, recalling being nearly drowned in a creek, and confessing to the killing of a cat at a place known as Smith's Field. Lodge himself knew nothing of such incidents nor did anyone else who was present. He wrote Uncle Robert, requesting confirmation or denial, and the uncle replied at once that there had indeed been a snakeskin, but he could recall neither the cat nor the drowning. Even if the story ended there, it would be a triumph for Mrs. Piper. Out of a thousand possible names, she had said, "Jerry." Of many possible relationships, she immediately said, "Uncle." And a snakeskin is an unusual enough object to suggest more than a lucky guess.

84

But the story of Uncle Jerry was by no means over. A third uncle, Frank, came forward to announce that he clearly recalled the near-drowning, the death of the cat, and, yes, the name of the place had been Smith's Field.

Such uncanny accuracy could not be coincidental, yet there seemed no possibility that a secret accomplice had uncovered the information and coached the medium. Nevertheless, Lodge sent an investigator to the village where Uncle Jerry had lived to determine if the facts could be learned from old residents and if anyone had recently attempted to ferret out details of the family. The errand was fruitless, except in exonerating Mrs. Piper. This result was, in fact, predictable. James, Hodgson, and others had long ago made certain that Mrs. Piper had no acquaintances in England.

One cannot but wonder what the lady herself thought of all these investigations, the endless questioning of her honesty and probing into her private affairs. She seems to have endured it all with great patience, although she was rather bewildered at finding herself the center of so much attention. Since she herself could not remember what took place during the trances, it is understandable that she was less impressed than others were. She thought her English visit was "very nice."

At the end of the series of séances, Lodge, Walter Leaf, and F. W. H. Myers made a report to the Society. Aside from the startling story it tells, the document is interesting because it reveals the attitude of the investigators. They succeed in keeping their scientific aplomb, they strike the correct note of objectivity; yet there is an undertone of awe. The gentlemen had never before encountered anything like Leonora Piper.

Although the modest lady from Boston sailed through the investigation with flying colors, Dr. Phinuit fared badly. The report obliterates him as a separate individual of historical reality. The French doctor did not really speak French and accounts he gave of his earthly existence do not hang together. British physicians declared that Phinuit was often a brilliant diagnostician—

that is to say he agreed with them—but his medical knowledge was sketchy. It is suggestive that Phinuit's name seemed to be a variant of the name of the Control used by the Boston faith healer who initiated Mrs. Piper. The committee concluded that Phinuit was an *alter ego* of the medium, part of her subliminal self. (But the report, while demolishing the doctor, brings him oddly to life. The investigators were caught by the sense of Phinuit's presence, and the usage of "he" "him," and "the doctor" when Mrs. Piper is meant is often more than a convenient way to differentiate between the medium awake and the medium entranced.)

HOW DID SHE DO IT?

The "Uncle Jerry" test is typical enough of Mrs. Piper's work to merit a brief re-examination. The medium made seven bull's-eye hits in a row: the name, the relationship, the fact that Uncle Jerry was dead, the snakeskin, the near-drowning, the cat, and the exact name of the field. If we rule out spiritualism and ESP, we are reduced to only a few possible explanations:

1. *Lucky Guesses.* Such a run of luck is fantastic and impossible to accept.

2. *Secret Information.* Mrs. Piper knew nothing of England and had no connections there. She was guarded at every moment. Oliver Lodge decided to ask his uncle for "an object" on a sudden impulse. He himself did not know it would be a watch until it arrived. Also, since Lodge's hired sleuth, an experienced fact-finder, could not obtain the information, it seems unreasonable to believe that some unknown agent of Mrs. Piper's could.

3. *Fraud by the Investigators.* This seems as unlikely as coincidence. It would involve collusion among a great many prominent people who had no motive for dissembling and every reason not to. The Society for Psychical Research at this period can hardly be called prospiritualist. William Stainton Moses, an early member, resigned in a huff because he found the Society's attitude too rudely skeptical of professional mediums. Mrs. Henry

Sidgwick, wife of the Society's first president and herself no mean investigator, studied eight professional mediums during the years 1874 through 1886 and pronounced every one of them either fraudulent or mistaken. She reversed this opinion in the case of Mrs. Piper. Lord Rayleigh, who later won a Nobel Prize for physics, also studied Mrs. Piper and it is unthinkable that he was in collusion with her.

4. *Imagination or Suggestion.* The argument has been advanced that both uncles "remembered" because of later suggestion, that they were, in fact, mistaken. This objection, of course, applies only to the cat, the drowning, and the name of the field. No one seriously suggests that the uncles (and everyone else) merely imagined that the dead man's name was Jerry or that the watch belonged to him! Mrs. Piper's pronouncements about incidents and exact details were confirmed so often by so many different witnesses, that it is hard to believe that hundreds of skeptical imaginations were working overtime for her benefit.

The "Uncle Jerry" test defies all attempts at simple explanation. If Mrs. Piper had never given another séance, her place in psychical research would have been secure. But the first visit to England was only the beginning and by no means the greatest achievement of her career.

"NEVER SO UNCOMFORTABLE"

Unlike many mediums of her day, Leonora Piper was not a constant public performer. But when she did travel and appear in strange auditoriums before strange audiences, there were sometimes amazing results.

No doubt she also disappointed many of the spectators, people who identified mediumship with ghost shows and levitations. Tricks were beneath her and she would make no deliberate effort to please a crowd. Her mission, after all, was primarily religious. Mrs. Piper looked upon herself as a "bringer of glad tidings," not a performer in show business.

The more discerning members of her audience were astonished by what they heard. Their experiences in attending the medium were never forgotten, and they repeated them until the stories became family legends.

One such audience member was a Mr. Shaw, an inventor, a most practical man with a clear mind and a strong personality. His story, previously unrecorded, is typical of hundreds of Mrs. Piper's demonstrations.

Mr. Shaw had a document and other business papers which required the signature of a man who had disappeared. Leaving his own city, Shaw set out to track the man down and after difficulties found him in a cheap boarding house on the New Jersey coast.

The man had become an alcoholic and now lay in bed, suffering delirium tremens. Unaware of his companion or his surroundings, he constantly picked at the sheets, the pillow, and his own body as though removing imaginary vermin which seemed to crawl over him. For at least two days, Shaw waited patiently at the bedside, watching the ceaseless picking, hoping that a lucid moment would come. When the victim recovered slightly, Shaw whipped out his fountain pen and, guiding the weak hand, managed to obtain the needed signature.

The mission accomplished, Shaw began his homeward trip, which required an overnight stop in Washington. He learned, upon arriving in the capital, that Mrs. Piper was giving a public demonstration, and, having heard of the remarkable lady, decided to attend. When the call came for members of the audience to send small objects to the stage, Shaw, his curiosity aroused, sent up his fountain pen.

The medium, apparently in a very light trance, touched the pen, then, moaning, began to pick at herself, her fluttering hands running over her collar, her sleeves, the skirt of her dress in an uncanny imitation of the delirium tremens victim. Recoiling from the pen, Mrs. Piper announced that she had never been so uncomfortable in her life.

Shaw watched in amazement. There seemed no possible way for the medium to have known the pen's recent history—he alone knew about the man in the boarding house, yet he had just observed a re-enactment terrible in its accuracy. After the demonstration, Shaw returned home to tell his story, adding another bit to the legend of Mrs. Piper.

"G.P." RETURNS FROM THE GRAVE

A young friend of Dr. Hodgson, George Pelham (pseudonym for George Pellew), had once attended a sitting with Mrs. Piper. He was presented to the medium under an alias, and the séance was not especially notable. Mrs. Piper never knew she had met him, and she, in turn, could not have made any great impression on Pelham, for the young man remained a skeptic not just regarding spiritualism but about all religion. He had strong doubts about any existence after earthly life. This lack of any faith was a source of worry to his many friends.

Pelham died suddenly in February 1892, and about a month after his death a friend who assumed the name John Hart attended a séance with Mrs. Piper in Boston. Dr. Phinuit, in control, suddenly said, "There is another George who wants to speak to you." This spirit announced himself as G.P. and not only identified himself by his right name but revealed Hart's true name, which was unknown to the medium. He then mentioned various common acquaintances, and the following dialogue took place:

HART (*showing a pair of studs*): Who gave them to me?
G.P.: That's mine. I gave you that part of it. I sent that to you.
HART: When?
G.P.: Before I came here. That's mine, too. Mother gave you that.
HART: No.
G.P.: Well, Father then. Father and Mother together. You got those after I passed out. Mother took them. Gave them to Father, and Father gave them to you. . . .

This information, unknown to Hart, proved correct. G.P.'s stepmother had removed the studs from the corpse and asked her husband to present them to Hart. G.P., in this first appearance, made a number of references to James and Mary Howard, mutual friends of Pelham and Hart. At Hart's urging the Howards reluctantly agreed to attend Mrs. Piper, although they were not interested in occult experiments and the notion of attempting to contact the dead Pelham seemed distasteful to them.

The séance was held on April 11, 1892. James Howard wrote a verbatim report, later entered in the *Proceedings* of the Society for Psychical Research.

"G.P." made contact almost at once, and this time he did not speak through Phinuit, but in his own voice—or at least in a voice so like that of George Pelham that Mrs. Howard recognized the tone at once and was thoroughly frightened.

> G.P.: Jim, is that you? Speak to me quick. I am not dead. Don't think of me dead. I am awfully glad to see you. Can't you see me? Don't you hear me? Give my love to my father and tell him I want to see him. . . . I want you to know I think of you still. I spoke to John about some letters. I left things terribly mixed, my books and my papers; you will forgive me for this, won't you? . . .
>
> HOWARD: What do you do, George, where are you?
>
> G.P.: I am scarcely able to do anything yet; I am just awakened to the reality of life after death. It was like darkness. I could not distinguish anything at first. . . . I was puzzled, confused. Shall have an occupation soon. . . .
>
> HOWARD: Were you not surprised to find yourself living?
>
> G.P.: Perfectly so. Greatly surprised. I did not believe in a future life. It was beyond my reasoning powers. . . . Now it is as clear as daylight to me. . . . I want all the fellows to know about me. . . .

The conversation then veered to personal acquaintances, mention of a letter box, and other subjects. Howard attempted to ask G.P. two test questions he had devised, but after several false starts in the voice of G.P., Dr. Phinuit pushed his way into the séance and assumed control.

Although Howard later verified most of the incidents and details revealed during the séance, he remained in a quandary, torn between doubt, which was natural to him, and belief, which seemed impossible. After ten more sessions with Mrs. Piper, he was suddenly convinced of G.P.'s reality when, on a winter night in 1892, Mrs. Piper became submerged in a deep trance, her body apparently lifeless. The right hand began to twitch, jerk, then to write with great speed in answer to Howard's demand for proof. "Tell me," he insisted, "something known only to G.P. and myself."

That evening, Dr. Hodgson was recording the events. He took up several sheets of paper on which Mrs. Piper had written, read them aloud to Howard, who agreed that the statements were correct. Suddenly the medium wrote, "Private," and gently pushed Hodgson away.

I retired to the other side of the room, and Mr. Howard took my place close to the hand where he could read the writing. He did not, of course, read it aloud and it was too private for my perusal. The hand, as it reached the end of each sheet, tore it off from the block book, and thrust it wildly at Mr. Howard, and then continued writing. The circumstances narrated, Mr. Howard informed me, contained precisely the kind of test for which he had asked, and he said that he was "perfectly satisfied, perfectly."

We do not know, of course, what was written on the pages. Obviously it was the story of some private conversation or experience that Howard and Pelham had secretly shared. At any rate, it was enough to convince James Howard, whose earlier disbelief was now swept aside.

G.P. began to replace Dr. Phinuit, although at times they shared the medium in a remarkable manner: while Phinuit was speaking G.P. would use Mrs. Piper's hand to write about an entirely different subject. Phinuit's vividness, which had so impressed William James, waned as the power of G.P. waxed. More and more trance communications were in writing. Mrs. Piper, after trembling violently, would fall forward onto the table, where cushions had been placed to protect her. An invisible presence then seemed to seize her right hand and arm, using them to produce automatic writing, often at such a furious speed that the entranced lady could hardly keep up with the torrent of words.

Hodgson, feeling that more proof of the G.P. phenomenon was required, arranged for one hundred and fifty persons to attend sittings. They were carefully screened and as far as anyone could determine none of them had ever met Mrs. Piper. Of this group, thirty had been friends or acquaintances of G.P. and the remaining one hundred and twenty had not. The first task of the ghostly George Pelham was to identify which sitters had been his friends during life. The odds against a correct guess in any given case were four to one. Since Hodgson was familiar with Leonora Piper's uncanny talent, he fully expected that the number of correct identifications would be well above the mathematical probabilities of guesswork, but he was hardly prepared for the astonishing thing that happened.

When the shade of G.P. was asked to single out his friends, his score was exactly thirty out of one hundred and fifty. There was not one mistake!

Further, G.P. not only mentioned shared experiences to his friends, but in every case he treated the sitters with the same degree of intimacy George Pelham would have shown in life. He was polite to casual acquaintances, more relaxed with those he knew better, and cordial to old friends.

It was the most remarkable case of "something" ever recorded, although what the "something" might be remained an open question. The advocates of ESP declare that Mrs. Piper unconsciously read the minds of the sitters. If this is so, she must also have read their memories, for G.P. frequently mentioned incidents from the past which were accurate but which were not in the conscious minds of the sitters until G.P. talked about them. There are others who feel that the G.P. Control was exactly what he claimed to be: the spirit of George Pelham.

Since G.P. had indicated that his vision was not confined to the séance room, Hodgson invited the Control to look in on Mrs. Howard at home and report her activities. G.P. made contact that evening, this time through Phinuit. "She's writing, and taken some violets and put them in a book. And it looks as if she's writing to my mother. . . . Who is Tyson? Davis? . . . . I saw her [Mrs. Howard] sitting in the chair. . . . Saw her take a little bag and put some things in it . . . placed the photograph beside her on the desk. . . . Sent a letter to Tason . . . TYSON. . . ." And many more details.

Mrs. Howard, it turned out, had not done any of these things during the day in question. But she had performed every listed activity during the previous day and a half, and the descriptions were accurate to the least detail.

One of Mrs. Piper's triumphs was the conversion of Dr. Hodgson. As evidence accumulated, Hodgson's skepticism suffered one blow after another. He at last became convinced that Mrs. Piper was in touch not only with living minds through ESP, but with departed personalities as well. William James disagreed. Although he accepted a version of immortality, James believed that Mrs. Piper's "ghosts" were creations of her own unconscious mind and that her amazing fund of information came via telepathy.

Hodgson's conversion was partly based on proofs, arguments, and testing. But to a great degree he was overwhelmed by an undefinable certainty that he was in the living presence of George Pelham and other communicators who spoke through Mrs. Piper. The ghosts were real. They were human beings who chatted pleasantly of old times, recalled mutual secrets with friends, and chuckled at the memories of past incidents. (Indeed, a complete man with a very definite personality seems revealed in the extremely lengthy George Pelham transcripts. Brief quotations, such as those which have been given here, do not convey this sense of a whole man.) Hodgson wrote, "I cannot profess to have any doubt but that . . . they have survived the change we call death, and they have direct communication with us whom we call living through Mrs. Piper's entranced organism."

It must not be thought that the crusty doctor had in any way gone mellow or turned credulous. He considered Mrs. Piper a magnificent exception in a fraudulent world. During the time of his growing faith in Mrs. Piper, he was launching his most vitriolic attacks against Eusapia and other practitioners. Armed with sealing wax, thermometers, and measuring tapes, Hodgson invaded several supposedly haunted houses. The least skeptical report he ever made was the Scottish verdict "Not proven."

In January 1906, Hodgson suddenly dropped dead while playing handball. We do not know if he achieved the immortality he believed in, but it is a fact that the doctor underwent a surprising metamorphosis of one sort or another. As early as February 9 of that same year, he himself appeared as a Control, first through "Mrs. Holland," a medium living in India who corresponded with the Society for Psychical Research in London. ("Holland" was the pseudonym of Mrs. Fleming, a sister of Rudyard Kipling. She adopted the alias because her conservative family was scandalized by her involvement in spiritualism.)

Mrs. Holland, whom we shall encounter again with Mrs. Piper in connection with the strange phenomenon known as "cross-correspondence," seemed to have an affinity for the ghosts of psychical researchers. It was she who received the warnings against Eusapia Palladino purportedly issuing from F. W. H. Myers, deceased president of the British Society for Psychical Research.

Soon after his introduction as a Control by Mrs. Holland, Dr. Hodgson began to appear frequently in Leonora Piper's trances. William James declared that the Piper-Hodgson trances revealed nothing that Mrs. Piper could not have learned from the doctor

94

during their long acquaintance and Oliver Lodge described the Hodgson Control as vague and unsatisfactory. This is perhaps too harsh a view. Frank Podmore, a psychical researcher and author of *The Newer Spiritualism*, wrote that the Hodgson Control "seems to have been one of the most lifelike and dramatic impersonations of the whole series given by Mrs. Piper, and many relevant statements were made of an intimate kind such as could scarcely have proceeded from Mrs. Piper herself."

Lifelike or not, the Hodgson Control made major blunders. One sitter, a Dr. Hall, fooled the medium by creating a fictitious niece, "the late Bessie Beals," and at one of the Hodgson-controlled séances the nonexistent girl communicated from the Other Side. When called to task for this error, the Hodgson Control tried to squirm out of the situation by saying he meant "Jessie Beals," a ghost who must be related to another sitter. It was a performance quite uncharacteristic of Dr. Hodgson in real life.

Except for her remarkable performance in "cross-correspondence," Leonora Piper's power was waning, becoming unsteady. At times she reverted to earlier Controls, including the celebrities and historical personages Phinuit had once replaced. One evening the ghost of George Eliot began to write with Mrs. Piper's hand, and the demonstration seemed remarkable until the phantom novelist announced that in life she had been a friend of Adam Bede.

The confusion in the later trances was compounded when the Imperator Band invaded Mrs. Piper's psychic life. The Imperator Band was a tribe of supposedly ancient phantoms who first appeared to the Reverend William Stainton Moses in England during the 1870s. They announced themselves as a hierarchy of spirits with a complicated social order, and their individual names— Imperator, Doctor, Rector, Theophiles—are reminiscent of Rosicrucian theology. Although less crude and unruly than John King with his raft of relatives, the Band members made little more sense, and their presence contributed nothing but murk to Mrs. Piper's mediumship.

The only valuable advice they gave was the recommendation that Mrs. Piper have fewer trances, since her health was obviously failing.

In November 1909, she made a final trip to England, where, for the first time, she experienced great difficulty in inducing a trance, and, more dangerous, she sometimes fell into prolonged comas afterward. Her last séance took place in July 1911, and even at the last moment of her career the shy lady from Boston had a new surprise to offer. Although she failed to reach a state of hypnosis, her hand moved convulsively, then began to write automatically when she was otherwise fully conscious. It is ironic that the only Piper séance she herself saw was the last one.

Leonora Piper died (she would have said, 'Crossed to the Other Side') not long afterward. The medium's death was widely mourned by spiritualists and workers in psychical research; there were a few newspaper obituaries which gave cautious reports of her achievements, and several rather sensational magazine stories. Then she vanished from the public's memory. Mrs. Piper was not a celebrity during her lifetime, and in death she has been ignored by general history. Her name appears on no list of distinguished Americans.

Yet her contribution to man's knowledge of himself was major. When scholars discuss other mediums, one question arises repeatedly: "Was she entirely a fake or was there a grain of truth in it all?" With Mrs. Piper there is no such speculation. Instead, the question becomes, "Did she receive messages from beyond the grave, or was it merely telepathy?" Mrs. Piper's amazing powers of ESP are simply taken for granted in the debate that usually follows the question.

If Leonora Piper's achievements were "merely telepathy," then all usual notions of ESP must be drastically revised and expanded. In one well-documented case after another, the medium demonstrated a power that appeared to range across great distances; also, she seemed to "tune in" on the minds of individuals with whom she was unacquainted. In the "Uncle Jerry" test her mind apparently traveled across England, seeking out and scanning the memories of two men, Uncle Robert and Uncle Frank, of whose existence she was quite unaware.

In the George Pelham case her accurate and detailed information about the source of the cuff links was not culled from the mind of sitter John Hart, who did not know the true story. And these are only two of a hundred possible examples.

If telepathy or mind reading is the explanation of Mrs. Piper, then we have encountered a force of ESP that flashes across great distances and, like a computer sifting cards, scans millions of minds until it finds the one containing the information needed at the moment. Such a power is strange and unfamiliar, and to most men its existence is improbable.

It is especially difficult to associate such supernormal mental power with Leonora Piper, the gray lady with the umbrella and needlepoint bag. She fades into the background while Dr. Phinuit and George Pelham take the stage. They are far more real, more vital than the plain, patient housewife who created or summoned them. One tries to picture thought waves streaking from Mrs. Piper's head like bolts of lightning, leaping across country to read the memory banks of unconscious strangers—and the picture is fantastic.

Yet the alternative the gentle lady from Boston has left us, the alternative in which she herself believed, also boggles most imaginations: she was in contact with ghosts.

There is still a third attitude one can adopt toward Mrs. Piper, and that is the attitude the world at large has taken. One can ignore the whole matter, saying that it is all madness and a mistake; that the witnesses and investigators, however distinguished and sincere, were really liars, dupes, or victims of hysteria. One can claim that the twenty-five years of Mrs. Piper's testing were inconclusive and things that really happened did not happen at all. But, of course, they did.

III

Occult Stars: Some Remarkable Gentlemen

We have compared great mediums to great prima donnas, and it is certainly true that in mediumship as in opera the greatest amount of attention goes to women, not men. On stage this may be a matter of glamour; in psychical research it is also a question of talent. Most of the astonishing mediums—and the really magnificent frauds —have been females. This has been the case ever since the Fox sisters' debut in 1848.

Nevertheless, male mediums claim their share of the spotlight, and, as we have said, at the present time the world's best-known medium is a man, Arthur Ford. He stands alone; before her death in 1970 Mrs. Eileen Garrett was his only possible rival. (We are speaking exclusively of mediums. Prophecy is another matter and even in that field Ford has a strong claim to pre-eminence.)

Ford has reached a vast audience and achieved most of his fame through appearances on television and in connection with the late Bishop Pike. The purported communications between the Bishop and his dead son are too familiar to be repeated here, and those interested in the affair are referred to Pike's book *The Other Side*, a work produced with the aid of Diane Kennedy Pike. Warning is hereby given that the book throws little light into the dark corners of spiritualism, and the reading of it is a sad experience. It is an unadorned narrative of the two and a half years Pike spent in desperate attempts to reach a son whom he felt he had failed in life. The Bishop's prominence brought international attention, but *The Other Side* is merely one of countless such chronicles. Most of these works have been privately printed, gained no readership, and can be found only on the obscure shelves of libraries to which they have been donated by their authors. Usually they are the works of widows who have sought (and always attained) communion with a dead husband. The pattern is almost invariable: there is the death of a loved one, helpless grief of a survivor, and a failure to find consolation in life or established religion. Then a "strange event" occurs. (With Bishop Pike it was the mysterious stopping of clocks in his apartment at 8:19, the hour of his son's suicide in New York.) Eventually a medium (or a psychic, sensitive, or seer) is consulted, and, after a few false starts, contact with the departed and a measure of happiness are achieved.

All these accounts are painfully subjective, the author's desperate will to believe is manifest, and there is no straw too frail for grasping. Since the stories are so intensely personal and the consolation so gratefully and uncritically accepted by the searcher, it is both pointless and unkind to examine them too closely.

Arthur Ford's fame long antedated the Pike séances, and his talents are better revealed in connection with other, calmer matters.

The Reverend Arthur Ford, ordained by the Disciples of

Christ, made headlines after a séance on January 8, 1929, when it was announced that through his Control, a French-Canadian named Fletcher, he had reached the spirit of the dead magician Harry Houdini. It was well known to the public that Houdini, just before his death in 1926, had whispered secret words to his wife, words that would be sure identification if in the future he made spiritualistic contact with the human world. Ford, entranced, uttered, "Rosabelle . . . answer-tell-pray-answer-look-tell-answer-answer-tell . . ."

The Control Fletcher then revealed that these apparently meaningless words came from a stage code developed by the Houdinis for a vaudeville mind-reading trick. The actual message from Houdini boiled down to: "Rosabelle, believe."

To the astonishment and delight of the press, Beatrice Houdini, the widow, promptly confirmed that "Rosabelle, believe" was indeed the secret password, and, further, part of the message was to be delivered in the stage code. She signed a witnessed statement to this effect, and again affirmed Ford's accuracy in a letter to the columnist Walter Winchell. Spiritualists rejoiced. Here was not only confirmation of their beliefs but a solid identification of an individual spirit. (The latter conclusion was scientifically unjustified. Since Beatrice Houdini knew the secret and was living, ESP could explain the matter.)

The revelation was hailed as a spiritualist victory, but then, several years later, Mrs. Houdini absolutely reversed her position, denying everything she had said. No, she had not received a message from her late husband. Nothing of the sort! The code was quite different; all that Ford had said was balderdash. The lady turned vituperative on the subject of *all* mediums, denouncing them as frauds, fakes, leeches, and swindlers. She planned to make a Hollywood film exposing these charlatans, but its potential producers were thwarted by the statement she had signed earlier.

There have been many attempts to explain the Ford-Houdini affair, and not one has been satisfactory. It was charged that the medium and the widow had connived in a hoax, a publicity stunt somehow to enrich themselves, and that afterward there had occurred something equivalent to a falling-out of thieves. No evidence of such conspiracy was ever brought forward. Mrs. Houdini was known as something of a virago, and, in the light of her volatile character, it seems probable that she would have claimed collusion with Ford had such a plot existed. She could easily have passed it off as a joke, a wry trick in the Houdini tradition played on the gullible public. Beatrice had nothing to lose and would have succeeded in discrediting Ford—a project in which she developed an intense interest. But she merely held her reversed position and offered no coherent explanation of the change in attitude.

Clearly Mrs. Houdini was lying on one occasion or the other. The facts do not admit the possibility of confusion or honest mistake. Spiritualists, of course, claim that she lied in recanting and point out that often people swear to a psychic experience, then deny it afterward when they find that a single communication from a departed loved one has failed to bring them total happiness. Like patients at a certain stage of psychoanalysis they turn on their mentor. This is indeed a common reaction and one of the stumbling blocks in psychical research. But the argument is not much help in determining when Beatrice Houdini lied. Still, the "Rosabelle, believe" revelation must be chalked up as a victory for the medium, even though a limited one, a triumph still unhappily open to question.

Ford is a distinguished platform personality, and some of his outstanding demonstrations were given at Lily Dale Assembly Camp, that venerable site of spiritualist activity in northern New York. Allen Spraggett, a Canadian writer on occult matters, has given a graphic account of a Sunday afternoon gathering in the camp's tabernacle. The description, which appears in his 1967 book *The Unexplained*, is highly enthusiastic and can be considered a testimonial.

The medium that day followed the common practice of explaining to the audience of about two hundred that he was an intermediary between two worlds, "a kind of telephone operator." Then, going into a self-induced trance, Ford began to call out names which were one after the other identified by listeners. A quantity of personal information was given, some of it quite specific, including one spirit's angry denial that he had committed suicide: he had not drowned himself, as many believed, but had accidentally fallen overboard.

Although Spraggett is inclined to rather quick acceptance of occult manifestations, he is not unaware of the skeptical point of view, and at the very moment when he was thinking that some doubters would claim that the audience was packed with dupes and plants, Ford called out Spraggett's name. A communication from a fellow Canadian churchman, recently deceased, followed. "The burden of the message to me was that I should pursue my explorations of the psychic world because there were few things in life more important."

Spraggett had arranged to have the entire demonstration filmed and recorded, but he reports that the film and soundtrack mysteriously vanished from a photographer's studio. This is a regrettable loss, for another reporter, an elected public official who prefers to remain anonymous, observed a Ford demonstration and had rather different reactions:

> I arrived early at the hall and had time to strike up conversations with several of the faithful. The atmosphere reminded me of a Broadway opening night when some great star is appearing in an ideal vehicle, a sure-fire hit. Great excitement, high hopes, the certainty that something magnificent would take place. . . . Later, when more people arrived, I felt a rising tension and became somewhat uncomfortable. I remembered visiting Lourdes as a tourist, how faith and the longing for miracles deluded pilgrims into temporary recoveries. I could not quite call this audience the lunatic fringe, but there were certainly many fanatics, many emotionally disturbed persons present. [In contrast, Spraggett described the audience around him as "honest, sincere people, and not unduly cred-

ulous."] Ford's entrance was relaxed and disarming, there were no theatrics, yet his personality conveyed itself strongly. He was very much in command.

After a few remarks about what he would endeavor to do, he took a moment to relax, but it did not seem to me that he ever went into a "trance," as I understand the term. Ford frequently inquired of his audience if he was giving accurate details. He made a number of correct hits, but the information conveyed was of a general nature. One woman wept openly, and I thought happily, when she recognized her dead son's nickname, and an elderly man sitting next to me, who had been nervously clenching and un-clenching his hands for a quarter of an hour, suddenly shouted "Yes! Yes!" when the medium pronounced the name "Miller."

There was a feeling of hysteria in the hall, but it was repressed and bore no resemblance to the frenzy of a revival meeting. I thought Ford was skillful, clever, quick to pounce upon the slight-est reaction of a listener. His success in calling out familiar and sometimes unusual names impressed me. . . . It *did* seem telepathic. But I have grave doubts about the reliability of many of the people who confirmed his hits. . . . I myself received no communications. I would not care to repeat the experience. Whatever Ford's pow-ers, there is something morbid about listening to the names of sup-posedly dead persons called out and then hearing a survivor shout confirmation as though his number had just won first prize at a lottery. . . .

These two evaluations of Ford's work are in extreme contrast, but the actual events they describe are almost identical. Public séances held in auditoriums all tend to be very much alike. In studying works about psychical research or experience, some-times the reader is enveloped by a sense of *déjà vu*. Repetitions are constant.

Harold Sherman is the highly successful author of *Your Key to Happiness* and *How to Make ESP Work for You*, the latter being a self-help book with test questions for the reader at the end of each chapter. His first encounter with a psychic medium occurred in Detroit in 1920 and has much in common with

Spraggett's experience at Lily Dale. The medium in the earlier case was John Slater, who made an international name for himself giving mass séances in large auditoriums. (Two thousand attended the demonstration Sherman watched.)

Slater, like Ford, began with a brief explanation of what was to take place. While Ford referred to himself rather modestly as a "telephone operator," Slater described himself as "a man standing on a mountaintop, looking down into two valleys." From this elevation he could see both this world and the next. Names were called, revelations given, and there were so many confirmations that Sherman and his companions, exactly like Spraggett, began to think of dupes and plants in the audience. At precisely that moment—again like Spraggett—Harold M. Sherman heard his own name called out. Some seemingly amazing revelations followed.

Slater's Detroit performance, as written, is far more spectacular than anything Ford did at Lily Dale, but the difference of the two reporters must be taken into account. Spraggett, although searching for marvels, is nevertheless an explorer of psychic mysteries. Sherman is a totally convinced and hard-selling occultist.

Such men as Ford and Slater are noteworthy whether considered as clairvoyants or performers. But for color, spectacle, and astonishment, no male of the twentieth century has come close to the figures of earlier days, some of whom seem to have been more like warlocks than mediums—which brings us to the most remarkable gentleman of all, Daniel Dunglas Home.

The Flying Scotsman

If we imagine Mrs. Piper creeping on stage as a gray shadow and Eusapia Palladino charging into the arena with lowered horns, then Daniel Home must make his entrance flying through an upstairs window of one of those stately homes of England, whose inhabitants are, at the moment, in a state resembling shock. Home, seventy feet above the ground, floats into the room, dapper and gracious, his wavy hair unruffled by the self-created air currents of flight.

Landing gently on the carpet, he smiles winsomely, the boyish smile that won the hearts and fortunes of three high-born ladies. "It was really nothing. Nothing at all." Daniel is a modest young man, his handsome head quite unturned by command performances before the Czar of Russia. We will not attempt to estimate his physical height at this moment—it had a way of changing radically and just now we do not know whether he is elongated or not. The whole introduction is most unsettling, but carried off with grace, charm, and beautiful manners.

Daniel Dunglas Home (whose surname was originally spelled Hume) was born to a family living just outside Edinburgh in 1833. The Homes were not exactly impoverished but were definitely working class, and the only notable fact about them is that Daniel's father was a clairvoyant of sorts, a finder of lost objects, interpreter of dreams, and an occasional fortuneteller. His reputation went no further than his superstitious neighbors and he could hardly be called a success either financially or psychically. Nevertheless his gift influenced the son and is yet another example of the apparent hereditary quality of psychic talent, which is so often passed from mother to daughter and sometimes from father to son. (Some people will insist that the tricks of the trade are handed down as a family craft.)

Home took care never to lose a slight but charming burr in his speech, but his upbringing was as much American as Scottish, since an aunt took him to the United States when he was only nine years old. The boy was fourteen when the Fox sisters, with their clicking knees and cracking knuckles, launched the spiritualist movement, and young Daniel, deeply impressed by several séances, became a convert at seventeen and in a matter of months turned into a novice practitioner, thus beginning an international adventure and fantastic career.

Reports of his first few years as a medium are vague, undetailed, and even contradictory. The art of mediumship—or perhaps merely the practice of spiritist fraud—had burgeoned in every major American city. Daniel was an unknown newcomer among seasoned professionals, but he conducted séances in New York, Philadelphia, and probably in Boston, gathering a circle of followers greater in devotion than in number. Even though he performed such feats as levitation of his own body and its elongation by nearly a foot, he remained an insignificant figure compared to such mediums as Andrew Jackson Davis, who was very little older and had begun his public career only a few years previously. Home was at a distinct disadvantage in that he did not attempt faith healing or mystical diagnosis. He believed himself "a teacher of the truth of immortality," and gave sermons while entranced. However, he was both a trance and physical medium—the dead spoke, inanimate objects trembled and flew.

And Daniel Home had two qualities that set him apart from rivals—extraordinary beauty and charm. Every contemporary who wrote about him was struck by his boyish handsomeness; he was winsome and would remain so for many years. Further, his attractiveness was of the kind with which Oscar Wilde endowed young Dorian Gray: innocence, kindness, and an eagerness to please. One hesitates to call Home "disarming," because the word implies that despite his winning ways, everyone should have kept their weapons handy, and that is not fair. No doubt Daniel Home traded upon his lovability. But those who gave him money did so gladly, and with one notable exception they always remained his devoted friends.

New York was his training ground, the finishing school where he acquired acceptable grammar and the social graces. By 1855 the twenty-two-year-old medium was ready for the larger stage of Europe and "friends" raised a considerable amount of money to send him abroad in style. Even if he had not possessed psychic talent and inborn showmanship, so ingratiating a young man as Home could hardly have failed anywhere. England welcomed him; so did France and Russia later. He immediately became friends with the rich and socially prominent; almost no one questioned his integrity. "But this is in no way surprising," writes Baron Johan Liljencrants, "if we consider the character of Home and his presence which won for him the personal affection and esteem of all those with whom he came in contact and *a priori* inclined his audience to look upon him as a man beyond suspicion."

But, apart from good looks and personality, how did Home make such an impression on London? A letter written by a Mr. Merrifield, who attended one of Home's English séances in August, 1855, makes the reason plain.

The first attempts of the evening were not especially successful. The sitters, none too happy, were preparing to depart when Home

. . . professed his willingness to give us another sitting. Accordingly, we took our places at the side of the table, the medium occupying the extreme right, and a constant associate of his sitting opposite to him. I sat nearly halfway between them, and therefore facing the windows. The table was circular, and the semicircle nearest the window was unoccupied. The lights were removed and very soon the operations began. It was about eleven o'clock; the moon had set, but the night was starlight, and we could well see the outline of the windows and distinguish, though not with accuracy of outline, the form of any large object intervening before them. The medium sat as low as possible in his seat. His hands and arms were under the table. He talked freely, encouraging conversation and seeming uneasy when it flagged. After a few preliminary raps somebody exclaimed that the "spirit-hand" had appeared, and the next moment an object resembling a child's hand, with a long, wide sleeve attached to it, appeared before the light. This occurred several times. . . .

There was a great deal more, but one sitter, at least, was unconvinced. The poet Robert Browning wrote testily that "the whole display of hands, spirit utterances, etc., was a cheat and imposture." Home was later lampooned by Browning in "Mr. Sludge: Medium." One wonders if the poet became less acid about such matters when his beloved wife began to dabble in the occult. Or were icy remarks exchanged between the writing of sonnets?

During his early years in England, Home was dependent on the financial generosity of his many friends. Since his work was "religious," he would not accept professional fees. Perhaps he also realized that a supposedly amateur status allowed him to remain a "gentleman," not an employee. Then, in 1859, he made a fortunate marriage to a Russian noblewoman, who supported him in luxury for three years until her death cut off his income. Home again became what might be called a "kept medium" and "kept companion." At thirty-two, Daniel Home could hardly be called an orphan, but he was nevertheless adopted legally by the elderly, very rich Mrs. Lyon. But this widow proved fickle and the signatures on the adoption papers had hardly dried when she had her "son" haled into court, charging fraud and demanding return of gifts and monies she had showered on him.

It provided a splendid Victorian scandal. Friends of Home flocked to court to testify about his absolute integrity; affidavits swearing to his occult powers came from prominent people. Malicious tongues wagged, insinuating that Mrs. Lyon had expected to enjoy a relationship with Home that was legally although not naturally incestuous and that when the upright young man refused to accommodate her, she turned on him. Everyone was sympathetic toward Home except the person who counted, the judge. The charge of fraud was not proved, but the court ruled that undue influence had been exercised over Mrs. Lyon, the adoption was annulled, and the gifts were to be returned. Since the lady took no further action, we gather that restitution was made.

The affair did no damage to Home's reputation. Five years later he remarried, again choosing a Russian bride with an independent income. If Home was a fortune-hunter, he was a lucky one. Both his wives were attractive women, young, highly eligible for marriage. Neither had to settle for a gigolo, and both marriages seem to have been happy. Ironically, a life filled with gaiety and adventure ended in Europe in 1886 after a painful and prolonged illness.

He remains the most charming figure in psychical research and far and away the greatest physical medium the world has seen. One contemporary account will show why. The following was written by the Master of Lindsay and submitted for the archives of the Committee of the Dialectical Society in 1872:

> I was sitting with Mr. Home and Lord Adare and a cousin of his. During the sitting, Mr. Home went into a trance and in that state was carried out of the window in the room next to where we were and was brought in at our window. The distance between the windows was about seven feet six inches, and there was not the slightest foothold between them, nor was there more than a twelve-inch projection to each window, which served as a ledge to put flowers on. We heard the window in the next room lifted up, and almost immediately after we saw Home floating in the air outside our window. The moon was shining full into the room; my back was to the light, and I saw the shadow on the wall of the window sill, and Home's feet about six inches above it. He remained in this position for a few seconds, then raised the window and glided into the room feet foremost and sat down.
>
> Lord Adare then went into the next room to look at the window from which he had been carried. It was raised about eighteen inches, and he expressed his wonder how Mr. Home had been taken through so narrow an aperture. Home said, still entranced, "I will show you", and then with his back to the window he leaned back and was shot out of the aperture, head first, with the body rigid, and then returned quite quietly. The window is about seventy feet from the ground.

Small wonder that Lord Adare was happy to press loans on Home and have him as a frequent bed-and-board guest. Such entertainments are hard to come by!

Home appeared to defy gravity like an astronaut. One witness, Sir William Crookes, was casually watching the medium, who sat in a large, upholstered chair. Suddenly Home rose into the air, chair and all. To allay any suspicion of trickery, Home then knelt in the chair and repeated the performance. It was an anticlimax when he simply rose from the floor from a standing position.

Home's demonstrations of self-levitation were many and varied, and the reaction of one of his acquaintances, Lord Lindsay, reveals the concern the medium's friends felt for him. Lindsay, having learned that Home intended to leap from a window, then float through another, was greatly alarmed for Home's physical safety and tried to halt the experiment. Apparently he need not have worried.

Elongation is the ability of a medium to change his physical height, or, more precisely, to extend any part of his body so that a basic physical alteration has occurred. Eusapia was believed by some to have elongated both her arms and her legs. Home gave many demonstrations of this, but the best contemporary account comes again from Lord Lindsay. (*Dialectical Report* of 1872; also quoted by Frank Podmore.)

> On another occasion I saw Mr. Home, in a trance, elongated eleven inches. I measured him standing up against the wall, and marked the place; not being satisfied with that, I put him in the middle of the room and placed a candle in front of him, so as to throw a shadow on the wall, which I also marked. When he awoke, I measured him again in his natural size, both directly and by the shadow and the results were equal. I can swear he was not off the ground or standing on tiptoe, as I had a full view of his feet, and moreover, a gentleman present had one of his feet placed over Home's insteps, one hand on his shoulder, and the other on his side where the false ribs come near the hip-bone.

Home, it might be added, was not the only practitioner of sudden growth and diminution. There was the English medium J. Herne, who gave several demonstrations of apparent elongation, but he is really better known as a member of the famous séance to which Mrs. Guppy was transported from afar. Herne had a habit of suddenly vanishing from a room, leaving behind him only wisps of smoke, a marvelous performance which, alas, was proved bogus by Moncure Conway. Conway demonstrated that the sitters on Herne's right and left were tricked into holding each other's hands in the dark, thinking that they were touching the medium, thus leaving Herne free to manufacture all sorts of miracles. The smoke came from some burning substance concealed in a teapot, which he carried from the room when he made a quite ordinary exit through a door. Conway surprised the medium, teapot in hand, by igniting flash-powder.

This was not the only mortification the elongator Herne suffered. Keeping bad company, he joined forces with an American trickster, Charles Williams, performed in tandem with him, and managed to deceive English investigators with a series of fraudulent miracles. When the authorities threatened exposure Herne ran off to Amsterdam with a new partner, "The Mystic Rita." The methodical Dutch itemized the contents of their baggage: fake beards, phosphorescent liquids, treated gauzes for materializing ghosts, and other paraphernalia of deception.

Another elongator named Peters gave an Alice-in-Wonderland growth performance in the house of the Reverend C. J. M. Shaw. The Reverend Mr. Shaw was aided by his brother, and each gripped a foot and ankle of the medium, whose body wavered, reeled, and suddenly grew taller. His right arm shot out six inches beyond its normal reach; then the left arm followed suit. Peters all the while kept getting taller until he fell to the floor in a faint. Apparently the good Reverend and his brother were too astounded to make further observations, for there is no report of Peters' subsequent rate of shrinkage.

One searches futilely for records of elongation by females and for contemporary instances (perhaps, regrettably, this is another lost art). Ladies who have specialized in elongation, if there were any, made small impressions, so to speak. There are mentions of Eusapia's arms "apparently lengthening" but that is not at all the same as D. D. Home's adding more than half a cubit to his already considerable stature. The dearth of female elongators and the fact that the skill has apparently vanished in modern times leads one to consider an unkind suggestion made about Home's lengthening himself: some sort of jacking up devices could have been concealed in his boots. Since heavy boots would be noticeable today and always would have been when worn by women, this explanation is tempting. Building such an elevator, making it rise and then drop without detection, and having it small, silent, yet strong enough to support a heavy man seems, however, to present quite a problem. Nor is there evidence that Home was mechanically inclined or talented.

Like Eusapia, Home sometimes uttered spirit messages he received while entranced. They were vague and unverifiable, but unfailingly reassuring about perpetual happiness on the Other Side. But his fame rested on his talents as a physical medium, his amazing demonstrations of mind seeming to control matter.

An impressive performance was the Fire Ordeal. Lord Lindsay writes:

> I have frequently seen Home, when in trance, go to the fire and take out large red-hot coals, and carry them about in his hands, put them inside his shirt, etc. Eight times I myself have held a red-hot coal in my hands without injury, when it scorched my face on raising my hand. Once I wished to see if they really would burn, and I said so, and touched a coal with the middle finger of my right hand, and I got a blister as large as a sixpence; I instantly asked him [Home] to give me the coal, and I held the part that burnt me, in the middle of my hand, for three or four minutes without the slightest inconvenience.
>
> A few weeks ago I was at a séance with eight others. Of these, seven held a red-hot coal without pain, and the two others could not bear the approach of it; of the seven, four were ladies.

A similar demonstration, described by Sir William Crookes, in a report to the Society for Psychical Research, not only confirms Lindsay, but adds another brushstroke to the portrait of Home's character or pretended character: his emphasis on religion.

Mr. Home again went to the fire, and, after stirring the hot coals about with his hand, took out a red hot piece nearly as big as an orange and, putting it on his right hand, covered it over with his left hand so as to almost completely enclose it, and then blew into the small furnace thus extemporized until the lump of charcoal was nearly white-hot, and then drew my attention to the lambent flame which was flickering over the coal and licking around his fingers; he fell on his knees, looked up in a reverent manner, held up the coal in front and said, "Is not God good? Are not His laws wonderful?"

Frank Podmore, a pioneer psychical researcher and one of the most skeptical of all, made a belated attempt in 1910 to debunk Home by explaining the methods used by stage illusionists to create the impression of handling hot, even blazing objects. (Those who care to test Mr. Podmore's suggestions might try coating their tongues with confectioners' sugar, and overlay the sugar with soap; then they may eat fire or lick a glowing poker with impunity—so Mr. Podmore says. Other tricks involve coating the hands with various chemicals. Since one of the ingredients is sulphuric acid we hesitate to recommend it. Perhaps just picking up the hot coal is safer.)

Podmore learned from stage performers that a platinum sponge, part of it dampened with alcohol, then lighted, produced a very realistic blazing-coal effect and could be held without discomfort. But the investigator's arguments, so often convincing, fail in the case of Home. Obviously the witnesses who handled the coals themselves had not prepared their hands in advance; and most of them could certainly tell the difference between a coal and a sponge. It should also be remembered that Home, except in rare cases, conducted his séances in full lamplight. It is surprising that Podmore should be so incredulous of this particular demonstration. The famous "firewalks" by Fiji Islanders were well documented even in his day. Faith, leading to a form of self-hypnotism which apparently gives immunity to pain and burning, is involved. It is a classic "miracle" of great antiquity. Virgil mentions a similar case; so do Silius Italicus and Pliny. Modern reports have come from numerous Pacific islands, Japan, India, and even European countries. Tests have been made with thermometers, and it is well-established that faith, not trickery, works the wonder. In many countries, especially in Latin America, volunteers have been nailed to the cross in re-enactment of the crucifixion and the "victims" felt no pain in their hands.

It is interesting to note that two of the sitters at the one Home séance shrank from touching the coals and felt intense heat as they were approached. Lacking faith in the medium, they doubtless would have been burned, just as Lord Lindsay was when he made a skeptic's test.

Podmore's latter-day attack on Home, written twenty-four years after the medium's death, is merely a speculation about how things *might* have been done. He is determined to expose Home, he points out some weaknesses in the evidence, but he does not succeed in proving anything.

Many inquiries written just before and after the turn of the century suffer from an understandable bias. Podmore and a score of other researchers felt compelled to separate spiritualism from spiritism. There had been so many frauds, so much outrageous trickery, that the very investigation of occult phenomena was suspect. The Society for Psychical Research tried to protect its members by emphasizing that "membership . . . does not imply . . . any belief as to the operation, in the physical world, of forces other than those recognized by Physical Science." Even so, Mrs. Sidgwick delayed joining for two years, fearful that membership might cost her her position at Newnham College. The Verralls were equally reluctant. Kipling's sister used a pseudonym and early records constantly refer to "Mrs. A.," "Mr. L.," "the Misses G."

Everyone would have felt more comfortable and respectable if physical mediumship could have been dismissed altogether. It smacked of the fraudulent, the superstitious, as it still does today. Unhappily there were such characters as D. D. Home. Since he could not be ignored, we have Podmore's attack, which really boils down to "it could possibly have been done some other way. The witnesses must have been unreliable. Besides, I simply don't believe it."

Although in the flight through Lord Adare's window Home doubtless reached the literal height of his career, he made his major contribution (some would say "did his worst damage") to psychical research during a series of experiments conducted by Sir William Crookes.

Sir William is a prime example of the unpleasantness that often ambushes a respected man when he ventures into occult research. His credentials as a chemist and as a physicist were impressive. He discovered thallium, invented the high-vacuum Crookes tube (which is still in use), and was a brilliant pioneer in the study of radioactivity. Today his name is best remembered in connection with the tube and with a juicy scandal involving a medium named Florence Cook. It is a scandal that refuses to die and enjoyed a public revival only a few years ago.

Miss Cook in the early 1870s made a great success in London by completely materializing our old acquaintance, the ghost of Katie King. The black-clad medium was bound to a chair inside a curtained cabinet and the knots were sealed with tape. Soon afterwards a ghost, dramatically dressed in contrasting white, would glide from the cabinet to chat cosily with the sitters. The whole performance was done by gaslight. Late in 1873 a skeptic named Volckman seized the ghost, determined to expose Katie King as Florence Cook in disguise. Mr. Volckman was slapped and clawed for his impertinence and quite a struggle took place. (It should be remembered that Katie was the sister of a pirate and the battle-toughened veteran of many a brawl). The gaslight went out. The sitters, blind and in consternation, bumped into each other and one gathers there was general pandemonium. The ghost escaped, but afterward Miss Cook was found in the cabinet, still neatly tied, sealed, and unscarred.

The medium, feeling that her reputation was besmirched, appealed to Crookes to conduct whatever experiments he chose and, she hoped, to verify her psychic power. The scientist obliged.

The extensive tests involved the use of a galvanometer, which indicated that the medium did not move during the séance, and photography. The ghost was observed by electric light. All the Crookes-Cook-King séances were eventful, to say the very least, but the final one, a farewell scene, is a classic.

Katie, according to Sir William, "invited me into the cabinet with her, and allowed me to remain there to the end." (The "cabinet" was actually his library, which had been curtained off from the adjoining room.)

> After closing the curtain she conversed with me for some time, and then walked across the room to where Miss Cook was lying senseless on the floor. Stooping over her, Katie touched her, and said, "Wake up, Florrie, wake up! I must leave you now!" Miss Cook then woke and tearfully entreated Katie to stay a little time longer. "My dear, I can't; my work is done. God bless you," Katie replied, and then continued speaking to Miss Cook. For several minutes the two were conversing with each other, till at last Miss Cook's tears prevented her speaking. Following Katie's instructions I then came forward to support Miss Cook, who was falling on to the floor, sobbing hysterically. I looked around, but the white-robed Katie had gone.

There seem only three possible conclusions one can draw from this story: It really happened that way and a ghost did appear. Or, a fraud was perpetrated by Miss Cook and an accomplice with a gift for quick disappearances. Or, Sir William Crookes was a dreadful liar. A great many of Crookes's colleagues and contemporaries took the third viewpoint. Miss Cook was young and attractive, and Crookes himself had written that he had once embraced Katie the ghost and found that she was "as material a being as Miss Cook herself." Surely a dead giveaway!

None of this talk was pleasant for the scientist, but his reputation was otherwise so impressive that gossip did not prevent his election as president of the Royal Society.

This ancient scandal burst forth again in 1962, revived by a book called *The Spiritualists* in which Trevor H. Hall denounced Crookes's experiments, charged conspiracy between the scientist and the medium, and claimed that the so-called séances were actually assignations. Crookes, however, had the last word. His ghost promptly contacted the celebrated automatic writer, Grace Rosher of London, and his denials, written by a pen propped against Miss Rosher's fingers, were vehement. ("I cannot imagine how such an absurd suggestion could be made.") The handwriting was uncannily like Crookes's own.

Sir William's experiments with D. D. Home were conducted before his involvement with Florence Cook. These tests too have been attacked on various grounds but so far, at least, no one has suggested a love affair between the medium and the researcher.

In the Crookes-Home demonstrations we have one of the earliest attempts to apply laboratory methods to occult phenomena. Crookes, aided by a colleague identified only as Dr. A.B., constructed a weighing device: a wooden board one yard long had one end resting on a solid table and the other connected to a self-registering scale. The board, thus suspended, weighed three pounds. Home touched the board at the point where it lay on the table and, although his fingers did not appear to press down, the weight changed dramatically. Crookes then climbed on the table and stood on one foot at the spot Home had previously touched. The scientist's weight of one hundred and forty pounds caused only a two-pound change on the register. As a check against finger pressure a tap bell and a small cardboard matchbox were put between Home's fingers and the board. The scale at once showed a six-pound increase. Repeated testing brought the same result.

Crookes made the apparatus more delicate and complicated and first tested Home by having him place the fingertips of one hand in a bowl of water resting on the board and the table. Assistants grasped Home's feet and other hand. Still, the scales showed that Home's touching the water changed the weight of the board. The *minimum* recorded change was more than ten ounces. Actually, Crookes need not have bothered with the water-bowl experiment. When Home simply held his hands a few inches above the apparatus its weight mysteriously increased although he did not touch it at all.

The demonstration was repeated in different ways using different and more sophisticated equipment. Always, in some unknown way, Home seemed to affect gravity. There were usually three witnesses besides Crookes himself.

Since Sir William was a physicist, it is not surprising that most of his testing of Home involved weight and measurement. He was not seeking any spirit contact but hoped to discover an unknown natural force at work. He wrote

The spiritualist tells of flowers with fresh dew on them, of fruit, and living objects being carried through closed windows and even solid brick-walls. The scientific investigator naturally asks that an additional weight (if it be only the thousandth part of a grain) be deposited on one pan of his balance when the case is locked. And the chemist asks for one-thousandth of a grain of arsenic to be carried through the sides of a glass tube in which pure water is hermetically sealed.

Yet some of the Home-Crookes sessions are entirely observations. At one séance a two-foot length of lath rose from the table and floated in air ten inches above the surface for an estimated minute. Home was seated a yard away. Another occasion produced more startling results: a wire cage containing an accordion was put beneath the table in such a position that Home, with his left hand, could touch one end of the instrument, but not its keyboard. Suddenly the accordion began to play, then flew from its cage and hovered unsupported in air while the music continued.

This was not the last time the accordion (or another) was heard:

> Home was the medium. A phantom form came out of a corner of the room, took an accordion in its hand, and then glided about the room playing the instrument. The form was visible to all present for many minutes, Mr. Home also being seen at the same time. Coming rather close to a lady who was sitting apart from the rest of the company, she gave a slight cry, upon which it vanished.

It is in keeping with Home's character that he should materialize a gay, entertaining ghost who gave a mini-concert. There is a lack of eeriness about Home's mediumship, a sociability. Doubtless he apologized profusely and charmingly to the lady who was frightened. Only once in the records of Crookes's experiments does the supernatural seem at all ominous.

> In the dusk of the evening, during a séance with Mr. Home at my house, the curtains of a window about eight feet from Mr. Home were seen to move. A dark, shadowy, semi-transparent form, like that of a man, was then seen by all present standing near the window, waving the curtain with his hand. As we looked, the form faded away and the curtains ceased to move. . . .

With this exception, incidents of Home's career do not resemble scenes from *The Turn of the Screw.* This was undoubtedly one reason for his great success, for the welcome he received from nobility and even royalty in Europe. And, of course, there was his own ingratiating personality, which Lewis Spence describes as "artless and spontaneous and very affectionate, of pleasing manners and generous disposition. He won the hearts of all with whom he came in contact. . . ." At the risk of arousing yet another scandal, we quote Sir William's words about Home: "One of the most lovable of men."

D. D. Home's career extended over many years and he gave scores of astonishing demonstrations. During an era when mediums were constantly being exposed as frauds, the Scotsman remained unsullied. A committee appointed by the Dialectical Society studied Home's work, but although they were not convinced of his power and entertained the gravest doubts about all mediumship, their report was not an exposé—they could neither believe in him nor disprove him. No hidden threads were detected, no tricks of releasing a hand or a foot. It is true, of course, that he was a rather early figure in the story of psychical research. Observers were not so experienced then as later, test conditions were in a pioneer stage, and, despite Sir William's precautions, Home was probably not subjected to as rigorous examination as more modern psychics.

The Scotsman's performances on the Continent were even more successful than those in Britain. We have earlier mentioned the impression he created at the court of Napoleon III and Eugénie. His séances in France were given almost exclusively for royalty, nobility, and other persons of high rank—plus an occasional clergyman. The empress kept a detailed record of the marvels Home wrought in her presence and in later years enjoyed reading those accounts aloud to friends. She was especially thrilled one evening when only Napoleon III, the Duchess of Montebello, Home, and Eugénie herself were present. A ghostly hand seized a pen which was lying on the table, dipped it in an inkpot, and inscribed the signature of Napoleon I. The facsimile was excellent. "Might I kiss this wonderful hand?" asked the emperor. It rose to his lips, moved to the empress, then to Home. Snobbishly it ignored the Duchess of Montebello. The emperor kept this autograph as a memento of his famous ancestor, and commented that the hand had been warm and soft.

From France, Home went on to Holland and gave spiritualism a royal sendoff at The Hague. Queen Sophia patiently sat through six unsuccessful séances, but on the seventh night the spirits appeared in abundance. The queen was convinced and gave support to Home, which, we may suppose, included money. (Home did a thorough job of planting seeds of occultism in the royal gardens, for a century later they would blossom into a fine scandal about mediumistic influences at the court of Queen Juliana.)

Since his death, a number of critics have assailed him, although it is more accurate perhaps to say that they have assailed his testers and witnesses—all those who believed in his powers. All this is natural enough, since it is virtually impossible to attack a man never caught in deceit in his entire life. The critics are forced to say, "But he *must* have been cheating!" and then to assault the test conditions and attempt to show how he might have accomplished a colossal fraud.

If Home was a genial faker, he surely must have mastered conjuring tricks far more sophisticated, far more subtle than the methods the debunkers have suggested he used. They ignore the fact that Home usually worked in full light; they proffer cumbersome arrangements and gadgets that seem impossible. Podmore, who is typical, tries to explain away the surprising accordion demonstrations by suggesting that Home had concealed a music box on his person, that the accordion never played at all and was somehow moved by a black thread. It is difficult to imagine a music box hidden in Home's clothing that could clearly play "several notes and then a simple air" sounding like a wind instrument. If the levitation of the accordion was done with a thread (while Crookes had an assistant stationed under the table) then Home was a marvelous prestidigitator indeed.

The flight through the window is dismissed as an illusion; Home "somehow" escaped one room, slipped behind the curtains of another (which was occupied) and made a grand entrance. There is always the "somehow." One does not have to believe in Home's mediumship to acknowledge his victory over the critics. If he is not completely convincing to a skeptical mind, neither are they. An impasse is reached: "Home didn't do these things because they can't be done. Everyone involved was deluded, hallucinating, conniving or lying." And this, too, is hard to accept.

J. N. Maskelyne, the great stage conjurer noted for his feats of levitation and a formidable exposer of mediums, once said, "There does not exist, and there never existed, a professional medium of any note who has not been convicted of trickery or fraud." Maskelyne forgot the amazing Daniel Dunglas Home. And so has almost everyone else.

Spirits in Vermont: the Eddy Brothers

Today a vacationer traveling in rural Vermont would pay little attention to a rather large, fairly handsome white house that faces away from the road not far from the small community of Chittenden. There is little to attract notice. It is a remodeled nineteenth-century farmhouse, not only typical of New England but common in many parts of the United States—wooden, rectangular, with two stories and a central ridgepole. It is solid and symmetrical; five downstairs windows match five upstairs windows, which overlook the lawn. As the house itself is somewhat obscured by trees, so is its antiquity obscured by the modern additions of a roomy front porch with Doric posts and a flat-topped extension built at one side. The whole effect is commonplace, pleasantly shady but utterly unromantic, a most unlikely residence for the hordes of spirits and odd characters who once congregated there.

No house in America has a more peculiar history, for this was once the home of the strange Eddy brothers and a mecca for the international occult set, including the astonishing Madame Blavatsky. It has been described as the "Spirit Capital of the Universe," and if this is an exaggeration, it is not a very great one. More than five hundred individual ghosts reportedly materialized on the platform of its séance room.

William and Horatio Eddy, who were once the less than genial hosts to these spirits and visitors, are practically unknown today, although ninety years ago they were a famous pair. Even the monumental *Encyclopaedia of Occultism* omits them. Yet in their day they had no Yankee rivals in the field of physical mediumship, and, like D. D. Home's, their careers are not blemished by their being caught in fraud. A number of reporters investigated them, but the best account is that of Colonel Henry S. Olcott of the New York *Sun,* who visited Chittenden near the end of the summer of 1874. Modern studies have been done by the late Alton Blackington and John Mason.

The childhood of William and Horatio was as bleak as a Vermont stone quarry. Their mother, Julie Ann MacCoombs before her marriage to Zephaniah Eddy, was some sort of mystic, a woman subject to trances and given to the utterance of prophecies. This prophetic gift came from her mother, she said, who was also a seer. According to a romantic but not well-confirmed legend, Julie MacCoombs was the great-great-grandaughter of a condemned Salem witch who had returned to her native Scotland after a jail break. Unfortunately, the occult roots of the family tree are untraceable.

Zephaniah Eddy, unimaginative, brutal, and probably illiterate, seems to have had no concern about matters preternatural until after the birth of his sons. Even as babies they seemed to attract forces that Andrew Jackson Davis would have called "magnetic." Invisible hands rocked their cradles violently, they were physically transported, and Zephaniah claimed that later he frequently caught them consorting with ghost children, playmates who vanished into the air.

The spirits followed the little boys to school as faithfully as Mary's little lamb but with less docility. Slates and chalk were snatched from the boys' hands while their desks resounded with raps and thumpings of unknown origin. The one-room school became a madhouse and the two haunted pupils were sent home permanently.

At this time, Zephaniah Eddy looked on all these goings-on as great naughtiness. He beat William savagely when the boy fell into a trance, poured water from a hot teakettle on his son's body, and scarred the child for life by putting burning coals in his palms. None of these punishments awakened the entranced William or cured him of his "fits and spells."

At about this time the youthful Fox sisters were going from hall to hall giving psychic demonstrations while money rolled in. Other young psychic prodigies were also drawing crowds, and Zephaniah slowly developed the idea of exhibiting his freakish children. Abetted by a theatrical manager, William and Horatio and their two small sisters went on tour—a long series of performances which can be described only as demonstrations of sadism run rampant.

As part of their act, they were bound and gagged. Sometimes their lips were sealed with hot wax. All four children were nailed into suffocating boxes resembling miniature coffins. To prove the depth of their trances, they endured pinching, twisting, and the prick of needles and sharp wires. These were only the horrors of the stage. Outside the auditorium, other dangers and cruelties awaited them.

Infuriated mobs attacked them and their promoters for every reason except the justifiable one of stopping further child torment. Some of the protesters were religious fanatics; others were skeptics who felt they had been bilked of their money and had watched a performance of trickery. They barely escaped Danvers, Massachusetts, with their lives. Stones were hurled at them, guns fired. Besides scarred hands, William Eddy now had legs marked by buckshot wounds. Being the eldest of the performers, he was a special target. In Cleveland an angry crowd seized the lad, rode him on a rail, and only a last minute rescue saved him from the pain of hot tar and feathers. In some of the larger cities such as New York and Philadelphia they were safer from mobs, but still subject to threats and indignities.

Nevertheless, the children gave performances so sensational

and so profitable that only the death of Zephaniah Eddy ended their tours and their sufferings. But by then the brothers were warped men, hostile and suspicious, trusting no one but each other. Colonel Olcott's description of them in later life reminds one of a pair of fear-biting dogs, cowering and snapping at the same time. He says they were dark in hair, eyes, and complexion —". . . stiff joints, a dumpy carriage, shrink from advances and they make newcomers feel ill at ease and unwelcome."

However unsociable they were, their occupation at that time, 1874, was a peculiar sort of innkeeping. The Eddys took in spiritualist (or more accurately, spiritist) boarders and seldom had vacancies. The believing and the curious flocked from all parts of the United States and several European countries to attend séances nightly except Sunday. The Eddys charged ten dollars a week, a fee which for its time was fairly high but not exorbitant. Overflow visitors must have been accommodated in neighboring farmhouses, or in Chittenden and have made special arrangements to pay for the séances. Though the house was large, it could not have served the large numbers who gathered on certain nights.

It was far better to stay in the Eddy house itself, and Colonel Olcott, although a self-announced "investigator" (his connection with the New York *Sun* is given as "Special Correspondent"), obtained a second floor room and, like all visitors, was given the run of the house. Apparently all the guests used this freedom to search the premises, hoping or fearing to find the theatrical props of legerdemain. Where did the taciturn brothers hide the mirrors, wires, and gauze? Where were the costumes stored, the springs, threads, and devices? The colonel prowled from cellar to attic and was as unsuccessful as every other searcher. Secret panels? Unknown rooms? He took architectural measurements and satisfied himself that there were none. (This opinion was confirmed years later. After the brothers died, new occupants had the house moved, turning it sideways, away from the road. No secret cellar or other such chamber existed.)

Since most of the incredible report which follows relies on Colonel Olcott's observations, we might well begin by investigating the investigator.

Henry Steel Olcott was a versatile and learned man, fluent in half a dozen languages both classical and modern. While still a young man he became a prominent authority on agriculture, founding a progressive American school of agriculture based on Swiss methods. The United States government invited him to become Chief Commissioner of Agriculture, which was at that time the country's highest position in that field. He refused, and continued private activity as agricultural editor for the New York *Tribune*, working for Horace Greeley. He joined the Union forces in the Civil War, participating in a great deal of action, reached the rank of colonel, and received an honorable (and medical) discharge with citations for meritorious service. During the last year of the war Colonel Olcott was a Special Commissioner for the United States War Department.

His career up to this point is a typical American success story —solid, respectable but hardly imaginative or nonconformist. It is startling to learn that in 1875 Colonel Olcott, along with the frenetic Madame Blavatsky, founded the Theosophical Society. It is quite a leap from heading an agricultural school to teaching neo-Buddhism in India along with Annie Besant, but that is just what the colonel did. There is no doubt about Olcott's high intelligence and no doubt about his eccentricity. Later in life he wore a white, flowing beard which, combined with his bushy black eyebrows and steel-rimmed spectacles, gave him the look of a latter-day Jeremiah. The colonel was impressive.

But was he a reliable reporter in 1874 when he investigated the Eddy farm? Although his subsequent involvement with a branch of mysticism makes him superficially suspect, there is a world of difference between the teachings of Theosophy and the markedly physical demonstrations given by the Eddy brothers. In many ways they are in direct conflict. Colonel Olcott may have leaned toward the occult and may have been well and cleverly deceived, but there is no reason to doubt the sincerity of his report about events at Chittenden.

Olcott, like Madame Blavatsky and many less famous people, was drawn to Chittenden by rumors he had heard. The village itself disappointed him ("plain, dull and uninteresting . . ."), but he soon learned from a local inhabitant that Satan—no less—had invaded the Eddy household and firmly controlled it. Having taken up residence in "the devil's abode," Colonel Olcott searched the house as thoroughly as possible and waited to observe supernatural events. He found the other guests to be no more attractive than his hosts and commented acidly on long-haired men and short-haired women, describing some as "cranks."

The séance room was furnished with uncomfortable straight chairs for spectators and dimly lighted by a shaded kerosene lamp in one corner. A typical curtained "spirit cabinet" stood on a platform stage. If we imagine ourselves in Colonel Olcott's place, we enter the shadowy room and find a chair among a dozen other spectators. William, the more talented of the brothers, shambles in awkwardly, mounts the platform, and sits on a chair in the cabinet, then, reaching up, draws the curtains. There is complete silence while—we have been told—William sinks into a deep trance. Then there is music, distant, faint, combined with indistinct voices. Tension mounts in the room as some invisible band approaches. Several discs float in the air above the platform and their clanking sound identifies them as tambourines being shaken and thumped.

Hands appear. Faintly luminescent hands, disembodied, armless. A dozen of them flutter in the dimness, clutching and extending; some of them are tiny, the fingers of ghostly children; others are large, menacing, and a woman in the audience cries out faintly as a hand seems to reach for her hair, but then it vanishes. All the hands fade, disappear as a shrouded figure emerges from the cabinet, the figure of a crone who has been gathering kindling. She mutters incoherent words, then sings a folk ballad in a cracked, piping voice. She steps backward, toward the cabinet but not into it. Slowly the form dissolves, merges with the air around her until nothing is left but her hands waving good-by.

Other spectral figures arrive in rapid succession, each emerging from the cabinet, a structure so small that it seems to hold only the entranced William Eddy, a big man whose slumped body almost fills the box. A fashionable man in evening clothes says, "Good evening." There is a yellow gleam from the head of his cane as he dances about the stage, seeming to float above its floor. A small, excited gasp arises from the audience as he fades away, to be replaced by a familiar phantom, the spirit of an Indian girl called "Honto." Honto, tiny and fragile, is a frequent visitor. Speaking in a sing-song voice, she brings messages, utters prophecies. Honto is at the end of the platform, very, very near, and a woman seated in the front row, Mrs. Cleveland, says, "May I touch you?"

"Yes," replies the spirit.

Mrs. Cleveland, rather frightened, steps forward and timidly puts her hand on Honto's bare arm. She hesitates a moment, then recoils, stumbles back to her seat. "Cold," she murmurs. "Cold."

By now a score of phantoms have arrived; an ill-lighted fashion show displays the costumes of a dozen countries and centuries. Then, again, the sound of the tambourine and thin music, but this time it is receding, not approaching. The ghosts have departed, some vanishing instantly, others taking leave slowly, their bodies becoming transparent, invisible until only an arm, a head, or a foot remains; then that, too, is gone.

Horatio Eddy, at the rear of the hall, lifts the lamp from the open drum in which it has been shaded, raises it high, turning up the wick. The spectators blink and William Eddy, fumbling, grasping the edge of the cabinet for support, draws back the curtain. He is bedraggled and unsteady, the shirt with its open collar is sweat-stained. Someone applauds but stops quickly when he notices the angry stares of those around him. This had been a religious demonstration, and applause is blasphemy. But prayer is always in order, and one lady, bowing her head, leads the others, "Our Father which art in heaven . . ."

Such were the evenings Colonel Olcott spent at the Eddy farm, and although he never felt welcome, his investigation was not directly hampered by his hosts. During the day, no one objected as he studied the cabinet, the platform, and the surrounding walls. He was even permitted to bring in a workman, who painted a big black-and-white measuring scale on the wall, one so large and clear that the height of all entering ghosts could easily be estimated even in the obscurity of the séances. By this device he determined, at least to his own satisfaction, that whatever the "specters" were, they were not William or Horatio Eddy performing as quick-change artists. Honto may not have been the ghost of an Indian maid, but she certainly was a girl, a small woman, or a feminine-appearing boy. The same applied to other seeming materializations. There was a great and quite natural variation in size.

(At this point one longs for a less gentlemanly investigator than Olcott—the brazen Mr. Volckman of London, who would have leaped onto the platform and tried to wrestle any spirit to the floor. Such an outrage seems never to have happened at Chittenden, or if it did, no report of the incident survives. The sitters were awed, reverent, and maddeningly docile.)

Neither spirits nor spectators lived an entirely indoor life at the Eddy farm. Much of the nearby land was timbered and in one glen was a great upthrust of rock which provided the setting for "Honto's Cave." The cave is shallow, arched, and the word "grotto" describes it exactly. On certain nights, the spectators would gather soon after moonrise, sitting on benches improvised by placing boards over boulders. At these gatherings, the cave served to shelter and conceal William Eddy while he was entranced, but, to assure the watchers that he had not effected a miraculous escape, he talked loudly and almost incessantly from the cave's darkness. Meanwhile, phantom figures appeared on the cliff, about twenty-five feet above, silhouetted against the sky.

Indian spirits, quite naturally, were the frequenters of this neck of the Vermont woods and an outdoor séance Olcott attended was devoted exclusively to them. Honto appeared several times; there came the impressive figure of the great chief Santum (a popular ghost and an audience-pleaser in his buckskins, feathers, and beads), and during the course of the evening, the colonel saw enough Indians of both sexes to have launched a raid on Chittenden. A drawing which illustrates this particular scene shows ten spectators. They were heavily outnumbered by the plumed and painted phantoms.

The farm, as we have said, attracted many international visitors, but none so flamboyant as Helena Petrovna Blavatsky. Madame Blavatsky had not yet reached the height of her worldwide fame, but already commanded great respect in occult circles in many lands. She had every talent for success and celebrity, a powerful personality, keen intelligence, and a flair for showmanship. Madame Blavatsky was theatrical. She astounded Americans by smoking cigars, and, although she was a stocky woman with a sturdy peasant's face and body, she could wear veils and shawls with the grace of Isadora Duncan.

Guests at the Eddy farm during the summer of 1874 were agog at the prospect of a visit from such a personage. They knew most of the facts and all the legends about Helena Blavatsky, knew that she was still in her early forties but had crowded her years with enough adventures for a dozen lifetimes. She was born in Russia in 1831 of German parents and had excellent social credentials; her father was a minor nobleman, and she was a granddaughter of Princess Dolgorouki. Such a lineage was most impressive to Americans. At seventeen she married "well," the bridegroom being an elderly Russian official serving as vice-governor of Erivan (Caucasia). The remoteness of Erivan, its wildness and romantic aura, also stood her in good stead later. Her husband must have had an eye for dramatic effect. It was said that he never moved without an escort of at least fifty gorgeously uniformed Asiatic horsemen, and his bride's personal bodyguard was a giant Moslem named Ali Bek, who protected Madame with pistols and a sharp lance.

He did not have the opportunity to protect her for long. The young bride deserted her husband within a few months and set off to conquer both the physical and spirit worlds, visiting oddly assorted places such as Canada, Texas, Mexico, and India. She attempted to penetrate forbidden Tibet and after one failure managed with characteristic boldness to enter the country, heavily disguised, her crinkly hair hidden, her light complexion stained dark. Unfortunately she became lost on the tortuous trails, and her first Tibetan sally was adventurous but brief. A band of armed horsemen found her, detected her as an intruder, and accompanied her, despite protests, to the frontier.

Madame Blavatsky then disappeared as completely as a ghost at the Eddy farm. These were the "veiled years," the decade from 1848 until 1858, when she *may* have spent seven years at a mountain retreat in Tibet. Her cloudy allusions to this period of her life were always indefinite, always intriguing. The mysterious period of retirement lent her an additional aura of mystery and romance. Only one thing is certain about the era. She learned a great deal about Indian mysticism and acquired more than a dabbler's knowledge of the Cabala, Jewish mystical writings dating back to the Middle Ages but based on much older traditions. From this learning she would later piece together the novel religion of Theosophy, a curious and not unenlightened mixture of many faiths and philosophies.

She entered the world stage again in 1858, home in Russia, where she combined the conventional performance of spiritualism with esoteric overtones from the East. Emigrating to the United States, Madame Blavatsky quickly established herself as one of the best-known practicing mediums and occult teachers in the country.

If Madame could attract attention in New York, she must have been nothing short of sensational in Chittenden, Vermont. She not only attended the séances at the farm but volunteered to play appropriate music on the pedal organ the brothers had recently purchased for the séance room. William and Horatio were quick to latch onto her donated services. Everyone expected something marvelous to happen—and they were not disappointed.

The group, tingling with excitement, gathered for what began as a usual demonstration at the Eddys'. Madame Blavatsky's stout legs were pumping the organ, her strong fingers playing a quiet melody. William sat entranced in his cabinet. The curtain suddenly swished aside to admit a curious figure—a tall, swarthy man brilliantly costumed in velvet, decorated with gold braid, bedecked with tassels, and shod in gleaming boots. Ali Bek, the bodyguard, to the life! He bowed, made gracious gestures of welcome, and advanced toward the electrified observers, a powerful hand pressed to his heart in a Kurdish greeting. Then, apparently from nowhere, there appeared in his empty hand a lance described as no less than ten feet long and decorated with ostrich plumes. He strode across the platform, returned to its center, and gave a military salute. Smoke or mist seemed to emanate from his form and he blended with this self-created cloud, disappearing into the haze, which also faded away.

Madame Blavatsky, unlike some of the spectators, regarded the materialization calmly. She was, after all, accustomed to oddities and was somewhat unusual herself.

The celebrated lady did not remain long at Chittenden. She had many things bubbling in her mind, great activities and achievements planned for the near future. In three years she was to publish *Isis Unveiled*, the classic textbook of Theosophy, and thus attract one hundred thousand followers throughout the world. (Their number is now estimated at three hundred thousand. There are no reliable figures.) Always drawn to India, she went to Madras in 1879, where she established the world headquarters of the Theosophical Society, and performed enough miracles to warrant an investigation by the Society for Psychical Research in 1884. The miracles collapsed under scrutiny, but her disciples rationalized that a few outward, even though spurious, wonders are necessary and justifiable to draw the masses to the true inner faith. The anniversary of her death in 1891 is still remembered yearly by many of her followers and is given the charming name "White Lotus Day."

So the Eddy farm's most famed guest left, headed for acclaim that far overshadowed her occasional embarrassments. Colonel Olcott departed to help found the Theosophical Society in New York the next year and to write his book *People from the Other World*. It caused quite a stir, added to the reputation of the Eddy brothers, then gradually passed into oblivion, becoming a collector's item.

Eventually the brothers closed their spirit carnival, turned away the spiritualist boarders, and, except for a rare séance, lived off the unyielding farmland and their savings. The glen at "Honto's Cave" became overgrown, and the grim Eddys were more or less ignored by their neighbors. Horatio died in 1922 and William followed him in death ten years later. Both were very old men; it is difficult to think of them as ever having been anything except old men or tormented children and somehow incredible that they were in their twenties when Colonel Olcott visited and described them.

In 1969 writer John Mason reported that almost no one living today in Rutland or Chittenden was familiar with the brothers' strange story. A few local residents recalled remarks by their parents, comments that the whole thing had been a hoax, an illusion.

These Yankee skeptics seem to have good sense on their side, for everything about the Eddy story appears redolent of fraud. Too many of its events and details are reminiscent of well-known deceptions, the works of tricksters who, unlike the Eddy brothers, were fully unmasked.

But how on earth did they do it? John Mason estimates that it would have taken "ten to twenty trunkfuls of costumes" to stage this continuing, long-run spiritist revue. His estimate is surely not exaggerated and perhaps too conservative. Between four and five hundred differently garbed characters appeared at different times. There were elaborate headdresses and scores of fancy hand props. Where were such things manufactured and stored? There was no rapid transportation, no calling on a theatrical warehouse to deliver immediately "one Kurdish guardsman's uniform complete with plumed spear."

The limited dimensions of the cabinet are known, and it is quite impossible that anyone besides William Eddy and maybe one other small person could have been concealed in it. We must rule out all forms of light projection and dismiss the clever use of mirrors. There were none on the platform, nor was there any place to hide them at the end of the séances. Every way we turn we are confronted with a choice between the impossible and the preposterous. And of course the happenings were truly both impossible and preposterous.

Whatever the truth was, the taciturn brothers carried it to their graves. It is unlikely that there ever will be a convincing explanation of what really occurred in the Vermont farmhouse. The mystery remains, another addition to that endless file of cases marked "Unexplained."

IV

Identifying Spirits

When the ghost in *Hamlet* says, "I am thy father's spirit," everyone in the audience takes him at his word. Only Hamlet himself fears that the apparition might be a disguised devil and he later devises a play to check the ghost's truthfulness. But the royal Danish specter is not badgered by endless personal questions, not required to divulge intimate and obscure information to establish his identity. Nor is he cross-examined by a dozen committees. Ghosts in drama have a far easier time than unfortunate phantoms who fall among psychical researchers.

Struggles to prove or disprove the identity of a ghostly communicator have produced some of the most fascinating stories in the field of occult study. The phantom speakers are persistent, and at times their demand for personal recognition is so desperate that one thinks of the cries and pounding of a child locked in a closet. It is difficult to pin down anything so elusive as a trance personality, and efforts to accomplish this have resulted in such disparate matters as spirit photography and the quite eerie and exceedingly complicated phenomena known as "Cross-Correspondence."

We have seen that Dr. Phinuit, vivid personality though he was, failed to convince British investigators that he had an individuality apart from Mrs. Piper. Amazing things transpired in the name of Phinuit, but he himself could not prove a previous earthly existence. John, Katie, and other members of the King clan were involved in some noteworthy occult feats, but there is not the least shred of evidence to support their historical reality as persons. The same is true of the whole Imperator-Rector gang. Although no one doubts the former existence of Handel, Bach, Napoleon, and Socrates, their reappearances as ghosts have produced nothing verifiable and a great amount of twaddle. Probably George Pelham has the best claim to independent life in a ghostly state, but even G.P. did not pass muster with William James—although many others accepted him as an entity apart from Mrs. Piper. The verdicts on most Controls are monotonously similar: "Probably a part of the medium's subliminal self . . . an alter ego . . . a secondary personality." The only exceptions seem to be cases of outright fraud where the Control has *no* existence.

After examining scores of instances where the medium seemed honest and talented in one way or another, one is struck by a significant oddity: almost invariably the best Controls and spirit communicators are the recently dead. They were contemporaries of the medium during part of their lives and were personally known to some of the sitters or at least to persons still living at the time of the ghost's appearance at a séance. This was one of Mrs. Piper's outstanding achievements. "G.P." was known and remembered by many. Even "Uncle Jerry," long dead, had not been forgotten by the living. The same pattern holds in the work of other mediums such as Mrs. Leonard, Mrs. Verrall, and Mrs. Thompson.

To some believers this might suggest that spirits recently "passed over to the Other Side" are more articulate because they have greater interest in contacting a world in which former friends and loved ones still dwell. On the other hand, persons inclined to ascribe all psychic achievements to the power of ESP should find ammunition for their argument in this pattern. If no one still living remembers a certain deceased personality, then there are no human memory banks to be unconsciously scanned by the medium, and hence no new or startling information can be revealed. Whatever the reason, all contacts with spirits who spent their earthly lives during a remote era have been unsatisfactory—and the famed *Search for Bridey Murphy* is no exception. It was far more a search than a discovery.

One example, admittedly an extreme one, will show the usual results and the absurdity that so often arise when historical figures invade the séance room. Helene Smith (a pseudonym) joined a spiritualist group in Geneva in 1892 at the age of either twenty-nine or thirty—her birthdate is uncertain. Like Mrs. Piper, she instantly attracted attention as a medium, but here the resemblance to the Boston lady ends. She was dramatic, forceful, and decidedly neurotic. In 1894 Professor Théodore Flournoy, a well-known psychologist at the University of Geneva, succeeded in gaining admission to the circle and during the next year made an exhaustive—and no doubt exhausting—study of Helene's purported clairvoyance.

Mlle. Smith, when entranced, was a name-dropper and celebrity hound. Two principal Controls vied to possess her, and the usual trance pattern began with the phantom of Victor Hugo taking command first. Passage to the Other Side apparently weakened the master's talent, for his posthumous literary productions, penned through Helene, consisted of doggerel religious verse and a number of banal epigrams. Then, after violent physical struggle, Hugo's shade was ousted by a ghost named Leopold, who later proved to be Joseph Balsamo, better known to the world by the professional name Cagliostro. This was a major blunder, for later scholarship has established that Cagliostro's name was not Joseph but Peter Balsamo and his being identified with a vagabond named Joseph Balsamo was a coincidence of last names.

Although Helene spoke and wrote automatically, much of her information from the Beyond was derived from table-tappings, and early in 1894 the table hailed Mlle. Smith as the reincarnation of Marie Antoinette. The decapitated queen and the bogus magician often spoke through the table at the same time while Helene, striving to keep up, impersonated them in pantomine. At last both ghosts found voices. Cagliostro made frequent use of archaic words and spoke with an Italian accent and a lisp. Marie Antoinette, surprisingly, had a vaguely English accent to her French. During sessions of automatic writing, both celebrities used modern spelling and though their calligraphy showed two distinct styles, there was not the least resemblance to the handwriting of the actual historical characters they purported to be.

Professor Flournoy set rather obvious traps for Helene and she avoided most of them, not being lured into saying that her royal relatives used the telephone or rode bicycles. Nevertheless, as Marie Antoinette she smoked cigarettes, a habit that shocked Helene when not entranced. Her Marie Antoinette also calculated distances according to the modern metric system.

Flournoy was convinced of Helene's sincerity, and the origin of her delusion is not far to seek. She had been holding séances at the home of a certain Mrs. B., who gave her an illustration from Dumas's *Memoirs of a Physician*. It showed a scene between Cagliostro and the Dauphiness, and Mrs. B. suggested that Helene might be a reincarnation of Lorenza Feliciani, Cagliostro's wife, who is represented as a medium in the Dumas tale. Helene *did* become Lorenza and continued this trance impersonation until informed that the character in *Memoirs of a Physician* was a creation of the novelist and had little similarity to the historical Lorenza except in name. Helene's mind then turned to the popu-

138

lar, and quite false, legend that Cagliostro was intimately involved with Marie Antoinette, and promptly elevated herself into the ranks of royalty.

The Marie Antoinette impersonation was impressive only because of Helene's showmanship. This period of Mlle. Smith's mediumship was called the "Royal Cycle" because she also beĉame a reincarnation of an Indian princess—Asian, not American—and gave a long account of "The Unknown History of India."

Before leaving Helene Smith, we must note that she far outdid any modern astronaut. One evening she felt herself sailing toward a brilliant star, and the table assured her that she was now visiting the planet Mars. Her Martian travelogues aroused widespread curiosity, causing her to repeat the trip many times. She discovered that the Martians traveled in rapid carriages which had neither wheels nor horses, flew about in Jules Verne–style flying machines, and enjoyed the cooling effect of fountains on the roofs of their residences. The men and women, who resembled earthlings, dressed alike in decorated long-tailed shirts, perhaps foreshadowing the unisex fad on our own planet.

Mlle. Smith's most remarkable achievement, however, was her rapid acquiring of the Martian language and alphabet. Professor Flournoy, in his "The Natives of the Planet Mars," has given a very rudimentary primer of the language, and here is a sample of the Martian tongue transcribed into Latin characters: *"Dode ne ci haudan te mess metiche astane ke de me veche."*

An English translation, made by Baron Johan Liljencrants, reads, "This is the house of the great man Astane which thou hast seen."

Students who propose to learn Martian will find their progress swift if they have a previous knowledge of French. Grammatical structure and all vowel sounds are identical in the two languages. But unlike the gibberish usually passed off as "speaking in tongues," Helene Smith's Martian was consistent in usage. She assigned fixed meanings to words and did not forget or vary them, thus showing that her subconscious powers of memory were prodigious. It is an impressive feat to create the vocabulary for an entire language in a brief period of time and to remember the whole thing afterward. Unfortunately, the lady had no other accomplishments.

Helene Smith's historical Controls and celebrity communicators are typical of the pitfalls awaiting sensitives who venture into the dangerous game of contacting persons long dead. Yet such a contact is precisely what spiritualism is constantly seeking, for it would confound the dissenters who claim that all unexplained psychic communications are derived from ESP.

It is easy to construct an ideal case in imagination: An untraveled and preferably not well-educated medium in some town in the United States claims contact with the ghost of William Shakespeare. Extensive questioning by experts reveals full knowledge of Elizabethan England and several beautiful sonnets are produced by automatic writing. Then the ghost reveals the locations of hidden documents in England—folios, letters, and manuscripts previously unknown. These are subsequently discovered and pronounced authentic beyond doubt.

Such evidence would by no means change the faith of diehard materialists, who are just as adamant as fanatical mystics, but it would prove to open minds the actual existence of the spirit communicator apart from the medium. Countless men and women have spent their lives seeking such an ideal case, but despite their dedication and longing, it has never been discovered, and no Control has ever established himself fully as a separate entity.

MULTIPLE PERSONALITY

The occurrence of more than one personality in an individual is hardly common, but the fact that it can happen is well known to the public. *The Three Faces of Eve* brought wide attention to a phenomenon familiar to psychologists since early in this century. As a theme, it has been used in numerous suspense novels and was treated in depth in the work of the late Shirley

Jackson. Robert Louis Stevenson's *Dr. Jekyll and Mr. Hyde,* although dealing with the forces of good and evil in one man's nature, is obviously inspired by thoughts of dual personality, and it is hardly surprising that the author wrote in a letter that his own "other fellow" seemed a separate part of his consciousness while he was ill.

Sensing the presence of one's "other fellow" is a mental experience and should not be confused with the more physical *Doppelganger* phenomenon, which involves seeing the wraith (or ghost or "spirit-double") of a person still living. There are hundreds of reports of people suddenly catching sight of an immaterial twin. The poet Shelley had such a shock, and Catherine the Great of Russia one day beheld her exact double sitting on her throne. The empress was so convinced of the reality of this presence that she ordered her guards to fire upon it. This type of illusion or haunting is not the same as that in which two "persons" seem to share one body.

Although it first appears that discussion of multiple personality is more appropriate to psychology than to a survey of the occult, the fact is that many trance personalities and Controls show evidence of being subliminal selves of a classic type. Also, multiple personality may account for many an old tale of demonic or angelic possession of an individual.

An example is the story of Rachel Baker, "The Sleeping Preacher," who was born in 1794 in Pelham, Massachusetts, and at the age of nine moved with her family to Marcellus, New York. From all accounts, she was an excessively unattractive child, given to brooding about such dour matters as infant damnation and the tainted heritage of Adam. She fretted over the inherent wickedness of her nature, yet her own sins appear to have been neither black nor scarlet but a quite uninteresting washed-out gray. (She sometimes found herself nodding in church and was afflicted with the vice of sloth when it came to household chores.) At fifteen she became a sleepwalker and suffered the most horrifying delusions and dreams, her shrieks arousing the house in the middle of the night. At first demon possession was suspected and various remedies including the "laying on of hands" by church elders were attempted, but nothing exorcised Rachel's "devil" and soon she was pointed out as a caution to other youngsters.

Then "The Sleeping Preacher" emerged full-blown. While the girl was entranced, an alter ego began to conduct daily religious services, always starting and concluding with a fervent prayer delivered in an unusual voice. Between prayers, she exhorted her listeners, who were soon coming from miles around, to greater piety, and she harangued them with abstruse theological discourses packed with a wealth of scriptural citation and lengthy quoting utterly beyond the mental capacity of Rachel Baker unentranced. There was, of course, no psychological examination of Rachel, but all evidence points to something other than simple religious hysteria. "The Sleeping Preacher" was unaware of Rachel and Rachel was unaware of delivering sermons.

The emergence and submergence of her secondary personality caused extreme physical suffering. She endured fits and spasms, which she vented by loud groans and weeping, until at last the trance subsided into normal sleep, from which she later awoke as herself. The following day the entire process would be repeated with a new or at least varied sermon. Many people, including some members of the clergy, declared her invested by the Holy Ghost, but apparently her family found the whole matter a trial and attempted to cure the girl by changes of scene. Nothing helped. Only opium could interrupt "The Sleeping Preacher's" entranced services. Eventually her sermons and discourses were published, and perhaps this compensated pious Rachel for her daily pain.

The landmark study of multiple personality, the case of "Christine L. Beauchamp" as observed by Dr. Morton Prince, does not directly touch the occult, but Dr. Prince's findings throw so much light on certain trance personalities and Controls that his report, originally made to the International Congress of Psychology in Paris, August 1900, was reprinted in the *Proceedings* of the Society for Psychical Research. It is given only a brief summary here.

Christine Beauchamp consulted Dr. Prince when a nervous breakdown had reduced her to a mental and physical wreck. She had been forced to abandon college and was rapidly becoming incapable of meeting the smallest problems of daily living. Early interviews revealed that she was a puritanical young woman plagued by all manner of repressions and the qualms of a New England conscience. In the course of treatment, Dr. Prince detected no fewer than three quite separate personalities within her, *B* I, *B* II, and *B* III. The everyday girl, *B* I, knew nothing of the others, but *B* II was acquainted with Christine. Only *B* III knew both of the other selves. *B* III was by far the most aggressive of of the three "Beauchamp girls" and eventually developed an independent life of her own, frequently taking over Christine's physical mechanism and demanding to be called "Sally Beauchamp."

Sally proved to be a carefree girl with radiant good health and an engaging, if somewhat flippant, manner. She loved jokes and amusements but was utterly bored with the religious ideals Christine attempted to practice. Although sympathetic and tolerant of most people, Sally felt only contempt for weak, complaining Christine and lost little time in demonstrating her scorn by small acts of mischief and malice. Christine would suddenly awake to consciousness on a remote country road, ill and without a penny in her purse, abandoned there by Sally, who had enjoyed the hike and then spitefully submerged herself, leaving Christine to make her way home as best she could.

Christine sometimes received gifts from Sally—live snakes and reptiles, which she abhorred. These were but a few of the discomforts and embarrassments Christine endured during the seven years before Dr. Prince succeeded in fusing *B* I and *B* II into a single entity whom he pronounced to be the true Miss Beauchamp. This new creation was a healthy woman, and it is perhaps a mistake to regret the exorcism and destruction of fun-loving Sally. It should be added that during the treatment a fourth woman, B IV, who was completely different, emerged briefly and then vanished.

Many Controls who appear in spiritualist trances are obviously similar to the various Beauchamp egos. Also, numerous instances of demon possession are explained in the light of Dr. Prince's findings. In 1903 F. W. H. Myers wrote of the affliction of Laurancy Vennum, a fourteen-year-old girl who became known in the press as the "Watseka Wonder." Laurancy suffered nervous seizures and was hypnotized in an attempt to alleviate them, but the hypnosis had the startling result of changing her into another personality, that of a girl who had died a dozen years before. She showed an astonishing knowledge of the dead girl's life, and acquaintances of the deceased found the impersonation uncannily accurate and quite frightening. The new personality did not seem to grow or develop—it simply burst forth like a genie released from a bottle. After nearly six months the original Laurancy resumed command of her own body, but even long afterward the "dead girl" would suddenly seize possession. "The Watseka Wonder" does not appear to be only a matter of dual personality. Observers were insistent that Laurancy's familiarity with the dead girl's life and habits could not have been acquired by any usual means. Naturally, ESP has been offered as an explanation.

Two other cases of apparent spirit-possession were studied by Professor Flammarion near the turn of the century. A certain Mlle. Cousedon of Paris developed great ability at the self-inducement of trances. In fact, she was not only entranced but enraptured, for she became the Angel Gabriel and flapped about with arms extended like wings. She was not, it seems, actually air-borne. Gabriel often lapsed into a peculiar language of unknown syntax. It must have struck Flammarion as a sort of pig-Latin, for he noticed a great deal of rhyming. We have no grammar or dictionary of the tongue—which seems to be a lapse of scholarship, since the language of angels surely deserves at least as much attention as that of Martians.

Mme. Hugo d'Alesi, another Flammarion subject, could not by herself induce a trance, but when hypnotized she remained in an inert state for a short period, then seemed to shake off the hypnotism and become fully awake. A good many spirits appeared to possess her, and there was no limit to her versatility. She was a foul-mouthed rake, a confused cleric, an arch young lady with an affected speech impediment, and a provincial man named Tetard who liked nothing better than guzzling cheap wine and chewing tobacco. The characterizations were of a quality to excite the envy of an accomplished actress. But when free of the trance, Mme. d'Alesi reverted to her own personality at once and had no recollection of what had transpired.

The examples we have given, all of which excited interest and conjecture in their own time, have not led us far on the road to isolating and identifying a "spirit." Only the "Watseka Wonder" gives evidence of an extraordinary force at work, and even there if we grant the girl a powerful ability at ESP the mystical aspects of the "Wonder" vanish. But another case of spirit-possession, that of Patience Worth, is a very different sort of affair and contains elements hard to explain.

MRS. CURRAN TRIES THE OUIJA

The strange career of Patience Worth was first detailed by Walter Franklin Prince and more recently reviewed by Rosalind Heywood in her excellent work *Beyond the Reach of Sense*. We have only one new scene to add to the story, so its retelling here will be briefer than that remarkable woman, spirit, or whatever she was deserves.

Mrs. Joseph Curran, with whom the Patience Worth tale begins, was an unremarkable housewife of St. Louis, Missouri, a woman who was untraveled, had read little, and had completed only a grammar-school education. Her peculiar adventure began when a friend asked her to experiment with a ouija board. At the time she was over thirty years old and had never been interested in the occult even as a game. Nor was she at all charmed by the ouija until on July 8, 1913, a "spirit" suddenly began communicating at a furious pace, announcing that she was Patience Worth, born on an English farm in the seventeenth century. In her life she had emigrated to the American colonies and there was murdered by Indian savages.

Redskins and farms in Merry Old England are such occult clichés that no one would have paid much attention to Patience Worth had she not revealed an unusual flair for literary production. She turned out three novels, which were published, plus a vast number of poems, dialogues, and poetic prayers. All three novels enjoyed limited but definite critical success, and reviewers who praised the books were almost all unaware that there had been anything extraordinary about the method of authorship.

It must not be thought that Mrs. Curran was a would-be writer who had thought up an unusual way of breaking into print. Her friends and family declared that she had never indicated the least interest in writing. On the contrary, her ambition had always been to be a singer. Mrs. Curran, we emphasize, had never displayed any more than average intellectual attainment and she was anything but witty. Yet Patience Worth had a quick, flashing intelligence. An example of her skill at producing instant epigrams is quoted by Mrs. Heywood: When asked to define "flapper," then a current slang word, she responded immediately, "They dare what the past hoped for."

Mrs. Curran was never blotted out by the personality of Patience Worth. The relationship between them was more that of a medium and a Control than a personality and an alter ego. The spirit, Worth, dictated and her secretary, Curran, wrote down the words. Since this was the nature of their association, it is no wonder that Patience took a haughty attitude toward Mrs. Curran and her middle-class friends, regarding them as intellectual inferiors—as, indeed, they were.

146

A good many people of intelligence and reputation were eager to meet Patience, and to do so it was necessary to invite the rather dull Mrs. Curran. An example of this is a small gathering held one evening when Curran-Worth was visiting Chicago. The Reverend Harold Cook, who at the time was teaching in the English Department at Northwestern University, recalls the meeting vividly after many years. "It was most extraordinary," he says. "Remarkable."

Besides Cook, the guests included Harriet Monroe, poet and founding editor of *Poetry* magazine, a psychologist, and university faculty members. Patience Worth, speaking through Mrs. Curran, held the floor most of the evening, producing quick poems on subjects suggested by the listeners. The "spirit" was facile and sharp-witted and expressed herself in an antique manner which impressed the very knowledgeable guests as being absolutely authentic.

The actual source of the Worth-Curran literary output remains unknown. The three books, all historical novels, required extensive research which Mrs. Curran, it is practically certain, never did. If a hoax, it was perpetrated with a cleverness that the St. Louis housewife gave no evidence of possessing, and, furthermore, as a hoax it is pointless.

Patience could well have been an unusual variety of a subliminal self, but she did not behave like one. Mrs. Curran was highly aware of Patience, and this is a rare occurrence in such cases. One can also speculate that ESP, vast and far-ranging, was in operation.

Then there is always the view that spiritualists will take: Patience Worth was exactly what she claimed to be, even though her historical existence cannot be proved by birth and death certificates.

At any rate, the affair cannot be dismissed by saying that Mrs. Curran had a hidden talent which for her own reasons she chose to conceal under a spiritualistic pretext. One novel, *Telka*, is a tale of medieval England, and a study by a philologist has shown that no less than ninety per cent of the vocabulary was derived from Anglo-Saxon. Since the King James Bible is only seventy-seven per cent composed of Anglo-Saxon derivatives, Mrs. Curran, if she wrote *Telka*, accomplished a philological miracle. Equally remarkable is the fact that *Telka* contains not one word which entered the language later than 1700! Whatever explanations one accepts for the Patience Worth case, everyday beliefs are likely to be stretched in some direction. There is no simple way of solving the riddle.

Spirit Photography

The desperation of believers to identify the strange shapes and voices produced at séances has led to a great number of tests and experiments. Of these, one of the most bizarre and probably the most tragic was the growth of a small and lucrative business called spirit photography. Reports about it are usually written in matter-of-fact language, but one can easily sense the heartbreak involved in this fraud.

In the city of Boston in 1862 a certain Dr. Gardner announced that a photographer named Mumler had taken a séance picture in which not only Dr. Gardner appeared, but, with him, the likeness of a cousin who had died twelve years previously. This news, naturally, caused a great stir among spiritualists, who seized upon the development as sure proof of their faith. Customers flocked to Mumler, usually bringing their own mediums with them, although he was happy to provide—at a substantial fee— a clairvoyant to summon the spirit whose likeness he would record. Mothers proudly displayed vague photographs of dead children, and for a little more than a year Dr. Gardner continued in a fool's paradise, believing the new discovery had brought immense consolation to a world that could now scoff at death. He was disabused of this illusion when he learned that a living model had posed as a spirit in Mumler's studio. Only two instances of fraud could be proved, but there were sound reasons to suspect that the trickster had also used other models who were unwilling to betray their employer. What followed is typical of the psychology of believers: Dr. Gardner could not bring himself to reject *all* the photos as frauds—it was too bitter to think that the whole thing had been a hoax. Still, to his great credit, he had courage enough to broadcast his findings in the two cases.

Although Mumler's business was not halted, it dropped off, and he decided to try to bilk the gullible of New York. The police soon swooped, but there was not enough evidence to convict him of fraud. Some witnesses were reluctant to testify because they did not wish to be exposed as fools in public; others, steadfast in faith, would have done anything to protect the man who had given them such great happiness. It is the old story.

Mumler soon dropped from sight, but other charlatans took up the business, and to this day spirit photographs can be found in family albums in the United States.

Spirit photography made its appearance in England through the efforts of the doughty Mrs. Guppy and her husband—who was also a medium. It is difficult to determine Mrs. Guppy's place in the annals of psychical research. We have already described one of her famous entrances, the astounding flight from home to the middle of the séance table. Her exits were equally dramatic. She was one of a school of mediums who specialized in "transportation." (Others included Miss Lottie Fowler, Mr. Henderson, and Mr. Herne.) Her séances were usually conducted in darkness with the charming addition of musical accompaniment. At some point in the evening she was likely to vanish from the room leaving behind nothing but a slight haze on the ceiling. Before her marriage to the medium Samuel Guppy, she was already famous as Miss Nichol, thanks in part to the publicity given her by the praise of Dr. Alfred Russel Wallace, who shares with Charles Darwin credit for the discovery of evolution. Miss Nichol lived for a time with Mrs. Sims, Dr. Wallace's sister, and it was thus that Wallace happened to observe her performances, which were indeed remarkable. In addition to personal levitation, the medium specialized in apports. Fruit, fronds, greenery, and flowers were mysteriously whisked into the séance chamber. She seemed quite able to invoke an earthquake, and Dr. Wallace declared that one night the entire room "shook violently."

After her marriage to Samuel Guppy, the couple became a team. Some of Guppy's associates and colleagues were dubious characters, to say the least. Among them were the fraudulent slate-writer, Dr. Slade, and Kate Fox, who had left the United States after her exposure as a fake and gone to London to practice her trade. (Later, Kate married an English barrister and became Mrs. Jencken. She had come a long way from the dreary rented house in Hydesville but had failed to amend her character. In 1874 she reported from Brighton that her six-month-old baby had already become a "writing medium.") The Guppys, for all their excesses and possible rascality, remained private mediums, and it was in a private capacity that they introduced spirit photography, using a lensman named Hudson after their own efforts to take pictures had failed.

Hudson duplicated the success that Mumler had enjoyed in Boston, and, to make matters worse, he was far more skillful at deception. His work reveals a fine sense of the dramatic: draped, diaphanous forms float behind more substantial living sitters; a pretty child, half-smiling, peeps from behind a cloud of ectoplasm, her face vague but clear enough to be recognized by her loving father, Mr. Enmore Jones. (Later Mr. Jones sadly admitted that he had been swindled and mistaken. Such disillusion was the common fate of all the victims except those so passionately determined to believe that no amount of evidence shook their faith. These, the resolutely blind, were undoubtedly the happiest of the dupes.)

The first experts to study Hudson and his work were frankly baffled, but the whole business was eventually exposed by the indefatigable Mrs. Henry Sidgwick in an article published by the Society for Psychical Research in 1872. This, however, did not succeed in halting the traffic. Two years later a Frenchman, Buguet, set up shop in London to produce portraits of beloved ghosts. His work was even better than Hudson's, and clients flocked to his door. Having skimmed the cream of the London market, he unwisely returned to Paris, where he was promptly arrested for fraud. Buguet's subsequent confession and explanation of his process did not daunt the faithful for long, but some of those he had bilked were shattered. Others, more credulous, insisted that the confession had been obtained by a nefarious group of Jesuits who had bribed an otherwise honest man.

Among Buguet's successors in the late 1870s was a man named Parks whose methods, on the surface, seem plausible. Hereward Carrington describes a visit to his London studio: "[The photograph] was taken on a plate freshly purchased and which had never been in Mr. Parks's possession. The plate had been prepared and placed in a shield, when a photographer who was present requested that it might be taken out and turned upside down before exposure." The results that day were somewhat peculiar: "On developing the plate, a rude outline of a figure, composed of *two* busts appears, the busts pointing in opposite directions."

Today the faked photographs that once deceived knowledgeable people would not survive even a cursory laboratory examination. But the heyday of spirit-photography occurred in an era when picture taking was still in an experimental stage. Equipment, paper, and developing processes were comparatively unreliable and this made fakery an easier task than it is now. Undoubtedly accidental double exposure created one of the most famous spirit photos. Both Frank Podmore and Mrs. Sidgwick independently report a weird event that happened at D—— Hall on the day of Lord D.'s funeral. A photograph was taken in the library of the mansion that morning and when the plate was developed six months later there appeared a faint but recognizable image of Lord D., apparently haunting the room.

Apart from accidents, the opportunities for fraud are legion in spirit-photography and sometimes the duplicity comes from an

unexpected quarter. A Mr. Beattie, a professional London photographer, was among the first to investigate the work of the
charlatan Hudson. For a long time his efforts at detection were
frustrated. The photos, he said, "were not made by double exposure, nor by figures projected in space in any way; they were
not the result of mirrors; they were not produced by any ma-
chinery in the background, behind it, above it, below it, nor by
any contrivance connected with the bath, the camera, or the
camera-slide." Intrigued by the puzzle, Beattie attempted to dup-
licate Hudson's effects. Several photos were eventually produced
which, owing to flaws in the paper and developing, had light
spots which might easily be mistaken for human figures. Then
came several astonishingly successful attempts which confounded
Beattie. The "successes" were soon traced to the work of an employee, an assistant who had doctored the photos for reasons
known only to himself.

Beattie's later investigations were more fruitful when he turned
to the use of a microscope to reveal skillful double exposures.
Zealots and true believers were unmoved by the new evidence.
They had defended Buguet by attacking the Jesuits, and now
they turned on Beattie, pointing out that he was an utterly un-
spiritual type who could hardly understand that during a séance
objects as well as people were likely to have an aura and what
the photographer mistook for proof of double exposure was in
reality spiritual emanations radiating from table and chairs.

When all the evidence has been examined, any possible truth
in spirit-photography depends at last upon the recognition by
friends and relatives of the faces of the dead appearing in such
pictures, and this is untrustworthy, since the same likeness is
usually given as many different identities as the number of believers examining it. A grieving widow will joyfully declare that
an obscure human likeness is positively her late husband. A son
will exclaim, "That's Mother, of course! How well she looks."

It would be pleasant to report that the spirit-photography
swindle has vanished, more doubly exposed than the film it em-

ploys, but this is not the case. In recent years there have been reports of "amazing" photos taken in London, Rome, and—not surprisingly—Los Angeles. The art has been so thoroughly discredited that it will undoubtedly never again find as many victims as in the past, but there remains every reason to expect it to survive among the bereaved and the gullible.

Minds Across the Sea

The long struggle by spiritualists and psychical researchers to establish or demolish the identities of communicators from the Other Side led, during what might be called the Golden Age of mediumship, to a curious and puzzling series of incidents which are known as Cross-Correspondence. Avoiding a complicated academic definition, we can best explain Cross-Correspondence by constructing a simple, hypothetical case.

Let us suppose that Mrs. Chicago, a medium practicing automatic writing in the city of that name, one night believes herself controlled by a spirit identified only as "Wolfe." Entranced, she repeatedly writes the words, "Church bell . . . cattle . . . plow." They are meaningless to her, but she follows the impulse given by her unknown Control.

At about the same time another medium, Mrs. London, living in England, pens automatically a script in which several key words appear over and over. "Abode . . . bosom . . . father." Then "general" is repeated several times, although it is not clear whether the word is a noun, adjective, or particular title.

None of this makes sense until a third sensitive, Mrs. Honolulu, receives the odd message, "Thomas Gray . . . Quebec . . . Mrs. Chicago and Mrs. London . . ."

The three communications are subsequently examined by a psychical researcher with a literary bent, and the Cross-Correspondence becomes immediately clear. The Chicago script refers to the first stanza of Gray's "Elegy," and the London message has reference to the last stanza of the same poem. The further key is the fact that on the eve of the capture of Quebec, British General Wolfe, an admirer of Thomas Gray, made the famous comment that he would rather have written the "Elegy" than conquer the besieged city.

Our imaginary Cross-Correspondence, like those recorded by researchers, depends to some degree on interpretation. The Chicago script is a paraphrase, "Church bell, cattle, and plow" for "Curfew, lowing herd, and plowman." Yet Wolfe obviously fits in with "general, Quebec, and Thomas Gray." The London words are exact. The whole thing goes together so neatly that, unless there has been collusion among the three mediums, it seems to show that a single communicator reached them all at widely separate locations. We do not yet know the communicator's identity, although it would seem to be either the general or the poet. For this, we must wait until the next communication, hoping (and praying, if we are spiritualists) that it will be plain and unmistakable, thus confounding the ESP and "subliminal self" advocates.

The most celebrated cases of Cross-Correspondence occurred early in this century, and several mediums, including Mrs. Piper, played major roles. But the central figure was Mrs. A. W. Verrall, a lady worth meeting, and one who, like Mrs. Piper, seemed an improbable candidate for mediumship. There are so many zanies, frauds, and cranks among occultists that it is a great pleasure to encounter a woman like Mrs. Verrall. She is one of the most attractive characters in the drama of psychical research.

One pictures her standing on a podium in a lecture hall, expounding learnedly and enthusiastically on the classics, perhaps speaking in Latin or Greek, languages in which she was not only literate but conversationally fluent. Her brown hair is upswept in the high pompadour favored by ladies of the late Victorian era, and her tweed suit is smart but sensible, befitting her station as wife of a prominent scholar and university professor. Altogether, she strikes one as a handsome woman, vital and self-confident. There is a touch of the Roman matron in Mrs. Verrall: integrity, energy, and an uncompromised perseverance. Had she strayed from the subject of her lecture—and one doubts she ever did this—Mrs. Verrall might have informed her listeners about obscure details of the Darwinian theory, the byways of anthropology, or the arguments for woman suffrage. Alert and inquiring, she would be an impressive personality today—and in her own era she was outstanding, an adventurous intellect who stood fast against the antifemale prejudices of her generation.

She was the daughter of an educated family and early in life she displayed unusual mental capacity. Although England at the time did not encourage higher scholarship for females, the girl decided to become a political scientist—a bold ambition considering that her countrywomen would not even be thought competent to vote until another half century had passed. Later her interest shifted to classical languages and she became a lecturer at Newnham. Another remarkable woman, Mrs. Henry Sidgwick, wife of the first president of the Society for Psychical Research and herself an excellent investigator, was Newnham's principal, and the two women became friends. They had much in common: both were married to celebrated academic figures, and both could claim scholarship in their own right; both had keen, inquiring minds that would accept nothing in science or philosophy without examination.

Mrs. Sidgwick, unlike Mrs. Verrall, was inclined to be a tartar. Between the years 1874 and 1886 she exposed no fewer than eight fraudulent mediums in England, writing reports that are cool, factual, yet seem somehow etched in acid. When other investigators were praising Eusapia Palladino, Mrs. Sidgwick raised skeptical eyebrows and said, "I am impressed, but not at all convinced." (Later she said worse.)

The Sidgwicks' enthusiasm for psychic matters affected the Verralls, and soon they, too, were attempting to put research into the occult on a scientific footing. Dr. A. W. Verrall, an authority on classic literature, held an important post at Cambridge, and for him and his wife to dabble in such affairs as thought-transference and table-rapping was hardly an activity to enhance their standing in the community. Nevertheless, with encouragement from the Sidgwicks and their good friend Frederic W. H. Myers, they took up the study of spirits and parapsychological phenomena. Both became highly informed, although her zeal was greater than his. One supposes that there was a good deal of gossip in conservative Cambridge.

Mrs. Verrall entered the new field with the same determination that had earlier enabled her to master four foreign languages. It must not be thought that she was a born heretic or a faddist. Her religious beliefs were casual but orthodox, although in philosophy she inclined more to the materialism of Lucretius than the mysticism of Plato. A product of her times, she had a sublime faith in science that was shared by most educated Victorians.

After wide reading and study, Mrs. Verrall decided that personal experiment was the only practical approach to psychical research. Some years before, a Mr. Gutherie of Liverpool had conducted a series of telepathic tests to determine whether such simple things as designs, colors, and objects could be conveyed from mind to mind. His results, although inconclusive, strongly suggested the reality of ESP.

Following Gutherie's lead, Mrs. Verrall attempted nine careful experiments in 1893. With some notable and dramatic exceptions, the best-authenticated cases of telepathy have occurred between individuals who were closely associated, often relatives, and Mrs. Verrall chose to work with her nine-year-old daughter, Helen. They sat back to back and, under observation, alternately acted as recipient and sender. No words were used. Mrs. Verrall felt it would be simpler for the receiver to draw whatever impression came to mind. In the nine trials mother and daughter scored four remarkable hits, four failures, and one doubtful result. It is characteristic of Mrs. Verrall that successes and failures were reported with equal emphasis. Unlike many clairvoyants, she never glossed over "negative experiments."

Although wary of generalizing, Mrs. Verrall felt that in this one case, at least, an unknown power or ability had come into play. Since there was no denying the results, skeptics resorted to the two usual methods of attack: it was suggested, not very politely, that there had been collusion between mother and daughter—a weak accusation when one considers Mrs. Verrall's career and character. Others merely shrugged off the matter as silly and beneath the attention of serious scientists. Undaunted, Mrs. Verrall persisted in experiment. Her neighbors and academic colleagues had found her interest in telepathy questionable enough, but the real shock came when the outwardly respectable lady began to indulge in crystal-gazing.

Her work in crystallomancy, which we shall examine later, produced no startling results for psychical research. Nevertheless, her self-analysis might have been a real contribution to psychology, had psychologists not chosen to ignore it. Despite the huge accumulation of evidence, the existence of any unconscious mind was as much doubted then as ESP is now. Mrs. Verrall not only explored her own inner mind but achieved revelations remarkable enough for Frederic Myers to devote a portion of his book *Human Personality* to her efforts. Further, he mentioned her by name, and many devotees of ESP are convinced that in so doing he unwittingly triggered what would become a deluge of telepathy and Cross-Correspondence.

A TRIUMVIRATE OF GHOSTS

At the beginning of this century, psychical research suffered twin blows in the deaths of Professors Sidgwick and Myers in 1900 and 1901. Their friend Edmund Gurney had preceded them in death by a decade. They had been an outstanding trio of investigators in the occult, and Mrs. Verrall felt the loss keenly.

All three had stated many times that if there existed any way to communicate from beyond the grave, they would make themselves known to their survivors, and Mrs. Verrall resolved to become the human instrument through which they might speak, although she was by no means convinced that such contact was possible.

The story of Mrs. Verrall's efforts has no parallel in psychical research. She was probably the world's only self-made medium. A psychic talent, or at least the ability to convince others of such a talent, invariably comes as a gift. Not so in Mrs. Verrall's case. Her early work in telepathy and her "visions" had revealed unusual sensitivity, but little more than that, and her rise to mediumship is an example of lifting oneself by the bootstraps. She developed skill in automatic writing in the same way she had once learned Latin conjugations—by patience and hard work. She chose automatic writing as the best method of communication because it somehow seemed less dependent on her own personality than speech. Further, it would give her exact records—and Mrs. Verrall liked exactness in everything.

This practice, automatism, might well be recommended to any novice who wishes to test his powers in spirit or telepathic communication. The potential receiver sits at a desk or table in a comfortable chair and in an atmosphere of complete relaxation. Nothing else is required except a paper and a pen or a pencil. The receiver, pen in hand, attempts to make his mind blank, usually concentrating on a nondescript color or closing his eyes and thinking of infinity. Some mediums fix their attention on a neutral object, such as a crystal, to aid semi-hypnosis. When the ideal state of passivity has been reached, the hand should write of its own will and without conscious direction by the mind of the receiver. The independence of the hand is vital in this experiment. When Mrs. Verrall wrote she was in a state of very light trance, unconscious of the language in which the words came, usually unaware of the purport of a message, although sometimes she had a hazy idea of individual words.

Such is not always the case. Another automatist, Mrs. Holland, never lost consciousness. In fact, she had to keep her wits about her just to move her pencil rapidly enough to keep up with the torrent of words pouring from her ghostly communicators. Mrs. Piper was completely entranced; on the contrary, Mrs. Curran was awake when she received dictation from "Patience Worth."

The most startling modern automatist, Grace Rosher of London, writes messages from her deceased fiancé, Gordon E. Burdick, and from other spirits when fully awake. The content of the Rosher communiqués is not remarkable, and they would probably have been dismissed as delusion or nonsense except for two mysterious facts: Miss Rosher does not hold the pen when she writes, but leans it against her clenched fist and it seems to move of its own accord. Further, graphologists have noted an amazing similarity between the writing of the Burdick Control and that of the living Burdick. One expert declared flatly that no forger could produce Burdick's handwriting with such accuracy. Miss Rosher received purported messages from Sir William Crookes, the eminent nineteenth-century physicist, and the signature by the Crookes Control was also uncannily like Sir William's actual calligraphy. It is a strange case, although its impact is slightly lessened by the fact that Miss Rosher happens to be a professional artist and, still more unfortunate, her specialty is miniatures, which have been displayed in many galleries, including the Royal Academy.

Although a common activity in séance chambers, automatic writing antedates modern spiritualism by centuries and has fascinated many celebrated persons who cannot be called spiritualists. Sardou, Victor Hugo, Goethe, Elizabeth Barrett Browning, Coleridge, and most notably William Blake all tried it with varying results.

Today, the largest single group of automatic writers is not, as one might suppose, spiritualists, but followers of the Moral Rearmament movement, who set aside a portion of each day to receive "divine guidance," which they record in notebooks. Their practice of a daily "quiet time" is not automatic writing in the strictest definition of the term, for the receiver is rarely entranced. Nevertheless, all other marks of occult, or at least mystical, practice are to be found in the "quiet time." The Moral Rearmament faithful are more inclined to skepticism about the messages so received than are many spiritualists. They check their written "guidance" against four standards pronounced by the late Dr. Frank Buchman: honesty, purity, unselfishness, and love. Any instruction not conforming to these "absolutes" is rejected as a whispering of Satan or a prompting from man's baser nature. The remaining messages are considered divine orders.

Mrs. Verrall's automatic writing demanded far greater concentration than that practiced by the Moral Rearmament people or by those who take up the occult as an interesting parlor game. She devoted hours to her work, seldom missing a day, and she would record nothing that seemed to come of her own volition. For several months nothing whatever happened, and it required stern perseverance to keep trying. Then, quite suddenly, her pen began to write, not in English but in Latin and Greek. The grammar and style of the first messages were deplorable. Nothing about them made sense except the repeated signature, "Myers." But gradually the scholarship improved, whole sentences, correctly written, emerged. Yet the meaning remained elusive. Still, Mrs. Verrall dutifully reported all findings to the Society for Psychical Research, even though she herself did not undertsand the writings.

Then the trance writings and utterances of Mrs. Piper were forwarded from America, and it was clear that the Myers Control was saying similar things to the Boston medium and to Mrs. Verrall. Also, Mrs. Verrall's daughter, now a young woman almost twenty, was receiving related messages independently in her own automatic script. Nevertheless, Miss Alice Johnson, secretary of the Society for Psychical Research, put the Piper and Verrall scripts in the society's archives, aware only that a peculiar coincidence had occurred. At about the same time she was reading manuscripts from Mrs. Holland of Calcutta, India, but did not yet see a connection between these and the other automatic writings.

Mrs. Holland, it will be remembered, was the sister of Rudyard Kipling who practiced her mediumship under a pseudonym because of family disapproval. ("My own people hate what they call 'uncanniness,' " she once wrote in a letter.) She usually attempted psychic contact at eleven a.m., because she felt that this was "a good commonplace hour when one is not likely to be over-imaginative." It also happened to be a time when her family was out of the house.

Several items in Mrs. Holland's manuscript startled Alice Johnson. There was a description of Dr. A. W. Verrall that can be called remarkable, considering that Mrs. Holland had never seen him. Also, the script contained a positive order that the material be sent immediately to "Mrs. Verrall, 5 Selwyn Gardens, Cambridge." This was the correct address and, presumably, Mrs. Holland had no way of knowing it. She herself had ignored this instruction because it seemed too preposterous. Her only knowledge of the Verralls came from reading Myers' *Human Personality* which, naturally, contained no address or physical descriptions. Baron Johan Liljencrants, examining the case a dozen years later, felt that Mrs. Holland might have seen the address in a magazine or newspaper and then forgotten it until it was resurrected by her unconscious mind. This speculation really has no evidence to support it except the will *not* to believe.

The third thing that impressed Miss Johnson was the odd signature on one manuscript, a slanting, scrawled "F," which had been Myers' usual way of signing notes and letters in life—another detail that seemed impossible for Mrs. Holland to know. (Mrs. Holland, in other scripts, made two more remarkable hits about the Verralls. She described their dining room in great detail, making only one mistake about a bust that stood in a corner. Also, the spirits were human enough to discuss fashions, and Mrs. Holland mentioned a new dress for Mrs. Verrall, "not a black one," at the very time when the lady was changing her mind and rejecting a black frock for a brighter one.)

There was now a trio of mediums, Mrs. Holland, Mrs. Verrall, and Mrs. Piper, all working with the Myers Control. Others, in various cities and countries, also received related messages from time to time. There were communications signed "Gurney" and "Sidgwick," and the whole thing had the appearance of a concerted effort by the three spirits to establish their personal identities and discarnate survivals beyond all doubt. There is a constant note of desperation in these manuscripts. The Controls describe the "unspeakable difficulties" of getting through. They are "behind a frosted glass," they attempt to "run the blockade." There is "a veil." The frustrated ghosts plead with the mediums to pay closer attention. They urge, cajole, and demand more time. The Gurney Control gives Mrs. Holland a tongue-lashing. "You annoy us bitterly."

Studying the records of the Cross-Correspondences is a formidable task. There are about thirty-two hundred separate scripts and the fraction of these that has been published runs to more than fifteen hundred pages, many crowded with Greek and Latin passages and classical allusions that only a scholar of the level of Myers or Sidgwick can understand. Of the countless cases only a few are simple enough for brief recounting.

One of the most famous is known as the *Ave Roma Immortalis* reference. On March 2, 1906, Mrs. Verrall received an automatic communication that was mostly in Latin, although it also contained a strong request in English that she sacrifice other activities to spend more time as a medium. Two days later she wrote:

> Pagan and Pope. The Stoic persecutor and the Christian.
> Gregory not Basil's friend ought to be a clue, but you have it not quite right.
>
> Pagan and Pope and Reformer all enemies as you think. Crux significationem habet. Crucifer qui olim fertur. The standard-bearer is the link.

The next morning there came another message, entirely in Latin, except, "Ask your husband, he knows it well," and, "No, you have left out something."

Dr. Verrall recognized a connection between the two Latin passages, but he kept silence about it, awaiting new developments. His wife recognized only the first message, which she knew was from the *Aeneid* and referred to the futile resistance of the Trojans against the Greeks.

Then, on March 11, extracts from Mrs. Holland's latest manuscript arrived and the prominent words were, *"Ave Roma Immortalis.* How could I make it any clearer without giving her the clue?" It was then plain that the messages were all allusions to a famous painting by Raphael, a scene in which Pope Leo meets Attila the Hun. A standard-bearer appears in the painting and "immortal Rome" is shown in the distance. Additional significance is added by the fact that the communicator, the Myers Control, died while visiting Rome.

In brief summary, both women, thousands of miles apart, had believed they were receiving messages from Myers and that Myers was apparently trying to convey by some means the same subject to both.

Another case, simple and striking, began when Mrs Piper began to repeat the Greek word *thanatos,* death, while entranced. Observers made careful note of this, since Mrs. Piper was ignorant of Greek and such a thing had never occurred before.

It was later discovered that only the day before Mrs. Holland in India, under the same Myers Control, wrote the Latin word for death and ". . . the shadow of death fell upon his limbs."

This could, of course, be coincidence. But eleven days later, in England, Mrs. Verrall, who knew nothing of what her colleagues in India and America were writing, was contacted by the Myers Control, who supplied a slight misquotation from Landor: "Warmed both hands before the fire of life. It fades and I am ready to depart." There were other references to death, the citation of a passage about early death in the *Aeneid,* and the Latin words, "Pale death." For once, Mrs. Verrall received a little praise from the spirit: "You have got the [key] word plainly written. . . . Look back."

The word "death" seldom occurs in Mrs. Holland's writing and even less often in the automatism of Mrs. Verrall. Mrs. Piper had never before resorted to the classics and her *Trance Utterances* are not studded with "death." On the contrary, she avoided the term.

And so we have three mediums, all under the same Control—or so they believed—all talking about the same thing at the same time.

The Hope-Star-Browning incident of 1906 is impressive but complicated and lengthy. Suffice it to say that Myers, in life, had been fond of quoting Robert Browning. In rapid sequence Mrs. Verrall, Miss Helen Verrall, and Mrs. Piper produced Browning references that could not be understood until all three scripts were taken together. It was Mrs. Piper, not surprisingly, who supplied the key that explained the work of the other mediums.

The "Sesame and Lilies" Cross-Correspondence is also complicated but so striking that some of its details must be given.

For some time the five members of an English family named Mac had dabbled with the ouija board and automatic writing. On July 19, 1908, Miss Mac, the daughter of the family, began to receive automatic messages signed "Sidgwick" that contained references to Mrs. Verrall. The spectral communicator was so persistent that in late September the Macs sent Mrs. Verrall a manuscript written two months earlier. It contained an amazing number of references to earlier writings by both Mrs. Verrall and Miss Helen Verrall, both of whom had been writing the key word "lilies" with unusual frequency. Miss Mac's message linked the communications by providing a clue, "Sesame and Lilies," the title of a work by John Ruskin. There were at least fifteen Cross-Correspondences in the Mac-Verrall manuscripts. For instance, Miss Verrall had written the title of Clough's poem, "Say Not the Struggle Nought Availeth." Miss Mac, who had no previous knowledge of the Verralls, obligingly comes up with an allusion to it. So does Mrs. Verrall, although she knew nothing about what her daughter was writing.

On August 19, 1908, Mrs. Verrall wrote:

". . . It is a literary allusion that should come today.
Think of the words
Liliastrum Paradise—liliago—no, not that.
Lilies of Eden—Lilith no.
Eve's lilies
all in a garden fair. Try again.
   Lilies swaying in a wind
      Under a garden wall
   Lilies for the bees to find
      Lilies fair and tall.
Then besides the Lilies there is to be another word for you and
    for her Lilies and a different word—
So that Lilies is the catchword to show what words are to be put
    together.
And your second word is gold
   think of the golden lilies of France
You will have to wait some time for the end of this story for the
    solution of this puzzle—but I think there is no doubt of its
    ultimate success.

We now compare Mrs. Verrall's writing with Miss Mac's manuscript, and at least part of the "solution" is at once apparent:

. . . Sesame and lilies . . . French . . . vase with lilies that grow by Sharon's dewy rose . . . Search the scriptures and the dust shall be converted to fine gold . . . A blue book bound in blue leather with ended paper and gold tooling . . . in a cemetery where lilies grow . . . Note that the words are a clue.

Many of the cross-references are obvious: Lilies, gold, France. Some, not exact, seem connected: Eve with "scriptures;" puzzle with "clue;" and the whole tone of a "literary allusion."

It should be added that the full title of the Ruskin book is *Sesame: of Kings' Treasuries, and Lilies: of Queens' Gardens.* "Gold," Mrs. Verrall's second catchword, thus occurs twice directly and once indirectly in "Kings' Treasuries."

Miss Helen Verrall was writing similar things at the same time, and while it is remotely possible that three automatists might come up with the same subjects and use the same key words within a short space of time—a month in this case—the fact that Miss Mac received instructions to forward her work to Mrs. Verrall, whom she did not know, throws a different light on the matter. It is hard to doubt the presence of a single, directing intelligence. Whether or not the message came from "Sidgwick" is another question. We come back to the knotty problem of a spirit's establishing its own identity, and the Mac case is not helpful.

Before leaving Miss Mac, however, it is interesting that her description of the book tallied exactly with the particular edition in the Verrall library.

One further Cross-Correspondence should be mentioned, if only because it was Mrs. Piper's farewell performance for the British Society for Psychical Research.

On August 8, 1915, Mrs. Piper, during a Boston séance, began to write rapidly and with unusual agitation. The message she recorded was addressed to Sir Oliver Lodge in England and purported to come from the phantom of Frederic Myers. ". . . you take the part of the poet and he [Myers] will act as Faunus. . . . Mrs. Verrall . . . Mrs. Verrall will know, she will explain." Mrs. Piper had no idea about the message. She thought, after her trance, that the name Faunus might be connected with "faun" but did not recognize him as a minor Roman deity, often identified with Pan, who guarded crops, herds, and—significantly— was a god of prophecy. "The poet" meant nothing whatever to Mrs. Piper, nor did it to Sir Oliver when the writing was forwarded to him.

Mrs. Verrall, as her fellow medium had predicted, had no trouble solving the mystery. The reference was to an incident in one of the Odes of Horace. The poet was strolling on his farm one day when a great tree fell, apparently burying Horace beneath its foliage. Escaping death by inches, the poet attributed his survival to the miraculous intervention of Faunus. Lodge still did not know what to make of the riddle, but was strongly inclined to believe that it was a grim prophecy, that some impending disaster would nearly destroy him, but Myers, acting from the spirit world, would come to his aid.

Five weeks later, Lodge's son, Raymond, perished in World War I. Sir Oliver did not link the death with the prophecy until his wife returned home after consulting the famous medium Mrs. Leonard. Lady Lodge was in a highly emotional state, for she had visited the medium anonymously at the request of a friend who had heard some remarkable revelations. Actually, Lady Lodge went as an informal investigator and had no thought of attempting to contact her late son. But Mrs. Leonard promptly gave messages from "Raymond," who said that on the Other Side he had met a friend of his father, a spirit named Myers!

Lodge, also shaken, then consulted Mrs. Leonard under an alias and almost at once a communication from "Raymond" mentioned that word had come from America in August. It seemed obvious that another remarkable Cross-Correspondence had begun, but Lodge, a bereaved father, was far more interested in establishing the identity of "Raymond" than in following up the Piper-Verrall reference. Thorough investigation was now needed, so Lodge jettisoned the encumbrance of anonymity in dealing with Mrs. Leonard and went directly to the heart of the matter.

Could "Raymond" identify himself as a discarnate individual? Mrs. Leonard's Control gave a clear answer. Lodge should look at a certain photograph, she said, a photo of members of the British Expeditionary Force in France. "Raymond" described his position in the picture. Sir Oliver and Lady Lodge were sadly disappointed because there was no such photograph. But then an apparent miracle happened. The picture, exactly as described, arrived by mail from the mother of one of Raymond's friends. Three weeks before Raymond's death it had been taken in France, although the Lodges had known nothing of this. Mrs. Leonard's description had been uncannily accurate.

Sir Oliver, now on the track of something that seemed truly

amazing, determined to check the Piper-Verrall-Leonard Cross-Correspondence. The Lodges, separately, arranged sessions with a clairvoyant, Mr. Browne (a pseudonym), once again assuming aliases. Both husband and wife heard Raymond accurately described and there were references to "the Society," to Myers, and to the other two members of the ghostly triumvirate, Gurney and Sidgwick, who were attempting contact through Cross-Correspondence. Aware that mind-reading might be at work, Sir Oliver took the precaution of sending an acquaintance to consult still another medium, who was given the key words "Horace," "Lodge," and "Myers," and then asked the connection. Although the clairvoyant had no background in the classics, as far as anyone could determine, "Horace" was immediately identified as a Latin poet, not an English or American given name. The Lodge-Myers link, according to the medium, involved a passage from the poet's work, a satire contrasting the quiet joys of Horace's villa to the troubled life in Rome.

This provided the cue for Mrs. Piper's farewell address to the British investigators. Eight weeks after Lodge was informed of the new Horace Cross-Correspondence, Mrs. Piper wrote an automatic message for him, providing a final key in a third passage from Horace that combined the themes of Faunus and country pleasures versus urban troubles.

Whether or not the identity of the spectral Raymond was established, the whole thing was an astounding performance. Four mediums were involved and there seems no possibility of a conspiracy transatlantic in scope. Sir Oliver and Lady Lodge were rather well-known figures and one cannot completely rule out the possibility that they were recognized either by Mrs. Leonard or Mr. Browne, but this seems unlikely. Neither of the mediums who came up with the Horace references had the least knowledge of Latin literature, nor did they know each other. And the correct identification of the photo taken in France, including the details of Raymond's position in a group, is either a startling demonstration of telepathy between unacquainted minds or one of the most marvelous coincidences that has ever been recorded—or was it something else? The voice of Raymond?

Lodge related these experiences along with later occurrences in a book called *Raymond*, one of the most remarkable and disturbing volumes to come out of the golden age of psychical research. The pain of bereavement is understated but implicit in the writing. Sir Oliver, like other anguished fathers, longed to believe in his son's survival of bodily death, and a skeptic might say that he found what he was seeking because of a desperate need for consolation, a need that would seize on any reassurance however improbable. Those elements are certainly present in the book, but they are only part of the story. Sir Arthur Conan Doyle was only one of the many prominent and thoughtful men who were deeply moved and impressed by *Raymond*. He wrote, "It is a new revelation of God's dealing with man, and it will strengthen, not weaken, the central spirit of Christianity . . . a revelation which alters the whole aspect of life and death."

It is doubtful that a reading of *Raymond* would convert any materialist into a mystic. Doyle, for example, was already a spiritualist. Nevertheless, there are enough unexplained facts in the book to cause even the most skeptical to have second thoughts before dismissing the matter as wishful thinking.

Modern parapsychology views the Cross-Correspondences as demonstrations of ESP operating at full power. There have been no performances so world-wide and dramatic in recent years and there are two possible explanations for this. Perhaps we lack sensitives with the talent of Mrs. Piper, Mrs. Leonard, and others. It might well be that many spring up in one generation and then there is a decline, as in the arts, letters, and sciences.

The second explanation, and perhaps the more convincing one, is that present-day research in ESP deals mostly with the rather prosaic transmission of pictures, shapes, and designs. The voices of the dead are not considered in laboratories. Scientifically this is better investigation, but the emotional factor that so often seems to release paranormal power is omitted. The remarkable sensitives who launched the Cross-Correspondences were not merely attempting to demonstrate a hidden force; their mission, they felt, was holy. There were voices on the Other Side struggling to break the barrier, to reach the world. It was the mediums' task to aid them. We cannot say that the task was fully accomplished, that even one "spirit" was identified beyond doubt. But it is amazing to consider how close they came.

⊙

V

Poltergeists

Haunted Clergymen

Poltergeists, the noisy, rattling ghosts held responsible for most hauntings, have a peculiar affinity for parsons and priests. Since members of the clergy deal professionally with matters spiritual, it is perhaps not surprising that many of them should become unwittingly involved with things spiritist as well—apparently it is a hazard of their vocation. Whatever the cause, for centuries men of the cloth have been plagued by troublesome phantoms. Unholy ghosts have tweaked their wives, pinched their children, smashed their crockery, and wreaked general havoc in manses and rectories.

Reports of the bedeviling of pious men date back to early centuries of the Christian era. Among the oldest accounts (A.D. 530) is a story told by Cyprian in his

171

Life of St. Caesarius of Arles. The Deacon Helpidius, a gentleman of high status and physician at court for King Theodoric, was besieged in his own house by invisible demons. Showers of stones rained from the ceilings. After ordinary prayer proved futile, official exorcism was successful in quelling the disturbance. Cyprian uses the story to buttress his argument that holy men have remarkable power over preternatural fiends. This may have been true of his hero, Saint Caesarius, but other priests have apparently lacked such potency.

The corner of Germany near Bingen has long been a favorite haunt of unruly spirits, and the first written account of dark doings in the neighborhood places a clergyman in a most unfavorable light. The hamlet of Kembden was the scene of an uproar in A.D. 856. Pious inhabitants were repeatedly awakened by noises described as "thunderous," while stones pelted down from both skies and ceilings. When a group of frightened citizens gathered for prayer, an accusing voice of uncertain origin began to excoriate them. Private scandals and sins were revealed, a priest being among those charged with villainy. The poltergeist, not content with earthly justice, caused the property of the worst miscreant to burst into flames.

Bishops and even saints have not been spared malicious assault by spirits. Nicholaus, the town clerk of Maus, noted that the house of Bishop Hugh was bombarded by rocks in A.D. 1138. Five centuries later another Bishop, Schlotterbeck, was haunted. His Reverence not only tried exorcism but also had a company of soldiers stationed around his palace. Neither guards nor rituals had the least effect. He continued to dodge flying stones and was dogged by mysterious footsteps.

Bishop Schlotterbeck may have taken comfort in the fact that personal sanctity is no guarantee against haunting. In A.D. 1170 an especially profane poltergeist beset the hermit monk Saint Godric. The ghost seized the horn in which the saint kept wine for celebrating mass and poured the contents over Godric's head. The dousing, although annoying, was harmless enough, but matters took a more serious turn when the poltergeist hurled a box full of altar beads at Godric and released volleys of stones against the hermitage. Since the saint had taken a vow of poverty, his cell contained few portable possessions—and this may have been his salvation. Every object in the room became a missile, and retreat was cut off by showers of stones.

In examining these five cases we have discovered a common habit of poltergeists: they hurl things. Anything movable may be thrown at a victim when a poltergeist attacks—especially stones. Rocks ranging from gravel to boulders rain from the sky or fall mysteriously from interior ceilings. In many cases, cordons of guards have surrounded a haunted building, yet a stony drizzle has continued to pelt it like hail.

Surprisingly, very few people are injured by ghost-hurled missiles and, except in fiction, poltergeists do not commit murder. (The sadistic "Bell Witch" of Robertson County, Tennessee, is an exception. There are perhaps others.) One concludes that ghosts have very poor aim or that they have no intention of causing serious hurt. The poet Robert Graves has complained that poltergeists behave in a fashion that is "humourless, pointless, uncoordinated." This is not quite fair. Many such ghosts have the childish humor of horseplay: they commit practical jokes and some of their performances have a Mack Sennett, pie-in-the-face sense of slapstick.

Their level of deportment is usually that of a naughty, not overly bright child who is trying to attract attention. As a matter of fact, attention-hungry youngsters are the most frequent perpetrators of what on the surface appears to be poltergeist work. Children, especially those approaching the unsettled time of puberty, are so often fakers of hauntings that case summaries invariably include the number of children present during a manifestation, and investigators seem delighted when they can write, "No children or young people were on the premises."

The late Frank Podmore, who was a sort of psychical-research muckraker and an inveterate skeptic, made an exhaustive study of eleven poltergeist cases with the intention of laying the noisy ghosts forever. Fraud or error, said Podmore, and usually there was a "naughty little boy or girl" at the bottom of the affair. But Mr. Podmore's debunking of ghosts was not entirely successful. Eight of the eleven cases certainly show evidence of human engineering behind the "phenomena." In the remaining three, the skeptic once again says, in effect, "It can't be true because it isn't possible." This tautology is small comfort to victims who hear strange sounds in the night.

If deceitful moppets cause most "poltergeist disturbances," then the children of clergymen must be a particularly mischievous breed. The number of clerical hauntings is strikingly out of proportion. Among reported cases, nearly one in ten centers around a clergyman or his residence. Half the so-called classic cases involve ministers or priests, and in examining Carrington's *The March of the Poltergeists*, a summary of three hundred and seventy-five typical reports, published in 1951, one constantly encounters such phrases as "in the Hamstall Ridware Rectory," "a rectory in Suffolk," "Askerwell Rectory," "the home of a parson," and "the home of the parish priest."

MYSTERY AT EPWORTH

The most celebrated clerical haunting took place at Epworth Parsonage, a childhood home of John Wesley, founder of the Methodist Church. A poltergeist invaded Epworth shortly before Christmas in 1716, a ghost who was more noisy than destructive. The plagued family heard rappings, crashes, and clacks. One night Mrs. Wesley, John's mother, was awakened by peculiar sounds on the lower floor of the house. She and her husband, clinging to each other, ventured down the stairs to investigate and, "Just as we came to the bottom of the broad stairs . . . on my side there seemed as if somebody had emptied a bag of money at my feet, and on his [side] as if all the bottles under the stairs—which were many—had been dashed in a thousand pieces." Luckily the bottles were not broken, although perhaps it did not matter much—since they were in the Wesley home they must have contained temperance beverages. Less luckily, no heap of coins appeared at Mrs. Wesley's feet.

The Epworth Poltergeist raised a racket for eight weeks, then became quiet. He had not, however, vacated the parsonage, but during the next year would suddenly assert his presence by poundings and thumps. Afterward, the case was reported in letters written to John Wesley by his mother and four of his sisters, and there exists a copy of a letter penned at the height of the haunting, a description sent to Samuel Wesley the elder by Mrs. Wesley—and it clearly reveals the lady's alarm. One of the five Wesley daughters, Hetty, did not record her experiences—a pity since much of the disturbance appeared to center around her. Hetty's failure to write an account has aroused the suspicions of persons who incline to the belief that the girl was secretly responsible for the Epworth uproar.

In 1965 two modern reporters, Douglas Hill and Pat Williams, stated in their book *The Supernatural* that the Epworth Poltergeist (along with other cases) has "largely been discredited due to flaws detected in the witnesses' testimony." This is rather a bold statement. The evidence of the Epworth haunting, while far too incomplete to convince any modern skeptic, hangs together very well. No court could convict Hetty Wesley of malicious mischief on the grounds that she failed to testify, and historically there is nothing else against her. Mrs. Wesley and her husband certainly believed the parsonage to be temporarily haunted.

John Wesley had a continuing interest in such matters, and is very probably the source of an article which appeared in the *Arminian* magazine, 1786, an account of the haunting of the Dixon sisters, gentle ladies who suffered the presence of a ghost in their house. This crockery-hurling spirit was not above chasing the women about the rooms, terrorizing them by brandishing chairs and vases.

YANKEE POLTERGEIST

The British Isles are dotted with haunted rectories and parsonages, and European priests and pastors figure in many celebrated cases of poltergeist activity. American clergymen seem to have been less often plagued, but the ghost who beset the Reverend Eliakim Phelps and his family ranks second to none for vigor, malice, and loquacity. He is one of the prize poltergeists of all time.

In 1850 the village of Stratford, Connecticut, was a quiet place —placid, respectable, and comparatively untouched by the Industrial Revolution that was changing neighboring towns. Prominent among Stratford's sedate inhabitants was Dr. Eliakim Phelps, the Presbyterian minister, a graying gentleman approaching sixty who had recently acquired a new family by marrying a widow much younger than himself. The Stratford Manse, although a religious household, was enlivened by the presence of two boys, one eleven and the other six, and two girls, six and sixteen. A frequent caller was Professor Austin Phelps, Dr. Phelps's son by his first wife.

Dr. Phelps appeared to be a model clergyman of his time and area, a man quite without eccentricities, although he had expressed a vague faith in clairvoyance and had on a few occasions undertaken experiments in mesmerism, including attempts to treat disease through hypnosis. These dabblings in the occult were mild and raised no eyebrows among his conservative flock.

No one thought it odd when a New York acquaintance of Dr. Phelps called at the manse on March 4, 1850, to suggest that he and the doctor attempt to contact spirits by means of knocks and rappings. Spiritualism was all the rage that year, the Fox sisters were the country's new celebrities, and thousands of people sat in dim rooms solemnly intoning, "Is anyone there? One rap for yes, two raps for no." Dr. Phelps, that night, was enjoying a not very serious experiment. But unlike other amateur occultists, he aroused a supernatural backfire.

At this first Phelps séance some tentative rappings were heard. However, the doctor felt that nothing extraordinary had happened. With no premonitions, the family went to church as usual on Sunday, March 10. It must be emphasized that everyone left the house at the same time, and every member of the family was observably present throughout a long church service.

They returned home in a group to be confronted by a scene of chaos. Tables and chairs had been overturned and scattered through the rooms, books tossed from shelves, the closets rifled. The house appeared to have been attacked by vandals; but one curious sight suggested something else: a mad sculptor had created eleven human figures made of clothing snatched from shelves, hooks, and drawers. They were arranged to represent a mysterious religious ceremony—kneeling and bowing before the central figure of a dwarf (a Christ child?) above whom hung another form, possibly meant to be a flying angel. The scene vaguely resembled a huge, grotesque crèche without animals. To remove any doubt about the religious nature of the tableaux, Bibles were placed near the figures and had been opened to passages referring to ghosts and spirit possession.

Although the occurrence might have been the work of a neighborhood prankster, the entire family was now alerted. Rooms were watched, many doors and windows kept locked. But despite all precautions the invisible sculptor continued his art. During the first weeks of the haunting, thirty creations appeared in the manse, and they were not merely tossed-together dummies. Dr. Webster, reporting the events in the New Haven *Journal,* describes the figures as ". . . most beautiful and picturesque. The clothing of which they were constructed was somehow gathered from all parts of the house in spite of the strict watch which was kept. . . . Some of them were so life-like that, a small child being shown the room, thought his mother was kneeling in prayer. . . ." Dr. Webster was completely convinced that a supernatural agency was at work.

The Stratford poltergeist, although as disorderly as one might expect an artist to be, had not yet shown his true, vindictive nature. Attempts to communicate by rappings were soon successful, but when Dr. Phelps began to receive blasphemous replies to his questions, he cut off all conversation, scandalized. Details of these shocking answers are lamentably lacking. We know, however, that they were so outrageous that Phelps not only stopped communicating but forbade his family to engage in any dialogue with the foul-mouthed ghost. The spirit was not so easily sent to Coventry. Messages appeared scrawled on the walls, written on scraps of paper, and letters dropped mysteriously from the ceilings. The ghost revealed a crude and scurrilous sense of humor: several of the messages were nasty lampoons of Dr. Phelps's fellow-clergymen.

The manse became a madhouse. When Mr. H. B. Taylor came to investigate the goings-on, he was treated to several unusual sights: "In my presence the elder boy was carried across the room by invisible hands and gently deposited on the floor. A supper table was raised and tipped over when the room was completely empty of people. . . ."

Dinner with the Phelps family could be a harrowing experience. Professor Austin Phelps has given a description: "In the presence of the whole family, a turnip fell from the ceiling. Spoons and forks flew from the dinner table into the air; and one day six or eight spoons were taken up at once, bent double by no visible agency, and thrown at those in the room."

We have noted that poltergeists seldom show homicidal tendencies. At least one incident in the Stratford haunting departs from this rule. The elder daughter suffered the terror of having a pillow pressed upon her face while she slept, and was nearly strangled by tape wrapped around her throat by unseen hands. The ghost had a particular dislike of this young lady. When a reporter from the New York *Sun* came to Stratford, he sat alone in a room with Mrs. Phelps and the girl, who suddenly wailed, "I am pinched!" Rolling up her sleeve revealed a bright red finger mark, apparently fresh, on her arm.

A sixteen-year-old girl is an ideal target for suspicion when poltergeists seem to be at work. Adolescent females, including the Fox sisters, have been responsible for countless fraudulent hauntings. But this does not seem true in the Phelps case. The phenomena centered more around Harry, the elder boy, aged eleven. It was Harry who was hung on a tree in the yard, it was Harry who floated across the room in Mr. Taylor's presence, Harry who was discovered in an unconscious state in a haymow quite unable to remember how he had arrived there. Dr. Phelps reported manifestations when he was alone with the boy and watching him carefully.

The New York *Sun* reporter, Mr. Beach, witnessed an eerie happening in the boy's bedroom on an evening in April 1850. Harry was sitting up in bed when, in the presence of several observers, a matchbox fell from the mantlepiece, striking the floor with a loud, metallic clatter which Beach described as similar to the noise of an iron bar hitting. "The box, untouched by any visible hand, slid toward the bed and disappeared under it." Harry leaped up, crying that he was burning, and Beach, rushing to the rescue, found a flaming scrap of paper beneath the bed.

There occurred another mysterious incident for which neither Harry nor his sister can be held responsible. Dr. Phelps, while sitting alone in a room, was momentarily distracted and turned away from the table where he was writing. When he turned back, only a few seconds later, he was amazed to discover that the sheet of paper before him was now filled with peculiar marks and writing, the ink still fresh and wet to the touch.

Conquering his moral repugnance, Dr. Phelps soon resumed communication with the ghost, who now revealed by rappings that he was actually not a Yankee but a Frenchman, in life a law clerk who had once drawn some financial-settlement papers for Mrs. Phelps. He confessed to fraud in the transaction and explained that because of this sin he was confined to hell (and, presumably, to the Stratford Manse). This matter of the dead law clerk is another rarity of the Phelps case. A poltergeist usually makes no attempt to reveal a worldly identity and on the infrequent occasions when one announces himself, he claims to be the victim, not the perpetrator of some crime. Also, these self-identifications by poltergeists are usually vague and impossible to verify.

Not so in the Stratford haunting. Dr. Phelps examined the papers in question and quickly discovered the fraud. Justice, however, must be harsher in the next world than in this, for the amount involved was not "sufficiently large to warrant prosecution." The ghostly law clerk remains an unclear presence in the story. Even if we assume—as few people will—that there were actual spirits prowling the manse, it is impossible to reconcile the first messages with the identification. More than one ghost, perhaps? Enough went on in Stratford to keep a dozen spirits busy.

At this point the town was startled by the arrival of a strange and dramatic figure. Andrew Jackson Davis, "The Poughkeepsie Seer," came to investigate and to determine by clairvoyance exactly what was going on in the bedeviled manse. The Seer, whom we last met in connection with the "New Motor" fiasco, is almost a forgotten man today. Almost nobody reads the voluminous and windy transcripts of his somnambulistic utterances— in fact, his complete works, running to thousands of pages, are practically unobtainable. Yet a century ago a great number of people in both America and Europe considered the Seer a major figure in prophecy, religion, and medicine.

Although his fame has plummeted, he has not quite passed into oblivion. Davis is prominently mentioned in *There Is a River*, the well-known biography of a more modern seer, Edgar Cayce. Cayce, according to author Thomas Sugrue, was shown a copy of Davis's *The Principles of Nature, Her Divine Revelations, and a Voice to Mankind*, published in 1847. After reading the introduction, Edgar Cayce said, "This sounds so much like me it gives me the creeps." There were, indeed, many similarities. Their methods and careers were so alike that some cynics have suspected Cayce of deliberately imitating Davis, although there is no evidence that he ever read *The Principles*.

Davis is by far the more striking of the two prophet–faith healers. Despite the best efforts of his biographers, Edgar Cayce remains a colorless personality. The Poughkeepsie Seer, on the other hand, was a born showman, as the citizens of Stratford must have realized when he arrived in their town, probably dressed in his usual natty jacket with velvet lapels. William Fishbough, who transcribed the 782 pages of Davis's first book, describes the Seer as possessed of "a bilious-sanguine temperament. His features are prominent and his head is of the medium size, and very smoothly developed, especially in the frontal coronal regions. The base of the brain is small, except in the region of the perceptives, which are prominent. The head is covered with jet-black hair. The expression of his countenance is mild, placid, and indicative of a peculiar degree of frankness and benevolence; and from his eyes beam forth a peculiar radiance which we have never witnessed in any other person." This does not do full justice to Davis. An engraving shows him to have been strikingly handsome, and the strong features remind one of the heroes of Gothic novels, a young Heathcliff or Mr. Rochester.

The Seer was only twenty-three years old when he probed the Phelps haunting, but he had already achieved celebrity, after having been discovered by a Poughkeepsie tailor, William Levingston. Levingston experimented with mesmerism as a hobby, and found that the boy, Andrew, an almost illiterate cobbler's apprentice, was an ideal subject. Entranced, the youth uttered prophecies and interpretations of the universe, and claimed power to cure the sick. Levingston and his protégé, after instant success in Poughkeepsie, took to the road as itinerant healers. Meanwhile, Davis, gifted with a quick mind and a retentive memory, was rapidly educating himself. His mystical dictations— odd blendings of Swedenborg, New England transcendentalism, and a belief in social revolution—gained him fame. But his income always came from healing.

For more than thirty-five years he gave "readings," interrupting them long enough to acquire a legal if somewhat dubious medical degree at the age of sixty. His new status as a physician did not alter his method of diagnosis, which involved touching a patient's palm with the tips of his fingers. In the last thirty years of his life (he lived to be eighty-four), Davis no longer bothered with trances. The touch of his fingers—psychometry—was enough. He is said to have "healed thousands," a statement which is impossible to verify or refute.

The young psychic, arriving in Stratford with a fanfare of publicity, added great glamour to the Phelps haunting. He spoke learnedly of "vital radiations," felt powerful emanations when he touched the Phelps children, and trembled as he received magnetic charges. Dr. Phelps, himself interested in mesmerism, must have been keenly watchful. He permitted Davis to poke about the house, inspecting closets and examining the rooms where phenomena had occurred, but the minister was cautious about expressing any opinions. Although Phelps showed a normal curiosity about the occult, he was still an orthodox Christian.

The Seer, at this period in his life, was fascinated by magnetism and electricity, and undoubtedly his thinking had been stimulated by a brand-new occult oddity known as the Electric Girls. The Electric Girls were not, as one might suppose, shocking young females, but women of all ages in whose presence strange forces seemed to operate. They were rather like physical mediums, although the phenomena they allegedly produced resembled the work of poltergeists. The most famed Electric Girl was Angélique Cottin, the daughter of a Normandy farmer. When Angélique was near a compass, the magnetic needle lost all sense of direction; various metallic objects seemed attracted or repelled by her, and heavy iron castings shifted position when merely brushed by her petticoats. At least such were the reports of the French investigator, Dr. Tanchon, and other witnesses. (Angélique turned out to be a boring failure when she performed for a committee appointed by the French Academy of Sciences. They noted only that the chair she sat in danced about, and attributed this to her own muscular efforts. Angélique was not only Electric but husky as well.)

A few years before the Phelps haunting, some Electric Girls had made American débuts, and Andrew Jackson Davis was quick to observe a connection between them and poltergeist activity. With this in mind, the Seer examined the Phelps household, concentrating especially on the elder boy and girl. He then pronounced both of them "electric," and was delighted with the precocious Harry, whose "organism released vital radiations," thus causing spirit taps unconsciously. The children were given to sudden changes of radiation, rather like an alternating current. When electricity was in the ascendant, objects were violently repelled; when magnetism held the field, objects were attracted. Obvious chaos would ensue if both were in the same room but operating, so to speak, on opposing wave lengths. Small wonder that dinner plates flew into the air to crash against the ceiling!

The Seer did not declare that *everything* in the affair was electromagnetically caused. There were also spirits staging the performance: he himself saw five of them.

Davis's conclusions about the haunted manse evoked a clamor from orthodox spiritualists, who insisted that the place was infested by ghosts and all twaddle about electricity was not only blasphemous but unscientific. Viewpoints were soon reconciled, however, and that very year Davis with his numerous followers joined the growing ranks of the spiritualist movement.

Meanwhile, the Reverend Dr. Phelps had come to the end of his rope. For more than eighteen months he and his family had endured the poltergeist onslaught, and some action was necessary to restore tranquillity to their lives. At the beginning of October, Dr. Phelps sent his wife and stepchildren to Pennsylvania for a much-needed rest. The manifestations stopped at once. Dr. Phelps, intrepid soul, remained alone in the house for five weeks and observed nothing unusual. Nor did the haunting resume when the family returned to Stratford the following spring.

The doctor, in a long interview with Harvard's Charles W. Eliot, gave a complete summary of the case from his own point of view. He appears to have suffered the haunting with a surprising equanimity, although he frequently harks back to the financial setbacks inflicted by the poltergeists. "The pecuniary loss [was] between one and two hundred dollars—while the spirit messages were valueless! Twenty window-panes broken . . . servants lost, valuable articles destroyed. . . ."

Were spirits at work? Phelps said, "I have never seen a spirit; I do not know what a spirit could do if it would, or what it would do if it could! The facts . . . render the idea of tricks or design and deception wholly inadmissible. . . . They were not produced by human agency and were absolutely inexplicable. Fifty-six articles were picked up at one time which had been thrown at someone's head. . . . Heavy marble-topped tables would rise on two legs and crash to the floor with no one within six feet of them. . . ."

Dr. Phelps was stanch in defense of his stepchildren, citing a number of incidents of which they could not possibly, he said, have been the perpetrators. He referred to a reporter from the New Haven *Journal* as an eyewitness to the innocence of the children.

In his presence, and that of three other witnesses, the following incident occurred: They were standing in the hall outside the chamber of the eldest girl, from which loud raps were proceeding. Hearing the girl cry out, they quickly opened the door and found that her face had a deep red mark on it where, she said, she had been struck. While the girl's hands were being held in an effort to quiet her, a huge porcelain jug was hurled against the door with far more force than the frail child could possibly have used, even had her hands been free. The jug was broken to pieces, this being accompanied by a loud report, and a half-inch indentation made in the door, showing the violence with which the jug had been thrown. One curious fact was that the line of flight was not direct from where the jug had stood, but in a semi-circle.

The children of the Phelps household were fortunate to have such a loyal stepfather. Other youngsters suspected of faking occult phenomena have fared badly, having been gagged, bound, chained, and locked in closets to prevent further mischief. Hereward Carrington gives a summary of one such case. "In the home of Captain Molesworth, Edinburgh, rappings and other poltergeists disturbances. Continued for some time. One of his daughters, then ill, was suspected of trickery; she was sewn in a bag, but the phenomena continued as before. She died soon thereafter. . . ."

In the Stratford haunting, the two elder children might well have abetted a fraud, but it seems impossible that they could have been the sole participants—assuming, of course, that fraud existed. Many cases, such as the Epworth poltergeist story, have a haziness about them, a lack of concrete detail that springs from incomplete reporting. At Stratford every incident was carefully noted. Accounts published in the New Haven *Journal and Courier* are precise, and, further, the *Journal*'s reporter was a witness to some remarkable happenings. The New York *Sun* also had a man on the scene.

Another corroborating witness is the Reverend John Mitchell, who frequently called at the manse. He testified to the levitation and hurling of objects, declared that he heard unearthly shrieks, and was emphatic that no member of the household could have tricked him. There were also neighbors and members of Dr. Phelps's congregation present during various unexplained upsets.

The entire family—but only the family—witnessed one of the earliest manifestations. On a certain evening what they described as a "vegetable growth" suddenly appeared on the sitting-room carpet. It spread and sprouted as though the floral pattern had taken root and life. Cabalistic symbols formed on the leaves, then the whole thing vanished without a trace. There were also the mysterious appearances of turnips, some used as missiles and some with writing on them.

The Phelps poltergeist has been studied by a number of investigators including Sir Arthur Conan Doyle, Frank Podmore, Hereward Carrington, and the Reverend Charles Beecher, but none of them has thrown much light on the murky affair. If it was all an elaborate hoax, then it is inescapable that the Reverend Dr. Phelps was the chief mischief-maker. The single incident of the strange writing appearing when he was completely alone is enough to establish his participation. But if he was a trickster, then both of his elder children were accomplices —perhaps tacitly, perhaps in acknowledged conspiracy. The younger children, ages three and six, were hardly old enough to be either witnesses or conspirators.

Mrs. Phelps at first appears to be the one member of the household who could be acquitted of complicity. Nothing seems to have happened when she was alone. But it would require astounding gullibility to go through a year and a half of violent haunting and not detect the hoax. Mrs. Phelps was an educated woman, active and capable in church affairs. It is hard to believe she could have been fooled so often and for so long.

If four members of the family were party to a fraud, why was there no breech of secrecy? Dr. Phelps, familiar with *Poor Richard's Almanac*, must have realized that "three can keep a secret if two of them are dead." The Fox sisters are a prime example of the eventual failure of such conspiracies. The three girls and their mother (and possibly the father, too) schemed together to hoodwink the public, but two of them at last admitted the truth.

The events at the Stratford Manse are astonishing no matter what view one takes, and questions raised by the haunting lead to fascinating speculations. Would respectable, strait-laced Dr. Phelps risk disgrace by initiating a preposterous deception? Would he trust two young children as accomplices? Perhaps a taut melodrama was being played within the family. If the step-children originated the haunting, did the doctor perpetuate it to prevent their exposure after the matter became public? Was everyone involved in the affair inflamed by a mass hysteria that caused them to see the carpet sprout, the pitcher fly, the fire-tongs dance across the room and fly through a window? Were four clergymen, a professor, three reporters, and a battalion of neighbors all mad, deceived, or lying?

Or was there a poltergeist?

BORLEY REVISITED

Borley Rectory, "the most haunted house in England," has been thoroughly publicized in books, magazines, and news-papers. Retelling the familiar tale seems superfluous, but there are two reasons for including it here. First, a tour of haunted houses and a visit with haunted clergymen that omitted Borley would be as incomplete as a trip to Paris without at least a quick view of the Eiffel Tower. Second, although many readers are aware of the investigations at the Rectory, fewer know about the subsequent investigation of the investigation.

A great deal of nonsense has been written about Borley Rectory. Many of the reports are exaggerations, and some of the most colorful are outright lies. Harry Price, the chief ghost-hunter at Borley, claimed that the affair was the "most fully documented case in the history of psychical research." This is true only if we take the word "case" to mean "haunting." Many examples of mediumship—for instance Mrs. Piper and Mrs. Leon-ard—have been much more thoroughly checked than the ghosts at Borley, and, unhappily for Price, some of the Borley docu-ments are doubtful at best. Still, after all the exaggerations and flights of journalistic fancy have been discounted, the story of the Rectory remains uncanny. Perhaps it is merely the greatest example of collective hallucination ever recorded. On the other hand, it may be more than that.

The obscure Rectory was catapulted into the news on June 10,

1929, when Mr. A. V. Wall, a reporter for the London *Daily Mirror*, wrote a sensational report that could hardly fail to catch the public's fancy.

Ghostly figures of headless coachmen and a nun, an old-time coach drawn by two bay horses, which appears and vanishes mysteriously, and dragging footsteps in empty rooms. All these ingredients of a first-class ghost story are awaiting investigation by psychic experts near Long Melford, Suffolk.

The scene of the ghostly visitations is the Rectory at Borley, a few miles from Long Melford. It is a building erected on part of the site of a great monastery which, in the Middle Ages, was the scene of a gruesome tragedy.

According to a local legend, a groom at the monastery and a nun from a nearby convent once enjoyed lovers' trysts in the woods behind the Rectory. "Then one day they arranged to elope, and another groom had a coach waiting outside the wood so that they could escape. From this point the legend varies. Some say that the nun and her lover quarreled, and that he strangled her in the wood and was caught and beheaded with the other groom for his villainy. The other version is that all three were caught in the act by the monks, and that the two grooms were beheaded and the nun buried alive in the walls of the monastery." The nun, or other ghosts, seemed to have reappeared recently to plague the present occupants of the house, a Reverend Mr. G. E. Smith and his wife.

The excitement of readers was further whetted a few days later when it was announced that Mr. Harry Price, England's most famous ghost-hunter and founding director of the National Laboratory for Psychical Research, would undertake to investigate the Borley haunting.

Price, accompanied by reporter Wall, set off for the Rectory carrying Price's professional kit, whose contents are curious and worth noting:

A pair of soft felt overshoes used for creeping, unheard, about the house in order that neither human beings nor paranormal "entities" shall be disturbed when producing "phenomona"; steel measuring tape for measuring rooms, passages, testing the thickness of walls in looking for secret chambers or hidey-holes; steel screw-eyes, lead post office seals, sealing tool, string cord or tape, and adhesive surgical tape for sealing doors, windows, or cupboards; a set of tools with wire, nails, etc; hank of electric flex, small electric bells, dry batteries and switches (for secret electric contacts); 9 cm. by 12 cm. reflex camera, film-packs, flashbulbs . . . a small portable telephone . . . notebook, red, blue and black pencils; a sketching block and case of drawing instruments for making plans; ball of string, stick of chalk, matches, electric torch and candle; bowl of mercury for detecting tremors in room or passage or for making silent electrical mercury switches; cinematograph cameras with remote electric control and films; a sensitive transmitting thermograph, with charts, to measure the slightest variation in temperature in supposed haunted rooms; a packet of graphite and soft brush for developing fingerprints. . .

Since meddling with ghosts may prove hazardous, he also carried "bandages, iodine and a flask of brandy in case a member of the investigating staff or resident is injured or faints."

These were the bare essentials for a quick inspection. Price had more equipment for longer jobs. Complete as this kit might seem to a layman, it is unsophisticated compared to present-day ghost hunting equipment. A modern tool kit would include an infrared image convertor; a beat-frequency oscillator with antennas, "trumpet," and transformers; and mechanical vibrators. There would also be highly sensitive sound-recording devices.

Although Price described the Rectory as "solid, unpicturesque, red-brick of two stories," he must have been pleased with his first impressions. If the building was not attractive, it was certainly atmospheric. Sixty miles from London, it rose from a low knoll encircled by trees—a gloomy, isolated spot. Across the road, the stone tower of a twelfth-century church added to the somberness. The Rectory itself was a monument to Victorian discomfort: twenty high-ceilinged rooms, drafty passageways, closets, stairs, and dingy cellars that seemed to serve no purpose. A window in the dining room had been bricked up, and other windows were barred to make sure that maidservants did not slip out at night. The Rectory was provided with other features familiar from ghost stories: great gables, a glass-roofed veranda, an eighty-foot well, and a garden gone to ruin. "Borley Rectory," said Price, "is rather like a rabbit-warren."

The structure was erected in 1863 by the Reverend H. D. E. Bull, who utilized the foundations of two earlier buildings which had stood upon that spot. Upon this gentleman's death in 1892, his son, the Reverend H. F. Bull, became the rector at Borley, serving until he died in 1927. The post was then offered to twelve different clergymen, all of whom refused it. At last a new rector was found, the Reverend G. E. Smith. Neither Mr. Smith nor his wife believed in ghosts, nor had they heard tales about the Rectory's being haunted. One incident, however, must have raised at least small questions in their minds. Before moving in, they found a fragment of a skull, neatly wrapped, in the library. (There is a conflicting version which says that the skull was unearthed in the basement.) At any rate, the rector and the sexton solemnly buried the grim relic in the Borley churchyard. The Smiths then took up residence in the house, "puzzled but not afraid."

It was not long before the couple learned of the Rectory's odd history; the neighborhood was rife with stories dating back to 1886, when a Mrs. E. Byford took sudden leave of the place after hearing "ghostly footsteps." Daughters of the Bull family saw the apparition of a nun on the lawn in daylight and then again in the garden. In 1916, Mr. and Mrs. Edward Cooper came to live in the cottage near the Rectory and night after night for three years heard the ghostly sounds of a padding dog. Mr. Cooper not only saw the nun several times but was astonished by a spectral coach and horses with glittering harness that galloped across the premises. One night both Coopers were alarmed by a "black shape" appearing in their bedroom, and shortly afterward they left the cottage. Meanwhile, in the Rectory itself, the Reverend Harry Bull informed friends that "spirits" were attempting to communicate with him. After the passing of Harry Bull and before the arrival of the Reverend G. E. Smith, the Rectory was vacant (except perhaps for ghosts), but Fred Cartwright, who lived in the neighborhood, saw the nun standing at the gate on four separate occasions.

The Reverend Mr. Smith and his wife found the house chilly, depressing, and almost impossible to manage without servants. They closed most of the upper rooms and tried to ignore the discomforts of their situation. Soon Mrs. Smith fell ill, and then the first events of an intensified haunting took place. The rector, alone in the house, heard sibilant whisperings as he passed through an archway. The ghostly voices seemed to follow him until he reached the private chapel. There they ceased abruptly "like a wireless set turned off."

During the following weeks eerie moanings echoed in passages and a woman's voice cried out, "Don't, Carlos, don't!" There were footsteps, bell-ringings, and the discovery of smashed objects—reported not only by the Smiths but also by a terrified maidservant. Most frightening of all were the dragging footsteps that moved through empty rooms. One night the Reverend Mr. Smith armed himself with a hockey stick and lay in ambush for the spectral walker. When the steps approached, he struck, only to find himself belaboring the air. (Perhaps a cross would have been a more effective weapon.)

Such was the situation when Harry Price and A. V. Wall arrived at Borley Rectory to begin their ghost hunt.

The first night of the investigation resembled a séance conducted by Eusapia Palladino. While standing in the yard and watching the building, Wall suddenly saw a ghostly figure which he identified as the mysterious nun. Price was not sure about the apparition—he had only a glimpse—but when they returned to the house, a half-brick smashed the glass roof of the veranda, landing only a few inches from the startled men. Racing to the second story, they searched in vain for a mischief-maker. All the rooms were empty. Meanwhile, a candle and a shower of pebbles were hurled down the stairs. With the Smiths and the maid, Mary Pearson, they retired to the library—seeking refuge, no doubt—and at once the keys of both the library and drawing-room doors fell from their locks simultaneously.

Price decided it was high time to hold a séance. There were raps, taps, and thumps. The late Harry Bull announced by table-turning that he was present. As the occupants of the house huddled together on one side of the room, a cake of soap leaped from a dish on the opposite side and bounded across the floor. This occurred at two a.m., and by now both ghosts and spectators were weary. Price writes:

> And so ended this very eventful June 12, 1929. A day to be re-membered, even by an experienced investigator. Although I have investigated many haunted houses, before and since, never have such phenomena so impressed me as they did on this historic day. Sixteen hours of thrills!

It is a pity that Price was too thrilled to put some of his equipment to use. A filming of the events would have been impressive. Instead, he reverted to table-turning.

Three weeks of quiet followed this outburst. Then, in early July, the ghosts renewed their onslaught. All the bells in the house—and there were a good many—pealed at once. A small table was hurled across a room, and the Smiths, deciding they had endured quite enough, moved from the Rectory. Their absence did not stop the manifestations. On August 7 a window was unlatched and thrown open from the inside, although the empty house had been locked.

During the following months the Rectory was not continuously watched, but report after report kept being made. Part of a fireplace was pulled to pieces and left on the main staircase,

Poltergeists

but there were no signs of forced entry. In the spring, the same staircase was strewn with stones. Meanwhile, villagers saw lights and heard "horrible sounds," especially during the full moon.

The Reverend G. E. Smith resigned his post at Borley in April, and not until October could a successor be found. On October 16, 1930, the Reverend L. A. Foyster, with his wife and children, was intrepid enough to take up residence at the Rectory. The ghosts quickly demonstrated that they had lost none of their vigor. A disembodied voice cried, "Marianne!" referring to Mrs. Foyster, and the shade of the Reverend Harry Bull, in a gray dressing-gown, materialized before her eyes. Objects constantly vanished, then mysteriously reappeared.

In early 1931 the haunting took an ugly turn. Mrs. Foyster was given a black eye on February 26, and the next night a hammer was hurled at the couple as they lay in bed.

The Reverend Foyster struck back by holding solemn rites of exorcism in the Rectory on March 7. Exorcism, one of the minor rites of both Anglican and Roman Catholic churches, seems incongruous in the twentieth century, but it is practiced more often than most people realize and is based on one of the oldest Christian traditions: the casting out of devils. The Reverend Foyster was following in the steps of Justin Martyr, who noted the miraculous results of Christian exorcism in the second century, and of Origen, who, a hundred years later, used the words "Jesu Christus" to banish malignant demons. Exorcism is mentioned in the Book of Acts and appears, without a detailed ceremony, in the Gospel story of Jesus purifying the swine.

Indeed, exorcism was one of the original selling points of Christianity, but was ordinarily used to remove demons (diseases?) from persons, not places. However, ceremonies to dislodge ghosts from buildings were common enough in early times, and the rites were formal and traditional when Saint Caesarius performed them in A.D. 530.

The Reverend Mr. Foyster at Borley was not as well prepared

193

for this job as a Roman Catholic priest would have been. The Roman Catholic Church has several forms of exorcism, some appearing in the Rituale Romanum in the section dedicated to consecrating given areas and purging them of evil; a more obscure form was used by the Spanish clergy in the 1600s, a violent denunciation and cursing of demons which ends with a reminder that one day the Lord will appear to judge "all the world by fire."

Episcopalians, although inclined to expel a ghost to "outer darkness," are usually more gentle. One rite invokes the aid of the Trinity and Cross while salt is poured into holy water in the shape of a cross. The priest then sprinkles the water in corners of haunted rooms, and afterward pours it upon the earth. (Householders who wish to take double precautions put up sprigs of yew, hazel, and mistletoe after the ceremony. These safeguards are admittedly pagan, but not all poltergeists respond to Christian appeals.)

The rector performed his ceremony—and was promptly pelted with stones hurled from invisible hands or catapults. Mr. Foyster got off lightly; he might well have heeded the example of three Irish priests who eighteen years earlier attempted to banish a ghost at Coonian, Ireland, and were first routed, then variously afflicted with facial paralysis, spinal meningitis, and a nervous collapse.

The Borley ghosts remained entrenched in the Rectory, impervious to prayer. The very day after the exorcism both doors of the Blue Room locked themselves. More objects vanished, then materialized.

The hectored Reverend Foyster doubled his efforts: this time *two* priests performed exorcism rites, and again the spirits retaliated with stones, although their aim was poor. Mrs. Foyster, lacking the protection of Holy Orders, fared very badly. She was struck on the head by a piece of metal, a flatiron was hurled at her, and on March 24 she suffered the unnerving experience of seeing the shade of the Reverend Harry Bull again. The haunting grew ever more dramatic: bells rang, pepper was dropped on beds, a room was set afire; Mrs. Foyster was three times hurled from her bed, a flying water jug nearly brained the sleeping rector, his daughter Adelaide was injured by a "nasty thing"; and Katie, the maid, working in the kitchen with the doors and windows closed, shrieked as bottles materialized around her in the air and smashed on the floor. Papers bearing Mrs. Foyster's Christian name, Marianne, appeared—enigmatic messages, nearly illegible, which seemed to plead for further holy rites. Traps caused occupants to stumble and the rector was struck by a hairbrush.

Upon the urging of Sir George and Lady Whitehouse, a Roman Catholic clergyman, Dom Richard Whitehouse, O.S.B., came to pray and investigate. While he was interviewing Mrs. Foyster, who was abed with her arms beneath covers, a stiletto was dropped into his lap. Calling for divine aid, Dom Whitehouse and Mrs. Foyster made a novena—prayer on nine successive days—and during the course of this, both became aware of a "presence." A mysterious message appeared on a wall addressed to Marianne. The scrawled words seem to say, "help, light, mass, candles." Under it, Mrs. Foyster printed, "I cannot understand. Tell me more." A reply came, but it consisted of more incoherent scribbles.

When Harry Price returned with investigators, wine miraculously turned to ink, doors were locked, and bottles were thrown. However, no casualties were reported, and Price used neither his brandy flask nor his bandages.

After the Foysters departed the haunted premises forever, Price launched the largest-scale ghost hunt ever recorded. He rented the Rectory and by newspaper advertisements secured volunteers to help in his search, since he himself could not live there all the time and, further, he wanted the observations of other witnesses, people from various walks of life who were not in any way connected with occultism of the spiritualist movement. This group included army officers, businessmen, physicians, and other professional men and women.

Not all of them were completely removed from psychical research. The first official observer, S. H. Glanville, was a draftsman, photographer, and consulting engineer—but as a hobby he invented gadgets for trapping ghosts. He went to Borley accompanied by his son, Roger. Like Price and Wall before them, these new investigators were not disappointed in their haunted house. There were thumps and cracks in the night, and new pencil markings, rather like the Marianne messages, were discovered.

During the next eleven months various volunteers who camped out in the Rectory noted one oddity after another. There was little to compare with the violence of the attacks on the Smiths and Foysters, but still no lack of unexplained events: a fifty-pound bag of coal moved eighteen inches, doors were strangely locked, bells rang, objects appeared and vanished; more pencil marks appeared; shuffling noises, crashes, and "extraordinary noises" were common. Mrs. Lloyd Williams observed the spectral nun and a "cold spot" was found just outside the Blue Room where investigators felt their flesh turn chill.

Price's tenancy, and the formal investigation, ended in May 1938, and the following December a new owner, Captain W. H. Gregson, R.E. (Ret.), moved into the house with his two sons, Alan, age eighteen, and Andrew, age fourteen. The captain, although he changed the name of the property to "Borley Priory," did not take the tales of phantoms very seriously—at least at first. "I liked to think that there was really something eerie," he said. "It added charm to the place." He was tolerant of sightseers, who dropped in frequently, and not annoyed when one visitor collapsed in the library because of "the malevolent influence which he said existed there."

The intensity of the haunting seemed to slacken under Gregson's ownership, but the disturbances did not cease. One night the captain's cocker spaniel went into the courtyard, mysterious footfalls were heard, and the dog appeared to go mad with fright. Shrieking, it raced into the darkness and was never seen again. Its successor, a pup, repeated the strange performance and was also lost for good. (Gregson did not know it, but dogs were sometimes used by early ghost-hunters because of their highly developed senses of hearing and smell. There are many records of dogs becoming terrified in "haunted" areas.)

The curious incidents of the dogs in the night were not the only peculiar events Gregson noted. A glass of water was shattered but the table on which it stood remained dry; footsteps were heard, small objects moved, and a heavy cover placed over the well was lifted and removed some distance during the night.

The end of the Borley Rectory was appropriately spectacular. It caught fire at midnight—perfect timing—on February 27, 1939. The conflagration was described by the *East Anglian Daily Times:* "Captain Gregson with the aid of an oil lamp was sorting out library books in the main hall when the lamp overturned and burst. The Sudbury Fire Brigade arrived and found the front ground-floor rooms and the bedrooms above already involved. Before the Brigade had obtained control, a portion of the roof fell in."

Even during the building's destruction the haunting did not abate. Two witnesses saw figures moving near the Blue Room window, and a constable claimed that a "woman in grey and a man wearing a bowler hat" stood in front of Captain Gregson during the fire, but it was later proved that no such persons were there. In the midst of the flames, several neighbors observed a girl and "a formless figure" on the second floor.

Afterward it appeared that fire was no more effective than Christian exorcism in removing the specters. Two and a half weeks after the burning a man named Herbert Mayes was bicycling toward his home at night during the dark of the moon. As he reached the grim ruins of the Rectory he heard a sound of stampeding horses approaching. Flattening himself against the Rectory fence, he waited for them to pass, but no horses appeared. The pounding of hooves grew louder, seemed to be within a few feet of him, then gradually faded in the distance. The whole experience lasted three to four frightening minutes. Years before, the Reverend Harry Bull and others had reported the same thing taking place on the same spot.

A less alarming but no less uncanny occurrence happened when Miss Rosemary Williams and Mr. Charles G. Browne went to see the ruins by moonlight one night in late March. Rosemary Williams, watching a gap in the walls where there had once been a window of the Blue Room, clearly saw a girl who seemed to be standing in midair. Mr. Browne caught sight of the same white-dressed figure as she was disappearing. Miss Williams was perfectly calm about the matter since "the apparition seemed so natural and unfrightening."

The Borley Rectory was Harry Price's greatest case and he made the most of it. His summary is impressive and convincing as he points out that there were no fewer than one hundred witnesses over a period of sixty years. Every person who spent any time in the house had unaccountable experiences, and this included five rectors and their families and servants. There were many other observers. Dom Richard Whitehouse, Sir George and Lady Whitehouse, neighbors, callers, Price himself, and A. V. Wall, to list only a few. The volunteer ghost-hunters Price collected were a varied group, most of whom had solid credentials—such as Mark Kerr-Pearse of the staff of the British Legation at Geneva, and Squadron-Leader Horniman of the RAF.

Price's book covers a ten-year investigation. It is packed with verbatim oral and written testimony, and a copious fund of original records are now deposited in the Harry Price Library of Magical Literature in the University of London. The evidence authenticating the haunting is formidable. Borley Rectory seems to be the perfect case to confound skeptics.

But is it?

If the Borley story is re-examined carefully a number of objections arise at once. We find embroideries of the truth that are most disturbing. Those who were determined to prove the presence of ghosts in the Rectory were not content to limit themselves to facts—glamour had to be added.

The Borley case was romantically enhanced by the legend of the nun. But, alas, there was never a monastery, medieval or otherwise, on the site. The Manor of Borley did in ancient days belong to the Benedictine monks, but they built no more than a small church there. Another part of the tale was demolished early in the investigation by Dr. Letitia Fairfield, Senior Medical Officer of the London County Council, when she pointed out that coaches were unknown in England before 1550 and, further, there is no historical example of the death sentence for breach of vows. She added tartly that men have been hanged, drawn, and quartered often enough for keeping their vows, but not for breaking them.

The "legend" seems to have been a product of journalistic imagination and is obviously based on Sir Walter Scott's *Marmion*, Canto Second. Scott, in an appendix, notes that stories of women bricked up with a jug of water and a loaf of bread date back to the time of Roman vestal virgins, and he mentions the remains of a female skeleton found in the ruins of the Abbey of Coldingham, Berwickshire. But it is romantic guesswork to say that a nun was entombed alive at Coldingham or anywhere else in England. There is no evidence.

So the legendary basis of the Borley story falls apart at a touch. This does not, of course, affect the testimony of witnesses who saw what appeared to be a nun or heard the mysterious coach—but it throws a different light on their reports.

The central question in the case is the reliability of Harry Price himself. How trustworthy was he? The answer seems to be, not completely. Price, despite a distinguished career, appears to have been a publicity hound. (On his first visit to Borley he was accompanied by a news reporter—a questionable beginning for a scientific investigation.) Aside from the Borley case, Price won his greatest fame by his "exposure" of the prominent Austrian psychic, Romi Schneider, a medium he had earlier pronounced authentic. Determined to prove Schneider a fraud, Price offered evidence in a misleading manner and may have distorted facts. Some of his own coworkers at the National Laboratory for Psychical Research thought that Price twisted the case against Schneider.

Did he do the same in his reports of the Borley Rectory? The Society for Psychical Research suspected that he did and arranged for three investigators to check on Price's work. These experts, T. H. Hall, E. J. Dingwall, and K. M. Goldney, compared Price's notes and journals to his published material and immediately found discrepancies. If a fact weakened the effect of a "miracle," Price ignored it. Also, in briefing his volunteer observers he thoroughly implanted certain expectations in their minds. Naturally many such expectations were realized. Further, he ignored the obvious possibility that Marianne Foyster might well have engineered many of the uncanny happenings.

Unfortunately Price had no opportunity to reply to the charges; he died before the critique was published. Perhaps he could have explained or at least clarified many of the doubtful points.

Several aspects of the Borley case encourage skepticism. The most glaring is the remarkable change in the character of the ghosts after the arrival of Price and Wall. All the early observations—by members of the Bull family and their friends and servants—indicate a traditional "English haunting." The nun appears frequently, the fantastic coach is both seen and heard, "a shape" is observed in a bedroom, mysterious lights shine in the windows of empty rooms. There is nothing that can be called typical poltergeist activity, little resemblance to the Phelps case and other poltergeist onslaughts. A. V. Wall's initial report in the London *Daily Mirror*, sensational though it was, indicated no evidence of a poltergeist except the sound of dragging footsteps. The Borley ghosts, up to this point, were neither childish nor mischievous.

But the moment Harry Price arrived on the scene the entire character of the haunting altered: a half-brick crashes down, pebbles and a candlestick are hurled, keys fall from doors and a cake of soap takes on a life of its own. The bouncy poltergeist behind this preternatural romp is very unlike the nun who appeared silently in the garden to beckon the Reverend Bull's gentle daughters. Everything has changed. The ghosts, basking in publicity and attention, outdo themselves to perform on cue. Price and the poltergeists seem to have arrived together. The haunting will never be the same.

The Hall-Dingwall-Goldney study of the Borley affair suggests that when the haunting was going full blast, Marianne Foyster was the creator of most of the phenomena. Mrs. Foyster, pretty and much younger than her husband, detested the Rectory. She felt lonely and isolated and was doubtless bored. The suggestion has been made that she stage-managed events either to enliven a dull existence or to persuade her husband to move the family into more comfortable and friendly surroundings. If so, she did it very cleverly. For instance, Dom Richard Whitehouse was positive that Mrs. Foyster's arms were beneath the bed covers when the mysterious stiletto was dropped into his lap. Later he said:

> When one is not acting in the strictly scientific capacity of a psychical research investigator, one does not feel obliged to regard everybody in the house at every moment of the day as a potential trickster. I had seen more than enough to convince me that the phenomena at Borley Rectory were preternatural, and I agree with Mr. Price in asserting that this place, which is now a ruin, was once the most haunted house in England.

If Whitehouse was mistaken, if nothing preternatural was at work, then dozens of observers must have been deceived or have imagined things they had been primed to expect. Others must be labeled outright liars and tricksters—and this list is a long one: Marianne Foyster, of course; Harry Price; A. V. Wall; Mrs. Smith and her maid, Mary Pearson; several members of the Bull family; Mr. and Mrs. Cooper; Herbert Mayes; the Foysters' maid, Katie; and a dozen more. It would indicate that an astonishing number of unconfessed rogues had collected at one place over a period of many years. Not one of the Borley observers later admitted trickery or error. Despite close questioning in some cases, they clung to their original stories.

Excluding ghosts, real or spurious, what explanation can psychical research offer for the events at Borley Rectory and similar occurrences? There are a number of theories and two are well worth considering. G. W. Lambert, after years of studying haunted houses, noted that nearly half of all hauntings take place not far from tidal waters. (In fact, one could show mathematically that the most likely subject for a haunting is a clergyman with a fourteen-year-old daughter who lives within three miles of the sea.) Unless we conclude that poltergeists are attracted by beaches and salt air, some other explanation is needed; population figures support Lambert's observation: there is a superabundance of hauntings in maritime zones. Lambert speculated that underground rivers, dammed by oceanic tides, might create pressures which would cause certain buildings to shift imperceptibly on their foundations. This could account for objects moving "by themselves," for doors opening and closing, dishes tumbling from shelves, and unexpected noises.

Lambert's study, complex and carefully documented, is not the pseudoscience it appears to be in brief summary. He is critical of dubious evidence and does not rush to conclusions. Borley Rectory is a poor test sample, because it lies outside the three-mile coastal zone on which Lambert concentrates. Nevertheless, it stood not far from the sea and the "hydraulic jack" explanation could be applied to many, but not all, of the Borley phenomena, including one of the final mysteries at the Rectory. Captain Gregson was at a loss to understand why a carefully stacked pile of books would suddenly fall over, upsetting the oil lamp and igniting the building. He had taken pains to make sure they were solid, yet the accident happened. A slight tremor, undetectable by human senses, could not only have accomplished this but could also have frightened the dogs and perhaps have moved the well cover.

Although Lambert's view is not untenable in some cases, there are serious objections to it. A pressure strong enough to move objects within a room should cause structural changes in the house itself, and this does not seem to have happened. Aside from this and other weaknesses in the "hydraulic jack" notion, most of the Borley occurrences were visual—the nun did not materialize because of the pressure of sea water. We must search elsewhere for an explanation.

Another and much bolder theory involves psychokinesis, often called PK, a very old idea which in modern times has been developed by W. E. Cox and J. G. Pratt of Duke University in the course of extensive investigations into the occult. A different and startling form of PK has been theorized by Dr. Nandor Fodor, a ghost-hunting psychoanalyst. We encountered PK previously in the case of Eusapia Palladino, but in her day it was called "telekinesis." PK is the power of the mind to move objects *by thought alone*, a notion which scandalizes materialists and others who "take the world as they see it." PK, when summed up in a sentence, sounds like magic or witchcraft and consequently has a bad name among conservative scientists.

Unlike sorcery, PK does not seem to be a conscious power that can be evoked at will, although a limited number of experiments indicate that it can be produced consciously in small ways over a period of time. Usually the persons who have seemed to exercise such a force have done it when entranced, asleep, ill, or otherwise highly disturbed. Cox, Pratt, and other modern researchers have observed cases where trickery was out of the question. Cox, for instance, was on the scene at Hartville, Missouri, when some strange force manifested itself in 1958. "The

Hartville Haunting," as it was dubbed by the press, was no dainty affair. A washtub filled to the brim rose in the air and accomplished a brief flight through the house. So did a heavy pail of water.

That same year Seaford, Long Island, came into the news when what was often called a poltergeist invaded a private home there. Investigators from Duke watched bottles make their way across a table and drop to the floor. No one was playing tricks; tests with precision instruments revealed no physical oddities in the house or its furnishings—yet phenomena of diverse character continued. However much skeptics may scoff at the reports from Hartville and Seaford, there is no denying that some very strange things happened.

We have noted the childish character of poltergeists; we have also noted that a young person is almost invariably on the scene of a haunting: Frank Podmore's "naughty little girl" who is so often the trickster behind a ghost story. Yet there are numerous cases where a child, although present, had no opportunity to do mischief or where the type of mischief was beyond the child's physical strength. (The former was the case at Seaford; the latter at Hartville.) How can we account for such events?

Modern parapsychologists suspect that PK is at work, and that children, especially those approaching puberty, sometimes have such power although unconscious of it. In three classic examples of clerical hauntings we have examined such could well be the case. Young Hetty Wesley suffered chills, palpitations, and other symptoms resembling shock before and during the peculiar events at Epworth. Harry Price, writing about Borley, commented that "young persons, especially young girls and adolescents, are admittedly good percipients." He was referring to the testimony of a youthful maid, Mary Pearson, around whom many events seemed to center. At the Stratford Manse everyone seemed to feel that the two older children were deeply involved with the "ghosts." In fact, if we strip the high-flown notions of magnetism and electricity from Andrew Jackson Davis's analysis, we find a description of PK as it might have been practiced by the Phelps youngsters.

"Mind over matter" is an ancient saying and an ancient faith, but only recently have investigators given it scientific attention. Research is in primary stages and in all the world there is but a handful of qualified men and women working in the field.

Gamblers have long insisted that they could "talk to the dice" and make the cubes come up with the winning numbers. J. B. Rhine thought this suggested a method of isolating and testing PK. His experiments with dice, after thousands of trials, seemed to show an element of truth in the old belief—the wished-for numbers appeared more often than was mathematically probable. Later studies, especially the work of R. H. Thoules, confirmed Rhine's conclusions. Naturally there came a chorus of objections. It is a giant step from peculiar odds with dice to the levitation of such bulky objects as a tub full of water or a bag of coal, said doubters. But this complaint somewhat misses the point. It is also a giant step from the first static-filled communications of Marconi's radio to clear conversation coming from the moon, yet the working principle is the same. Rhine and his followers have statistically shown that at times *something* is at work and the mysterious factor acts suspiciously like mind over matter.

Researchers studying PK are confronted with problems similar to those faced by the Italian investigators who probed Eusapia's mediumship. In all PK experiments, except for a few which have tried rather unsuccessfully to combine ESP with PK, a subject attempts to exert power over matter by a conscious act of will. Yet when apparent PK occurs under natural, nonlaboratory conditions (Hartville, Seaford, Stratford, Epworth, Borley, etc.) it seems to be the result of unconscious workings of the mind. If PK exists—and the evidence for it is not negative, merely inconclusive—it is such an elusive force that no one has discovered precisely how to pin it down in quantity for dissection. Parapsychologists are in the position of nineteenth-century physicians who knew that malaria existed and could study it but had no idea of its cause.

Will the PK theory account for the ghosts that have bedeviled clergymen and others from time immemorial? It could certainly account for all the early cases of saints and hermits who longed for mortification of their flesh. Their wishes were granted when the stones rained down. At Epworth, Hetty Wesley was the ideal instrument to unleash such force. Events in the Stratford Manse fit the theory nicely: children of an impressionable age were excited, perhaps alarmed, by their stepfather's dabblings in the occult. The statues and initial vandalism might have been a neighborhood prank, since the family was not yet on guard, but this event could have further aroused the emotions of the children and other things began to happen because they expected them to. The Borley Rectory, like the Phelps case, would also appear to be a chain reaction. Stories of a haunting triggered the minds of "sensitives" such as Mary Pearson; subsequent strange occurrences, the result of PK, caused collective hallucination and everyone soon began to see and hear things; then, enter a second unconscious practitioner of PK, Mrs. Foyster, and our case, despite loose ends, is complete.

Many people find it easier to believe in old-fashioned ghosts than in modern PK. Meanwhile, confirmed skeptics insist that fraud and error account for everything of a ghostly nature. But modern research, although painfully slow and handicapped, threatens to make absolute skepticism obsolete. In the long run it may be more rational to admit the existence of little-known powers than to cling to the improbability that there is *always* a naughty child, thousands of mistaken witnesses, and deceit by men who have little to gain by lying and much to lose.

Our review of haunted clergymen has been classic and representative rather than complete. Men of the cloth have such a powerful appeal to ghosts that a full report might run to a dozen volumes and still be lacking. Dr. Louis C. Jones of the Cooperstown, New York, Farmer's Museum, has collected between seven and eight hundred recorded cases, both antique and modern, and a good many of them involve ministers and pastors. In 1922 the French psychical researcher, Flammarion, did a full book on haunted houses, and priests play important roles. His countryman, Police Commandant Tizané, attempted to track down four hundred different ghosts, dozens of whom had been molesting the clergy. Tizané made an inconclusive report in 1951.

In England a vicar at Leigh unsuccessfully attempted to banish haunting spirits in 1963. Roman Catholic missionaries in Kambakonan, India, fared better in 1913. They effectively exorcised a stone-hurling demon who preyed on Sister André de Marie Immaculée and other religious. Borley was not the only haunted rectory in Suffolk: in 1934, a neighboring clergyman and his family were plagued by a noisy ghost, a spirit which seemed to transport dishes through solid walls, then smashed them. This particular rectory was an ideal environment for a poltergeist, since it had no fewer than thirty bells, all of which rang repeatedly and simultaneously even after the wires had been snipped to halt the racket. The case was investigated but never explained.

Terror in Tennessee

Although the clergy are the favorite victims of marauding phantoms, laymen are not spared, of course. In literature and folklore troublesome spirits usually lurk in castles, ancient manor houses, or dank residences hard by graveyards—places such as Borley Rectory. In life, hauntings are not always staged against such romantic settings. Tenants in modern apartments have been disturbed and even evicted by purported poltergeists—air conditioning and automatic elevators are no more effective than mistletoe and yew branches in discouraging invisible intruders. Even business places are not immune: in 1962 a supermarket in England was vandalized by a ghost who loved to play with bicarbonate of soda; the Municipal Hospital of Toten, Norway, underwent several days of onslaught as objects hopped, danced, and levitated; a coal scuttle in a school near Richardton, Canada, seemed to become demon possessed one day in 1944 and lumps of coal "started popping out of the pail like Mexican jumping beans." This occurred before the eyes of officials who arrived hastily after all the window blinds began to smolder although there was no evidence of ordinary arson.

No one knows how many poltergeist cases have been recorded. Their number certainly runs into the thousands. Despite this, it is not always easy for a private individual who is curious about occult matters to find a "haunted house." Mack Reynolds, an American writer whose specialty is science fiction, attempted to investigate some supposedly ghost-ridden places. In southern England he made no discoveries, but was urged to try certain castles in Scotland. In Scotland he was told that although dark legends existed in many places, he really ought to explore Ireland, where specters were more frequently encountered. But his Irish guides then encouraged him to go to England, where there were haunted castles, rectories, and manor houses by the dozen—or so they had heard.

Abandoning this wild goose chase, he returned to the United States to live in Taos, New Mexico, and was soon intrigued by the report of a haunted house in Oregon. He traveled to Oregon, had no success whatever in tracking down the ghost story, but local people interested in the occult were delighted to learn he came from Taos. "Tell us about the miraculous painting there," they said. "It weeps or something, doesn't it? Isn't it in a haunted mission?" He had never heard of such a thing, but returning to Taos did learn of a similar legend in the area. His own investigation brought no results—he saw nothing unusual, could find no evidence to support the tale.

Reynolds' report is not untypical, although he might have done better in England if he had followed an official guide printed by the government for the use of tourists. It lists dozens of places where ghosts have walked. But one difficulty does confront those who seek such locations. Such terms as "haunted house" and "haunted castle" are misleading. Extended hauntings of particular locations, with several noteworthy exceptions, are common in literature, but rare in life. Poltergeists seem as errant as gypsies. A house may appear to be haunted for a week, a month, and usually a year at the most. Mysterious activity may be vigorous, then suddenly cease altogether for no obvious reason. Owners or inhabitants of buildings where these outbreaks occur may, in some cases, enjoy the attention and publicity that follow first reports. But investigation and the arrival of curiosity seekers soon become burdens. Victims of uncanny happenings, unless they call such events miracles and wish to establish a shrine, are delighted when the whole thing ends and publicity wanes. A householder who reports the presence of a ghost is immediately branded a fraud or a fool by many of his neighbors. Nevertheless, testimonies of poltergeist invasions keep accumulating. Every country and every major religion is involved.

Whether the hauntings take place in Sumatra, South Africa, or New York, the behavior patterns of the ghosts are monotonously similar. There are, however, a few exceptional occurrences and among the most bizarre is the story of the Bell Witch who exerted malignant power in Tennessee during the nineteenth century. The tale has been called by Dr. Nandor Fodor "America's greatest ghost story," although it is by no means the best investigated and documented. Nevertheless the case calls for examination because of the rarity of a murdering poltergeist; also, it offers the best opportunity to consider Dr. Fodor's psychoanalytical approach to ghost hunting.

In 1817 John Bell, his wife, his daughter, and four sons lived on a farm in Robertson County, Tennessee. This farm, in the north-central part of the state, lay in an area which had long ceased to be pioneer territory, yet it was still rather wild, with great stands of timber and with rutted trails for roads and virgin thickets. Much of the land had been cleared for farming, but

accounts of the terror which struck the Bell family are overlaid
with a brooding atmosphere, a feeling of shadowy woods where
witches might dance in a Nathaniel Hawthorne story. And the
scattered homes were isolated: people who lived an hour's ride
distant were considered close neighbors.

The wooden farmhouse, sheltered by trees, stood at the edge
of somewhat rocky fields. It was a plain structure, two stories
with three rooms on each floor, small rectangular windows, and
a large stone chimney. There were a few outbuildings, including slave quarters. No one thought it worth recording exactly
how many blacks lived on the premises, but there must have been
few. Except for one preliminary mention and one disgusting
incident, they remain off-stage and invisible throughout the story.
The Bell family was neither poor nor affluent; their lives and
their home seemed typical of the age and area. They worked hard;
they were liked and respected by their neighbors; there was nothing peculiar about them.

The first signs that something odd was taking place at the
Bell farm were annoying but hardly alarming, and they gave
little hint of the melodrama to come. There were noises—scratchings, knockings, and bangs against the outer walls, doors, and
windows. Earlier, John Bell had seen an unfamiliar animal—like
a dog, yet not a dog—sitting between two rows of corn. When
he fired his gun at it, the creature disappeared. Now he wondered if this animal might be the cause of the nocturnal disturbances. Clearly something was seeking entrance. At last such
entry was effected: the noises were inside the rooms—a flapping
as of invisible wings, the gnawing of a bedpost by an invisible rat,
the sound of a dog's paws padding and scratching on the floor.

The power of the unknown invader seemed to increase nightly.
Soon the farmhouse trembled with the clank of great chains
being dragged through the rooms; what had once been mere
raps became crashes and, more frightening, utterances were
heard—not words, but muffled gurgles and gasps as though a
victim were being strangled.

The special sufferer was Betsy—Elizabeth Bell—the young daughter of the family, who slept alone in an upstairs bedroom. The covers were ripped from her bed; she was pinched and pommeled. John Bell, Jr., and Drewry Bell shared another second-floor room while Joel and six-year-old Richard Williams Bell occupied the third. One night Richard Williams was seized by the hair, lifted from bed, and shrieked as he felt himself in the grip of some force almost strong enough to tear his scalp from his head. At the same moment, Betsy Bell began screaming in her room that she, too, was being dragged by the hair.

The Bells, wary of public attention and possible ridicule, tried to keep the affair a family secret. But at least one neighbor, Mrs. Martha Dearden, later recalled curious behavior by John Bell. He had come to dinner at the Dearden farm, eaten nothing, taken no part in the conversation, but had sat in morose silence. The next day he returned to apologize for his unsociable conduct. "All of a sudden my tongue became strangely affected," he said. "Something that felt like a fungus growth came on both sides, pressing against my jaws, filling my mouth so that I could not eat or talk."

The haunting reached such a pitch of violence that the Bells could no longer endure it alone. Mr. James Johnson, a friend and neighbor, was summoned to the house and given the full story. Johnson, a pillar of Christianity and apparently something of a lay preacher, also heard unexplained sounds, witnessed the torments of the family, and then attempted an impromptu exorcism, invoking the Lord and bidding the troublesome spirit to be silent and depart. Like many another exorcism, the rite made matters worse. The invader was silenced briefly, then it vented its spleen on Betsy Bell. Red marks appeared where it slapped her, audibly, on the cheeks and she screamed as her hair was painfully yanked.

James Johnson decided that the mystery was beyond him and formed a vigilance committee of neighbors whose task—although he did not say so—was obviously to keep sharp eyes on the Bells in case one of them was a trickster. The presence of the committee did not deter the spirit from activity, and the watchers were as baffled as Johnson had been. The evil presence—and everyone was forced to agree that there *was* a presence—became known as the Witch, the term being used in an unusual sense. No one felt that a human practitioner of black arts was hexing the Bell family. They called the invader a witch because they had no other word they could apply without committing blasphemy. These people were puritanical Protestants who rejected the idea of ghosts or demons; but witchcraft, despite its scandalous history of sexual immorality, was an acceptable explanation.

Girls from nearby farms shared Betsy's bed in a futile attempt to protect her, and when she fled to neighbors' houses for the night, the Witch pursued. The girl, not yet thirteen when the haunting began, was already ripening into womanhood. She has been described as "the personification of robust health" and as being "very stout," which in the context seems to mean strong, not obese. Never had she shown a tendency to fits of hysteria. But as the Witch grew in power, Betsy began to fall into what witnesses called "fainting spells." These seizures, which came nightly, had all the symptoms of a mediumistic trance: panting, exhaustion, unconsciousness, long intervals between breaths. The haunting spirit was completely inactive while Betsy lay prostrate. After half an hour or a little longer, the girl would emerge from her entranced state, fresh and rested. Poltergeist activity would begin almost at once.

From far and wide curiosity-seekers flocked to the Bell farm, and the house must have appeared to be the scene of a perpetual box social—horses and wagons filling the yard, visitors arriving with provisions and crowding the parlor as they demanded that the Witch talk or rap or "smack its lips" or give any performance to satisfy their hunger for the supernatural. Gradually the Witch became able to oblige them. First there were whistles, then mumbles and gasps. The power of speech came slowly, but one night a voice spoke, distinctly yet in a whisper. "I am a spirit who was

once very happy, but has been disturbed and made unhappy."
This dramatic announcement electrified the listeners, and there
was more—and worse—to come. The haunting would not end,
the family would be given no respite, until the Witch had
achieved its goal: the death of John Bell. It was an ominous
threat; it would be carried out in full measure.

Once speech had been acquired, there was no end to the vocal
outpourings. The Witch proved to be a Jekyll and Hyde personality. It would quote scripture, utter pious platitudes, and
on Sunday nights could recite verbatim the sermons delivered
earlier that day in the local church—an astonishing feat of memory. But the hypocritical Witch also became the county's most
malicious gossip, reporting sins, scandals, and personal faults with
great relish. And never did it cease its jeremiad against John
Bell, calling him vile names, vowing to hound him to his grave.

The Witch, always referred to as "it," either had no sex or was
unaware of its sex. At first it announced itself as the spirit of an
Indian whose grave had been desecrated and whose bones were
scattered. "A tooth is missing and I must have it back." The
Bells, hoping that the discovery of the tooth would quiet the
invader, spent a day scouring the farm. They returned home that
night, bramble-scratched and muddy, only to be ridiculed. It was
all a hoax, the voice said, and now it claimed to be the witch of
Old Kate Batts, a local zany who was suspected of having the evil
eye and casting spells. This second self-identification, as fictional
as the first, was soon forgotten by the Witch. Since old Kate
herself, despite an unsavory reputation as a conjure woman, was
never attacked by the Bells or their neighbors, it is obvious that
no one really believed the Witch's claim.

The haunting was by no means confined to the farmhouse, and
the Witch's utterances were not limited to the séance-like hours
of the evening. It now spoke day and night, in the fields, in a
barn, crying out loudly and at length that it would soon destroy
"Old Jack Bell."

Although the inhabitants of the community were unaware of

the "naughty little girl" theory of poltergeists, suspicion fell on Betsy Bell as perpetrator of a malicious trick. There was no evidence against her, but people did not take kindly to girls who had fits and seizures. Betsy and the Witch seemed connected in an undiscovered way. Rumors of Betsy's mischief-making were persistent enough that years later, in 1849, the *Saturday Evening Post* published an account charging her with fraud and, by implication, with murder. After re-examining the evidence, the *Post*'s editors retracted and apologized. It is noteworthy that there seems to have been no other journalistic attempt to unmask the Bell Witch. If some trickster caused the events, he left no traces behind.

Ventriloquism was little understood in Robertson County at the time, and some people suspected that Betsy was "throwing her voice" to create the Witch's speech. A familiar test that many a medium, including Eusapia, has undergone was tried on Betsy. One night when the Witch was talking, a physician suddenly clamped his hand over Betsy's mouth. The Witch continued speaking; there was no change in volume.

One neighbor unaffected by gossip about Betsy was Joshua Gardner, a young man who intended to marry the girl. Their engagement had been announced and everyone agreed that it was an excellent match—everyone, that is, except the Witch. "Don't marry Joshua Gardner," it pleaded again and again. When pleas failed to change Betsy's mind, threats and physical torments ensued. Terrified, the girl returned young Gardner's ring. A violent renunciation scene followed, a scene which nineteenth-century chroniclers of the Bell story made the most of, jerking every last tear, playing with all stops out. Like Thucydides, these writers "put into each speaker's mouth sentiments proper to the occasion, expressed as I thought he would be likely to express them."

We may safely dismiss these Victorian theatricals and rely on the more prosaic account of Betsy Bell herself, who said that when Frank Miles, a friend trying to intercede on Gardner's behalf, cursed the Witch "the Spirit kept screaming at him to mind his own affairs, and to be careful or it would knock his block off." At any rate, Betsy sacrificed her youthful love, although later she married another man. Her brother Drewry, on the other hand, remained a lifelong bachelor because he feared the Witch would take offense at his marriage.

No one writer has given us a typical day in the life of the Bell family at the height of the haunting, but by comparing versions it is easy to reconstruct such a scene:

At the first sign of dawn the slave bell awakens the inhabitants of the farm. The blacks go about their chores and eat their breakfasts unmolested, but in the main house trouble has already started. A lay-abed member of the family is pinched awake, slapped soundly on the rump as he starts downstairs. While the Bells eat, the Witch makes frequent comments. It is tender toward Mrs. Bell, who—small wonder!—has not been well recently. "Luce, poor Luce, how do you feel now?" The Witch has no magic power of healing, but does sometimes offer medical advice.

Betsy and her mother serve the meal, since the Witch will not tolerate the presence of Mrs. Bell's household slave, a husky black girl named Anky. The Witch claims to be "a Spirit from everywhere, Heaven, Hell, the Earth. Am in the air, in houses, any place at any time, have been created millions of years." Such age and wide travel ought to have given the Witch a certain sophistication and urbanity, but such is not the case. The slave, Anky, has been banished because the Witch shares all the prejudices and folk beliefs of Robertson County. It expresses itself like an evil character in *Uncle Tom's Cabin*. "I despise the smell of a nigger; the scent makes me sick."

At the table John Bell stoically ignores the taunts of the Witch and struggles to force a little food into his mouth. His jaw is almost paralyzed, his tongue and palate feel swollen and coated with some horrible growth. As the boys are leaving for school, he walks toward a field to supervise the slaves.

"Old Jack, Old Jack! I will make an end of you!" The Spirit shrieks in the air above his head and suddenly he jerks convulsively; he is hurled to the ground and his shoes are torn off his feet. Richard Bell, some distance away, races to the rescue of his father, but it is useless. As Richard struggles to put the shoes back on his father's feet, they are twisted from his hands. John Bell shudders, twitches, recoils from a blow on the face. At last the attacker leaves in triumph, insolent and obscene songs echoing in the air, finally fading in the forest.

Late that afternoon, Richard and Joel Bell walk home from school with William Porter, a boy who will later become an important man in Robertson County. At one place on the roadside there is a dense tangle of hazel and briers, and when they reach this point on their homeward walk, a volley of sticks and stones is hurled at them, but they are not surprised. This, as Porter will recall in adult years, happens often, and the whole thing is more of a game than a menace. Sometimes they mark a stick and throw it back into the brush, and a moment later it will be returned. At first they believed this was the work of some prankster, but no longer. At night the Witch reports publicly about the stick and rock throwing, and claims responsibility.

Meanwhile, Mrs. Bell has spent an eventful afternoon at home. She is attempting, under difficulties, to entertain the ladies of her Bible Study Circle. The Witch has restrained itself until the highpoint of the meeting, the moment when refreshments are served. "Surprise!" it cries out cheerfully, as fresh fruits and nuts drop from the air into the laps of the startled guests. The ladies do not panic; they expected something like this. It has happened before, and some of them recall Betsy's birthday party, when a heaped basket of tropical fruits, rare in Robertson County, sailed into the room and landed gently on the table. "From the West Indies," said the voice of an invisible speaker. "I brought them myself!"

The Bible Study group leaves, thanking Mrs. Bell for her hospitality. (Do they also thank the Witch as cohostess and provider of extras?) The Bells eat an early supper, getting the food out of sight before the evening's curiosity-seekers arrive, as arrive they do, shortly after sunset. Betsy suffers no seizure tonight. Strangely, as her father's condition has steadily worsened, her own has improved. There are no fits, no spells. Still, the evening turns out to be a dreadful embarrassment to the Bells. The Witch has recently acquired a family of its own, a rowdy and vulgar clan which tonight is inflicted upon the visitors. Blackdog arrives invisibly, insulting the guests in a gruff, ·male voice. Blackdog's brother, Jerusalem, is younger, has a boyish tone but a vocabulary of obscenities beyond his apparent years. Their sisters, Cypocryphy and Mathematics, utter vileness in girlish voices. Tonight the whole quartet is drunk, and as the unseen but distinctly heard binge continues, the farmhouse begins to reek of whisky. Cypocryphy and Mathematics are maudlin boozers; in their cups, they weep. Blackdog and Jerusalem become abusive, yelling and threatening to break up the furniture, insulting the guests, who, despite their professed puritanism, seem in no hurry to leave.

Mrs. Bell slips quietly out and goes to the slaves' quarters, where she arouses Anky. "Go to my bedroom and hide under the bed," she orders the baffled slave. Mrs. Bell intends to find out once and for all if the Witch's aversion to Anky is actually based on a sense of smell.

The guests, having had their fill of shock and scandal, leave agog, and the Bell family prepares for sleep. Everybody is upstairs, doors are open and conversation is lively. Suddenly the furious voice of the Witch shouts from the lower bedroom, "There is a damn nigger in the house! It's Ank! I smell her under the bed, and she's got to get out!"

Amid wild commotion, Anky rolls from under the bed, beating aside the fringed spread which had concealed her. "Oh, Missus, Missus, it's going to spit me to death! Let me out! Let me out!" The terrified slave flees, racing to the quarters. Then the members of the family put on their night clothes while the Witch mutters further imprecations against John Bell, but coos over the dear child Betsy and her sweet mother. It has been quite a day. And so to bed. . . .

All the events given here happened during the course of the haunting and are reported directly from the records; they did not actually take place in the span of a single day, but there seem to have been many twenty-four-hour periods just as crowded with incident.

The worst morning of all was now approaching; the stage had been set for the murder of John Bell. Bell's condition was by now pitiable. Racked by convulsions, unable to eat, and hardly able to speak, he became completely bedridden. A physician prescribed some unknown tonic, which was kept in the family medicine chest and administered to the patient daily. But on the morning of December 19, 1820, Bell sank into a coma. Frightened, John Bell, Jr., went to fetch the usual medicine but it had vanished, replaced by a mysterious bottle of murky liquid. The family, now in panic, summoned the doctor and while they awaited his arrival, the Witch rampaged through the house, shouting in triumph. "I have got him this time! He will never get up from that bed again. . . . I gave Old Jack a big dose while he was fast asleep, which fixed him!"

Indeed it had. Bell, never emerging from his coma, died on the morning of December 20. Meanwhile the strange medicine was tried on the family cat, causing the animal to fall into convulsions and die almost instantly. (An oddity of the case: if the poison was so quick-acting, why did John Bell linger on for at least thirty hours after having "a big dose"?)

The family, and presumably the doctor, were so horrified by the deadly liquid that they hurled the bottle into the fireplace, where it exploded. There could be, of course, no later analysis of its contents.

The Witch, exultant, attended the funeral of its victim, and as the mourners filed away from the closed grave it burst into song: "Row me up some brandy, O! Row me up some brandy!"

Although the Witch became less active, it lingered at the scene of the crime for several months. Then one night a sudden cloud of smoke filled the room where the family sat, a cloud which seemed, according to Richard Bell, to burst from "something like a cannon ball which rolled down the chimney and out into the room." In the midst of this smoke pillar the Witch shouted, "I am going and will be gone for seven years. Good-by to all!"

Seven years later the promised return did indeed occur, but the situation at the Bell farm had changed. Betsy no longer lived there, having married. John, Jr., had also established his own home, and only the widow and her sons Richard Williams, Joel, and Drewry remained in the once-haunted house. These four were plagued for a fortnight, but the disturbance was comparatively mild. There were scratches and knocks, the pulling and twisting of bedclothes, but no voice spoke except to John, Jr., who was startled in his own home when the Witch announced a planned visitation upon his descendants scheduled to take place a hundred and seven years later. This threat was never carried out, and 1935 passed safely for the possible victim, Dr. Charles Bailey Bell.

A LOOK AT THE EVIDENCE

A story so bizarre and improbable as the Bell haunting needs strong support to command belief. Dr. Nandor Fodor, who studied the case and produced the most detailed and thoughtful modern recounting of it, states that "we may presume the records to be accurate as to the existence of The Witch." He offers a number of facts to enforce this conclusion. Still, it is a pity that almost everything known about the Bell Witch is derived from reports written long after the events took place. Richard Williams Bell was an eyewitness, six years old when the Witch descended upon his family's farm and ten when it departed. He did not write *Our Family Trouble* until twenty-six years later. He was no longer a child but a youth of eighteen when the Witch disturbed the farmhouse a second time. Bell, although probably writing in defense of his sister, Betsy, did not want to publish the manuscript. It was solely a record for members of the family. Nevertheless, his son, Allen Bell, in 1891 gave permission to an editor, M. V. Ingram, to print Richard Williams' recollections. Ingram was a journalist of the penny-dreadful class; the quietly titled book *Our Family Trouble* appeared with grotesque illustrations as *An Authenticated History of the Famous Bell Witch. The Wonder of the 19th Century, and Unexplained Phenomenon of the Christian Era. The Mysterious Talking Goblin that Terrorized the West End of Robertson County, Tennessee, Tormenting John Bell to his Death. The Story of Betsy Bell, Her Lover and the Haunting Sphynx, Clarksville, Tenn.* One marvels that the sensation-packed tale was never dramatized for the touring melodrama companies of the era.

Even though Ingram published with at least one eye on the cash box, he did make every effort to substantiate Richard Williams' report. Numerous witnesses, including all surviving members of the family, were questioned. There was agreement among them.

A later work, *The Bell Witch, A Mysterious Spirit,* was brought out in 1934 by Charles Bailey Bell, M.D., the son of Dr. Joel Thomas Bell. The author, a respected physician and certainly no sensation-monger, relied heavily on stories told by Betsy Bell, who related the dark history of the Witch at the age of eighty-three. Also, Dr. Bell's grandfather, John Bell, Jr., confirmed before his death that Richard Williams' manuscript was accurate. There is also the old *Saturday Evening Post* account, the intended exposé that backfired. The whole body of evidence, while not overwhelming, is surprisingly strong. Certainly *something* most extraordinary happened in Robertson County. Discounting exaggerations and romanticizing, the story remains a peculiar tale supported by many witnesses. We also know that local people had such faith in the Witch that everyone attributed John Bell's murder to the malignant spirit. No member of the family was investigated or prosecuted.

Regardless of how much is exact truth and how much is

legend, Dr. Fodor has used the case as the basis of a fascinating theory about poltergeist phenomena. (He credits the first stating of this theory, presumably about thirty years ago, to the English psychiatrist, Dr. Maxwell Telling.)

Let us suppose that Betsy Bell, around whom the entire gruesome case centered, had developed a secondary personality as in the famed *Three Faces of Eve*. But this personality, Betsy II, was not at all of the type known to psychology. It was incorporeal, a mental force without an actual body, yet gifted with both ESP and PK. It could exert physical force, but was not itself physical in nature. As Fodor points out, F. W. H. Myers, well before 1900, was fascinated with the notion that part of the "soul" might break loose and develop an independent, nonmaterial personality.

Since Dr. Fodor is a psychoanalyst, it is hardly surprising that his poltergeist theory would have Freudian elements. He speculates that "in some exceptional instances the human mind can be so split-off that part of it may function in apparent independence." Function physically? Could a psychosis make itself physically manifest in some unknown way, acquire independence from the body, yet still exert power over matter? If so, a deepseated hatred, even an unconscious one, would appear to be an avenging ghost.

Dr. Fodor ponders the Bell Witch and suspects that Betsy, at the onset of puberty, was sexually molested by her father. A two-headed psychological monster sprang from this incestuous union: John Bell suffered the torments of his own conscience, and the guilt engendered the physical suffering he endured. Betsy, tortured by shock, horror, and also guilt, gave birth to Betsy II, a disembodied personality who undertook the task of vengeance in the form of the Witch. There is no evidence that a sexual attack took place. Fodor, however, is drawing upon years of clinical experience, and although the whole matter remains a speculation, dozens of details fit neatly into well-established discoveries of psychoanalysis. Fodor is guessing, but it is an educated guess.

PK, as it is usually thought of, will not explain the case. The Witch not only moved objects but talked; it had a definite character, and its loves and hatreds seem to coincide with Betsy's emotions. The Witch resembled conventional splinter personalities in that it emerged slowly at first and had to learn things— to talk, to open doors, to make its way about in the neighborhood. From the first faint scratchings to the final assertion of power on the morning of the murder, the Witch was constantly growing and evolving. It is interesting to note that although the Witch itself was sexless, the bawdy members of its family were two males and two females. Since they appeared long after the Witch had arrived, one is tempted to think that they had sexual characteristics because Betsy's puberty, and hence her sexual awareness, was by this time much further advanced.

The theory of a secondary personality that is somehow discarnate yet potent fully accounts for all the more sensational "hauntings." And that the primary personality—Betsy, in the Bell case—remains unconscious of the secondary personality is precisely what one would expect. This is almost invariably true when splintering of the ego happens in cases that have no occult aspects at all. Betsy Bell would not have the least knowledge of what Betsy II was up to. On the other hand, Betsy II would know her creator perfectly.

The Myers-Telling-Fodor idea of combining psychiatry with ESP and PK is enough to set the imagination racing and the teeth on edge. One thinks of a Jekyll and Hyde story wherein the evil Hyde has become the Invisible Man. Such a creation, rising from the subconscious of a friend—or worse, an enemy—is far more frightening than any ghost ever described. Death wishes, hidden longings for vengeance, would take the form of unseen but powerful and evil personalities bent on the destruction of an unknowing victim: the stones that fall near the Reverend Foyster at Borley are hurled by an invisible figure, the creation of a young wife who unconsciously seeks to rid herself of an elderly husband. In Stratford, a strange creature sprung from the mind of the Reverend Dr. Phelps roams the halls of the manse, stalking his unwanted stepchildren, tormenting them, toying with thoughts of murder as he sets fire to a boy's bed or hangs him on a tree in the yard.

It is comforting that this theory has no solid proof behind it, and the best evidence in its favor is only that it explains such a vast number of cases so well—and we must grant it that much.

Certainly the extent of the power of the human mind—perhaps "psyche" is the better term—is unknown, unexplored, and what exploration has been done shows that its abilities are above all else unpredictable. Before dismissing the existence of an incorporeal Betsy II as impossible, one might reflect on Dr. Telling's remark: "Absurd facts require absurd theories."

And when it comes to hauntings the facts seem absurd indeed. But some of the events do stand as fact. In the midst of nonsense, hysteria, and fraud we suddenly come up against the unexplained, and it is difficult not to agree with Immanuel Kant. Although Kant himself had apparently received telepathic communication, on occult matters he remained a skeptic among skeptics. Yet, after considering the innumerable tales of specters, he could not deny "some belief in them all taken together."

VI

The Crystal-Gazers

Among occult practices, crystal-gazing is one of the least respectable and perhaps the most frequently satirized. A crystal ball is an indispensable feature of cartoons about fortunetelling, and skeptics who will consent to play games with a ouija board would be mortified if caught staring into a glass globe. The crystal's disrepute has been increased by fairy tales in which some wizard or evil witch casts a watery eye at a glass and observes, in miniature, the flight of Hansel and Gretel or the whereabouts of Dorothy of Oz. In popular belief, the occult crystal resembles those glass balls containing tiny houses and figures: if one inverts it quickly, a snowstorm is raised. This is a mistaken conception of crystallomancy.

Crystal-gazing is ancient and international. Among the

Hindus it has been an essential part of religious ritual at various periods, although Indian practitioners were often inclined to use ink, syrup, or jewels instead of globes of clear glass. A favorite stone was an unflawed aquamarine beryl. The Hindu ceremonies were elaborate, with mystic symbols inscribed on the crystal and on the floor of the room or temple where the gazing took place. The crystallomancer was required to fast and purify himself by ritual bathing, and then the hour for the actual work was chosen by astrology. Properties used in the ceremony—the crystal or its substitute, dividers and rod, and a sword—had all been prepared and consecrated during the waxing of the moon.

In varied forms, but with marked similarities, this ancient art was used in Rome, Greece, Japan, China, Assyria, Persia, Chaldea, Egypt, and Polynesia. American Indians, especially in Peru, had their own versions, as did witch-doctors in Siberia, Australia, and Africa. Indeed, it is hard to find a society lacking some form of crystallomancy. The impulse toward it is so universal as to seem instinctive in man.

Of the thousands of crystal-gazers in the United States today, Jeane Dixon of Washington, D.C., is undoubtedly the most famous. Concentration on a glass globe has played a major part in her well-publicized prophecies. The crystal is not essential to her "visions" but seems to give them a focal point. In trying to determine the date of a coming event, for instance, she has seen the pages of a calendar changing swiftly, then pausing. But although Mrs. Dixon speaks of seeing things in the crystal it is clear that she does not mean there are things inside the glass. We must again avoid thinking of tiny Swiss houses and snowstorms.

In England crystal-gazing has been familiar since earliest times, but the rise of the spiritualist and psychical research movements brought it into popular vogue in the late nineteenth century. Andrew Lang discussed it in *The Making of Religion,* and the practice is frequently mentioned in reports submitted to the Society for Psychical Research.

In those days the crystals were sometimes a bit cloudy. At one séance a group of sitters all concentrated on the name of a public figure while the medium, without knowing the name, attempted to visualize the person in the glass globe. The medium saw "black trousers, a white hat, red coat, black waistcoat . . . [a person] having whiskers and presenting a glass tumbler." Unfortunately, the public figure the sitters were attempting to convey was Queen Victoria. During a similar experiment in America a clairvoyant lady described George Washington "wearing a hoop-skirt covered by a muslin pinafore, with something bulging at the back, either a flounce or a bustle."

Mrs. A. W. Verrall, whom we met earlier in connection with Cross-Correspondence, has given us the clearest idea of the experience of crystal-gazing in its modern form. She used a sphere about four inches in diameter, and although the room was dim, the globe remained partly enveloped by dark cloth to prevent the reflection of nearby objects. Adhering to the instructions of the ancients, she did not attempt to gaze when she was fatigued or distracted. In her case, as in the cases of other crystallomancers, nothing occurred during the first ten to fifteen minutes of gazing. Ten minutes may not seem a great length of time, but anyone attempting to keep his attention riveted and his mind passive for that period will quickly discover how difficult a task it is and how slowly the minutes pass. In general, crystallomancers agree that after a certain time the crystal becomes cloudy—not a filming over but an interior clouding, the forming of a nebulous shape that has been variously described as "whitish," "gray," and "luminous."

Mrs. Verrall attained a semisomnolent condition during which her unconscious was released and given free rein.

> I believe that with me the crystal picture is built up from the bright points in the crystal, as they sometimes enter into it; but the picture, when once produced, has a reality which I have never been able to obtain when looking into the fire or trying to call up an imaginary scene with my eyes shut.

Visions came to her and, although she does not precisely say so, they seem to have resembled the pastoral landscapes and classical idylls then popular in art galleries. There were also rather start-ling patterns and designs, but forms from nature were more common.

> Landscape, large piece of still water in evening light, beyond it mountains and hills, two snowy peaks, one sharply defined dark hill in front . . . Steamer passing from right to left till it touched shore and was lost to sight.

Mrs. Verrall carefully defined the difference between "move-ment" and "change." A change was a shift of an entire picture; a movement a shift of an object within it. Although in a state of light hypnosis, she was later able to recall details. Her experience was unusual in that she saw pictures *within* the sphere, as Jeane Dixon does. Most mediums use the globe chiefly as an aid in in-ducing a trance. Visions appear to grow from the glass but are not long contained inside it.

At times Mrs. Verrall saw written words, not always legible, and household objects and animals. But the visions were often ambiguous.

> . . . A flower like a convolvulus, which I knew to be pink though I saw no color, first sideways, then facing with a hard round knob in the middle. Then I knew it was not pink, but metal. I knew this from the hardness of outline, not the color.

Words failed her when she attempted to describe the exact difference between a crystal vision and a mental impression. Mainly, it seems to be a difference of degree rather than kind. The visions were "far more vivid" and not like "imaginings." They had reality of a sort, yet were not exactly real. One con-cludes that it was rather like looking through a stereoscope which lends apparent dimension to flat photographs. She made no ex-travagant claims about her results and does not suggest that ghostly personalities invaded the glass. Nor did she pretend an ability to locate lost objects or fugitive criminals—practical purposes for which the crystal has often been tried in modern times.

Throughout Latin America today there are *divinas* who gaze into a glass, a jewel, or a bowl of water in attempts to find the missing property of clients. Sometimes they have remarkable results, as in a Mexican village near Lake Chapala, where a *divina* announced that a lost watch would be found wrapped in a blanket—and this proved to be perfectly true. In another Mexican case a ring, supposedly stolen, was described as being lodged in a drainpipe—and so it was. Despite numerous correct hits and the continued popularity of *divinas*, there has been to date no really scientific study of this facet of crystallomancy.

Dr. John Dee

English crystal-gazing reached its height—or perhaps the height of its excess—in the person of Dr. John Dee, one of the strangest figures ever to create a footnote to the world's history. His bizarre biography is shot through with the clichés of Walpole, Bram Stoker, and Mrs. Radcliffe.

So far we have dealt with the comparatively modern oddities of the nineteenth and twentieth centuries. Dr. Dee takes us far back in time to an earlier era, to another kind of occultism. Spirits are there, a tribe of them, but they are seen in a different light.

The major concerns of Dee and his contemporaries in mystic arts, the philosopher's stone and the elixir of life, are now dead issues except among the most lunatic members of covens. John Dee was a dupe, the gull of a mountebank, and perhaps he himself on at least one occasion abetted a swindle. This sets him apart from all other leading figures in this book. The great occultists we have met so far were either persons of extraordinary power or clever frauds (although in many cases the deception, if it existed, was surely unconscious). Dee was very different: he was a victim.

Yet Dr. Dee cannot be ignored. In some respects he was the first "modern" occultist; he provides the perfect example of the psychological compulsion to believe in miracles; and Dee better than anyone else illustrates an affliction that has bedeviled students of the occult in all centuries including our own. His story is worth examining.

John Dee, born in London in 1527, was a marvel of Renaissance versatility: a mathematician, astronomer, writer, diarist, and experimenter in primitive chemistry. His early brilliance is as well established as his later eccentricity, and throughout the following account it must be borne in mind that the man was a genius in several fields. Dee's calculations were important in persuading England to adopt the Gregorian calandar; he contributed to the study of navigation and to the world's knowledge of comets and eclipses.

A precocious youth, Dee took his Bachelor of Arts degree at Cambridge before he was eighteen, then went abroad for higher study in astronomy and mathematics, living in Holland and later in France. The young scholar quickly gained fame among European savants and in 1550 was offered a chair of astronomy at the Sorbonne as a result of his giving several lectures on Euclidian geometry. Unfortunately for him, he returned to England to accept a post as rector at Upton-upon-Severn. Dee's father had been a gentleman server at the court of Henry VIII, and this connection with royalty earned Dee the assignment of writing schoolbooks for the education of young Prince Edward.

Dee liked the prince, but his real devotion was to the fiery, red-haired Princess Elizabeth, and most unwisely he cast a horoscope predicting her early ascent to the throne. When Edward died and Mary Tudor came to power, Dee had cause to regret his forecast. He was promptly clapped into prison at Hampton Court on the capital charge of attempting to murder the new queen by black magic. There was no evidence that the doctor performed any sorcery against his sovereign, but pessimistic fortunetellers have always run grave risks when their prophecies indicated woe to the powerful.

This was only the first of several brushes with the headsman, the hangman, and the stake. Although Dee was released unharmed, an awesome reputation clung to him forever afterward, and he protested being calumnied as "a companion of hellhounds." His accusers were not as slanderous as Dee claimed, for his own diaries show that he constantly attempted the practice of magic, even though his sorcery was intended to be white, not black.

As a young man he was considered handsome in a dark, Welsh way, but later his features acquired a sinister aspect which undoubtedly added to his notoriety. The most famous portrait of Dee, an engraving by an anonymous seventeenth-century artist, reveals an El Greco face, razor-nosed, hollow-cheeked, thin-lipped and altogether frightening—exactly as one would imagine Merlin or Dr. Faustus. It was easy to suspect that such a man was in league with the devil, and in 1576 he narrowly escaped death at the hands of a mob.

We cannot pinpoint the origin of Dee's occultism, but his first major achievements were in astronomy, a science then linked with astrology, and from the casting of horoscopes it was a small step to other realms of mystic art. During his European travels he came under the influence of disciples of Paracelsus, the Swiss physician and alchemist whose career preceded Dee's by only a generation. The two have so much in common that one is tempted to believe that Dee patterned some episodes of his life on that of the older occultist. Both were brilliant, both renounced the conventional superstitions of science and immediately fell into new superstitions of their own. Both came to ultimate grief in vain pursuit of magic.

Paracelsus has been called the "father of modern medicine," and although this stretches truth rather far, no man has a better claim to the title. While still a medical student, he realized that most practitioners of medicine were Pharisees, and he rejected all traditional teachings to study the "great open book of the universe written by the finger of God." This credo, written long before Francis Bacon laid down what is generally thought to be the first description of the scientific method, served Paracelsus well. In pursuit of knowledge he set out to explore most of the known world, often living like a gypsy. It is certain that he spent time in Egypt and Arabia, and seems probable that he visited what is now West Pakistan. He noted and remembered the practices of Islamic magicians. In 1524 he returned to his native Switzerland and became a lecturer on medicine at the University of Basel, where he caused a storm of controversy when he publicly burned the works of Galen and Avicenna. The infuriated medical faculty made attempt after attempt to drive him from the city, but he proved a difficult opponent, having demonstrated his brilliance by discovering laudanum and introducing sulphur and mercury into the practice of medicine. But at last he fell afoul of the authorities and had to flee. Paracelsus lived out his remaining years as an impoverished vagabond and died in 1541. Like many a man before and since, he was poisoned by a group of physicians.

Fifteen years later John Dee in England was covertly studying the work of Paracelsus. When Elizabeth I came to power, he was freed of the shadow of the scaffold. Elizabeth remembered the darkly romantic Welshman who had cast such a favorable horoscope for her and sent Lord Dudley to Dee to learn "a propitious day for her coronation" according to the stars.

Following the example of Paracelsus, Dee now visited a number of far-away places, including the island of St. Helena. It has been suggested that Dee, during his many travels, was acting as a spy for Elizabeth, and that his activities in astrology, alchemy, and magic were merely a cover for his real role as secret agent. Documents exist to show that Dee was at least a part-time spy, but during his era most traveling Englishmen were. His writings burn with a fervor of mysticism that cannot have been assumed and whatever spying Dee did was incidental to his lifelong quest for the strange and miraculous. We do not know all the experiences he lived through during his journeys, but at this time something changed Dr. John Dee from an astronomer who dabbled in the occult into a fanatical mystic.

Returning to England, he set up housekeeping in a forbidding residence at Mortlake, a town whose name is perfect for Gothic romance. It is on the Thames and has, appropriately, its share of fogs and mists. In these gloomy surroundings he pursued all manner of dark arts. Dee now had a wife, a much-suffering woman whom he refers to as his "painful Jane." We are not quite sure whether the lady was filled with physical pain or caused mental pain to the doctor, but the former seems to be the case. She suffered in childbirth, suffered from undefined ailments, and no doubt suffered loneliness when her husband isolated himself from the family to brood over his mysterious experiments.

The doctor was not sociable with the inhabitants of the village, and they, in turn, harbored grave suspicions about him. He was a local celebrity, but not a welcome one. When, in 1572, an unknown star appeared in the sky, alarm spread through the land, and a stream of visitors came to hear Dee's explanation of this change in the heavens. Five years later Elizabeth herself consulted him about the meaning of a comet. Dee took this opportunity— and every opportunity—to try to convince the queen that she should finance him in elaborate and expensive attempts to transmute base metal into gold. Her majesty listened courteously, but granted no funds.

In the isolation of Mortlake, Dee grew ever more solitary, giving himself to study of Talmudic and Cabalistic mysteries, and increasingly to crystallomancy. There is no detailed description of his laboratory, but one can reconstruct it from the few facts we have and the requirements of Dee's experiments. It was a large, lofty room with open beams and a stone floor. One leaded window, facing west, offered a view of the Mortlake graveyard across the road. Tables, cupboards, and shelves were filled with curious objects: the brass staff of an astronomer, dividers for measuring the heavens and charting the houses in astrological forecasts; celestial charts, mortars and pestles of various sizes; and a small, smoky furnace for smelting. Dee owned heavy gloves made and blessed by the great geographer Gerhardus Mercator. (Besides revolutionizing mapmaking, Mercator performed occult experiments. Like Dee, he had trouble with the authorities. In 1544 he was charged with heresy, and although he managed to escape, forty-two other people arrested with him were all burned alive.)

The Mortlake laboratory also contained vials of powder and liquids, some of them poisonous, such as the distillation of foxglove. Other substances were exotic: the dust of an Egyptian mummy, a grainy white powder supposedly the ground horn of a unicorn. A crucifix, a Bible, and a flask of holy water were at hand to protect the sorcerer from a sudden onslaught of demons and devils; and, of course, there was a crystal on a wooden stand shrouded by black cloth embroidered with Cabalistic symbols.

The distinguished men and women who made the pilgrimage to Mortlake to call on Dee were made uneasy by these weird trappings. The callers were many and eminent, among them Sir Francis and Lady Walsingham, Sir Christopher Hatton, and the knightly poet Sir Philip Sidney. A medieval touch was provided by the visit of Mrs. Tomasin, the queen's dwarf.

In March, 1575, Dee wrote in his diary, "The Queen with her most honorable Privy Council and other Lords, Ladies and nobility came riding across the fields from Richmond." Elizabeth had arrived at an unfortunate moment. Dee's wife had been buried only four hours before, and, upon learning this, Elizabeth declined to enter the house but asked to see the famous crystal. "Her majesty being taken down from her horse by the Earl of Leicester, Master of the Horse, at the church wall of Mortlake, did see some of the properties of the glass to her majesty's great contentment and delight."

The queen's visit seems to have impressed Dee far more than his wife's death. Her majesty's arrival, not "painful Jane's" burial, concerned him that day.

Alone now, he began to see visions. In May 1591, spirits of blinding radiance sprang from his crystal ball. One of them resembled Queen Elizabeth, at least vocally, and another was patterned on Edward VI. "His hair hangeth down a quarter of the length of the cap [cape?], somewhat curling, yellow." These angelic visitors, impressive though they appeared, were merely heralds of the wonders to come. A year and a half after the first vision Dee was praying in his laboratory when the angel Uriel, dazzling, robed in light, appeared at the window amidst the blaze of sunset and gave the doctor a new crystal, promising that heavenly beings would reveal themselves within it.

THE GREAT CRYSTALLINE GLOBE

Dee's story of receiving the crystal from the hands of an angel is the only false note in his diaries. He was often deluded, often gullible; but only in the matter of acquiring the crystal does he seem to tell an outright lie.

It is probable that Dee, by fasting, constant prayer, and self-hypnosis, had strained a fragile psyche past the breaking point. He may have received the crystal from some ordinary source while in an entranced state, and later believed the miracle himself. Considering his character, this seems the best explanation. Such "forgetfulness," which seems related to some form of hysteria rather than to multiple personality, is characteristic of many people who have believed they have performed wonders. Dee has much in common with the Reverend William Stainton Moses, that Victorian tower of respectability who claimed he was frequently transported through his own house by spirits. Everyone testified to the clergyman's honesty, yet he reported the preposterous. Such cases occur repeatedly, and the victims of this aberration are not otherwise mad. William Stainton Moses was a capable man; John Dee was a brilliant one. His tale of the angelic gift is archtypical and revealing.

But the crystal proved a disappointment. Dee found that tremendous concentration was required to reach the entranced state when angels and phantoms shimmered in the glass, then leaped from it to whirl about the stone-walled laboratory. His experiences, when successful, bear a striking resemblance to reports given by the users of LSD and other hallucinatory drugs. Colors and lights were gloriously intensified; limbate spirits glowed in the shadows while music echoed inside his head and the winds seemed to speak or sing to him. Those who reach such a height of sensitivity, however it is induced, and later try to describe their experiences are unanimous about the inadequacy of words and similes to express their feelings. Ordinary conscious life seems to have few parallels to the entranced state.

Dee's reactions, noted in detail in his diary, are the oldest known descriptions of an entranced state written by a man who had actually experienced it. (We may except parts of the Bible and certain Oriental religious writings. Such visions and the visions of mystical Christian saints are not presented as studies of personal reactions.) Dee recorded not only the content of the trances but also their nature and his own feelings. We can forgive the doctor for not being so coolly analytical as Mrs. Verrall: he anticipated her descriptions of a crystal-induced trance by more than three hundred years.

Dee suffered a difficulty which has plagued many mediums. Spirit utterances, heard clearly at the time, vanished from his mind before he could record them. (He was also a pioneer in recording this fact about hypnosis.) Dee was forced to employ a "skryer," an assistant who could invoke the spirits while Dee, unentranced, sat to one side and noted what occurred. He first hired a lout with the Dickensian name Barnabas Saul, but the gloomy surroundings and weird nature of the work affected the lad, and on the night of October 8, 1581, Saul was terrified by a "spiritual creature" who seized him at the witching hour. Nevertheless, Saul continued to stare into the crystal and in early December he beheld an angel named Anael. When spring came, Barnabas Saul, his meager imagination spent, lost all power as a skryer. Upon his dismissal by Dee he vanishes from the history of the occult. Considering the fate that befell Dee's next assistant, Barnabas Saul must be counted lucky to have escaped.

The new skryer was called Edward Kelly, but his real name may have been Edward Talbot. He was slippery, hard to pin down, and "Kelly" could well have been an alias. Twenty-eight years younger than Dee, he was already wiser in worldly experience. He turned out to be a deep-dyed rascal, lecher, and swindler.

Kelly's physical aspect added to the weirdness of the house at Mortlake. Convicted of uttering counterfeit money in Lancaster, he had undergone the usual punishment of having both his ears cut off, and he disguised the loss by wearing a tight-fitting black cap with long flaps. Since Dee affected the flowing robes of a magus and a turban-like hat, the costuming of the scene in the alchemist's laboratory would have been enough to please a designer of Hollywood horror films.

Other elements accentuated the gruesome atmosphere. Before he joined Dee, Kelly's specialty had been drawing secrets from corpses. One of the haunts where he practiced necromancy was a park, Walton le Dale in Lancaster, a place frequented at night by only bats and owls. We do not know how many bizarre rites he performed in this park during the full moon, but there is a detailed description of at least one such occasion.

A certain gentleman with more wealth than sense was taken to the park by the necromancer and nearly frightened out of his few wits as he listened to Kelly's fearful invocations of the dead. Turning to the servants who had accompanied them, Kelly inquired who had been recently buried in a nearby graveyard. They replied that a local resident had been laid to rest only a few hours before, and Kelly then led the trembling band to the moonlit grave. He drew a wizard's circle, cried out a ghastly incantation, and proceeded to disinter the coffin. Prying it open, he performed a ritual over the exposed corpse, managing to add to the general terror by the use of ventriloquism. The body, held bolt-upright, appeared to speak prophecies.

The ghoul Kelly had little respect for the ancient traditions of sorcerers. Many magicians in various centuries have claimed the ability to draw speech from a corpse, but always—with a few dreadful exceptions such as Kelly—they have shunned this practice, reflecting a belief which was summed up by a classic historian of the occult, Eliphas Lévi:

> The care taken by the ancients over the burial of the dead protested strongly against necromancy, and those who disturbed the sleep of the grave were always regarded as impious. To call back the dead would condemn them to a second death, and the dread of earnest people . . . was the possibility that the corpses might be profaned and used in witchcraft. After death the soul belongs to God and the body to the common mother, which is earth. Woe to those who dare to invade these asylums. . . . Necromancers are makers of vampires, and they deserve no pity if they die devoured by the dead.

Edward Kelly had no such fear. But, then, Kelly was a prophet who could not foresee his own grim future.

A PECULIAR UNION

It is hard to conceive of a more unfortunate combination than Dr. John Dee and Edward Kelly. Dee, the scholar, the lover of science, pursued his strange arts with sincerity, and sought the miraculous as a saint seeks God.

Kelly, on the other hand, was a born crook and gallows bird, utterly without scruples. An engraving used to illustrate an early eighteenth-century edition of Dee's writings shows Kelly standing in a graveyard beside an ashen-faced client, calmly inspecting a body he has just resurrected. A skeletal man, tall and emaciated, Kelly is far more sinister than the imagined zombie he has called from the tomb. Although the engraving was done long after the necromancer's death, its details are based on contemporary accounts and descriptions. Such scenes certainly took place.

No confidence game was beneath Kelly: he sold bogus remedies, faked religious relics, and cast horoscopes without even an elementary knowledge of astrology. Nevertheless, Kelly and Dee became inseparable. They are always linked in the history of the occult, as they are linked in rhyme by Samuel Butler's *Hudibras:*

> I've read Dee's prefaces before
> The Devil and Euclid o'er and o'er,
> And all the intrigues 'twixt him and Kelly,
> Lescus and the Emperor would tell ye.
> Kelly did all his feats upon
> The Devil's looking-glass, a stone;
> Where playing with him at Bo Peep
> He solved all problems ne'er so deep.

Kelly was a far more talented skryer than Barnabas Saul. He could hear the crystal's spirits speak, not merely see them, and mystic writing appeared before his gaze. To spice up the sessions of crystallomancy, Kelly sometimes turned pale as observing "hell-fiends," "Satanic imps," and "goblins damn'd."

Acting upon heavenly instructions, he and Dr. Dee journeyed to ruined Glastonbury Abbey and there they unearthed a flask containing the priceless elixir of life. The elixir would make men immortal or at least prolong life greatly—three hundred years was a common estimate. It would also restore youth, beauty, and sexual prowess, and serve as a remedy for all ailments. The search for the elixir is less absurd if one considers the zoological beliefs of the time. Everyone was sure that the stag rejuvenated himself by eating serpents and that the serpent, in turn, became young by shedding his scales. Ravens were supposed to survive for centuries, and few doubted the near-immortality of the phoenix. In such a context the hunt for a miraculous nostrum is a good deal more sensible than the monkey-gland craze in the twentieth century. Paracelsus thought that the main ingredient of the elixir must be a mercury derivative, but since he died at the age of thirty-seven he is a dubious authority.

John Dee seems to have had no suspicion that he unearthed his treasure from a mine previously salted by his assistant. He bore the elixir home to Mortlake in triumph, while Kelly broadcast word of the discovery. Streams of eager visitors arrived at Dee's house as they had in former times, but now the efficient Kelly was on hand to take their money.

Soon the roles of master and servant were reversed. The doctor's dependence upon Kelly and his blind faith became so absolute that Dee was terrified that his skryer might suddenly vanish to take employment elsewhere. In a foolish and pathetic passage in his diary, Dee tells of a terrible day when he begged Kelly to remain, promising to pay him fifty pounds a year. The money was persuasive, and both men swore undying fidelity upon a Bible. "And so we plight our faith each to the other, taking each other by the hand, upon these points of brotherly and friendly fidelity during life, which covenant I beseech God to turn to His honour, glory, and service, and the comfort of our brethren, His children, here on earth."

Dee's income was now enormous, but expenses rose to meet it. He was supporting Kelly in grand fashion and spending huge amounts on his quest for the philosopher's stone to transmute metals. Once more he became a familiar figure at Elizabeth's court, where he appeared regularly and futilely, attempting to win subsidies for his research. During a visit to Whitehall, Dee met Albert Laski, Count Palatine of Siradz, a Polish nobleman who had come to England to meet the celebrated queen and, not incidentally, to interview the famous Dr. Dee, whose reputation had crossed the North Sea and half the continent of Europe. Laski was fascinated by the doctor's talk of metaphysical matters, for the "Polonian," as Dee called his new acquaintance, embodied every superstition of a superstitious age, and he was soon journeying to Mortlake, where both his greed and gullibility were exploited by Kelly.

Previously, Kelly had preyed only upon country squires and credulous yeomen. The distinguished Pole presented a far greater challenge, and Kelly rose to it. Apparently he had picked up some tricks of stage illusion, for the wonders now performed in the Mortlake laboratory were obviously produced by mirrors and wires. It is impossible to determine Dee's role in the tricking of Laski. He must have suspected that skulduggery was afoot. The laboratory could hardly have been rigged for the staging of Kelly's spirit charade without Dee's knowing it, but still the doctor said nothing. His silence reveals a weakness of ethics that has been common among occultists of every generation: he believed that the end justified the means. Dee was desperate to get money for his noble research. Further, he *knew* the reality and power of the spirits who sprang from the crystal. He himself had seen and heard them. So why not give the spirits a little mechanical help?

Missionaries of mysticism, honest and sincere most of the time, often yield to this temptation, and any student of psychic matters would do well to remember Dr. Dee's weakness. Three hundred years after Dee and Kelly hoodwinked the count, Helena Blavatsky resorted to childish tricks to speed up conversions to Theosophy, a religion in which she genuinely believed. Harry Price at Borley Rectory succumbed to the same temptation in a different way. Once he became convinced that the haunting was real, he weighted the scales of his investigation on the side of the poltergeists. Some present-day writers, especially authors of books on prophecy and faith healing, commit still another version of this traditional sin. Convinced of the over-all truth of their own reporting, they omit or distort any facts that might weaken their thesis. In his tolerance of deception to aid his cause, Dee is once again typical of the zealots of occultism, both ancient and modern.

In Mortlake angel voices, audible not only to Kelly but to others, proclaimed the Polish count the new savior of Europe, predicting a career to surpass Charlemagne's. Laski would conquer Moslem Europe and free Turkey from heathen grip. But before this grand design could materialize, it was necessary to return to Poland and spend a little time transmuting baser metals to gold.

A strange entourage set out for Europe: the doctor with a new and attractive wife and his children; Kelly and his wife; the nobleman with Polish and English servants. They were encumbered by an immense heap of baggage—all the sundry equipment for a laboratory, including minerals, powders, charts, globes, and a library. Their progress across the Continent was leisurely, and they lacked no comfort that the count's liberal supply of money could buy. After a pleasant month in Lübeck "gathering strength," they continued to Stettin to enjoy Christmas and three more weeks of luxurious idleness. Throughout their journey the voices from the crystal gave favorable prognostications, keeping Laski agog at the prospect of future magnificence.

Arriving at the nobleman's chief estate, Lasco, Dee set up the laboratory and a smelting shop. The area had an abundance of iron, and the doctor, with preternatural advice, decided this was the base metal for transmutation. To him, the opportunity seemed heaven-sent in every way. Now in his fifty-seventh year —old by Elizabethan standards—he had at last complete freedom and capital to put his theories to the test. He fell to work with the vigor of youth, confident he was on the threshold of a miracle. Formula after formula was tried, varied, then tried again. The first attempts seem based on instructions from Paracelsus: antimony, fired and purified, was then dissolved in vitriol, a liquid known in alchemy as "the stomach of the ostrich." The product was strengthened with "the sharpness of the eagle," which meant essence of mercury. Many subsequent distillations were necessary. After this lengthy process a brilliant red fluid was supposed to be obtained—the philosopher's stone.

Anyone attempting to follow Paracelsus's instructions should be warned that "no one can understand or attain such an arcanum without the help of God: for its virtue is ineffable and divine." It was not only divine but expensive. The ingredients were costly, and a torrent of fuel flowed into the furnace day and night. When Dee seemed on the verge of success, failure followed. The ancient alchemists who wrote about the stone had an irritating habit: like jealous cooks, they always omitted one essential ingredient when they gave out their recipes. This was what they meant by an "open secret." It was "open" to those learned enough to detect the omission.

When alchemists refer to "the help of God" one feels they are merely tipping their pointed hats to the Eternal. They actually relied on chemical processes combined with magic that could supposedly be produced by given methods. Although Dr. Dee followed the steps of his predecessors in many ways, he also broke away from tradition. The crystal-dwelling spirits were his chief mentors, and he was sure their instructions would lead him to triumph. He usually called these spirits "angels," but this is a peculiar use of the word. They seem more like the "shells" described by some modern theosophists—bodiless beings, yet not ghosts.

Count Laski mournfully watched the forests of his estate dwindle under the axes of a dozen woodsmen. He paid for more mercury and more vitriol, and bought gold to "bait the crucible." He mortgaged his land and fell into the clutches of money-lenders. Meanwhile his flagging hopes were kept alive by the prophecies of two angels, Madinie and Uriel, who gave reassurance through the lips of Edward Kelly. But then one day the angels changed their tune, pointing out that Laski's funds were exhausted and the great work would have to continue elsewhere. Everyone involved, both divine and mortal, had reached the same conclusion.

The measure of Laski's faith is that he neither had them arrested nor sent them packing. The two were provided with money for a journey to Prague and letters of introduction to Emperor Rudolph. They set off for the imperial capital, Dee's disappointment alleviated by spiritual consolations which Kelly administered.

Kelly's avarice was so insatiable and Dee's missionary spirit so blinding that neither seems to have considered the grave danger of their position. The Holy Inquisition, whose agents were everywhere, had pounced upon more than one alchemist and diviner, and once in the toils few escaped alive. Noblemen who held the power of life and death were equally dangerous to men such as Dee, because there was no possibility of satisfying them. If an alchemist proved to be a failure, he faced the dungeon or gibbet for fraud. Still, any indication of success was as perilous as its opposite. If a prince believed that a certain alchemist could produce limitless gold, he would not be fool enough to let the man go elsewhere to enrich a rival.

The fate that Dee and Kelly now courted can be appreciated when one considers what befell Alexander Seton only a few years later. Seton, a Scotsman, supposedly discovered the secret of the philosopher's stone in the Netherlands. He was either the greatest of all alchemists or an adroit illusionist, for Seton even convinced the great physician Zwinger of his prowess. Then the unlucky alchemist fell into the hands of Christian II, Elector of Saxony, who demanded that Seton reveal the gold-producing secret. The Scotsman refused, either because of dedication to noble principles or because there was no secret. Christian II imprisoned him in a tower dungeon, where forty soldiers kept a day-and-night guard. Alexander Seton's body was stretched on a rack, the soles of his feet were burned almost fleshless, and he was repeatedly flayed until insensible only to be revived for further torture—all of which gained Christian II nothing. A Moravian named Michael Sendivogius, also greedy for the fabulous stone, managed at great risk to engineer Seton's escape, but it was too late to save the alchemist, who, crippled by his torments, soon died in the city of Cracow, where he had found sanctuary. Rescuer Sendivogius was no more successful than

243

Christian II in learning the prized secret from Seton, and he, too, came to ruination, prison, and an unhappy end.

Oblivious of danger, Dee and Kelly went to Prague "in right good spirits" and they were received graciously by Emperor Rudolph, who indicated interest in their work but, like Elizabeth I, was unwilling to invest. The intellectuals of Prague greeted Dee as a distinguished scholar and the nobles were impressed by his erudition. Kelly was an outsider and it appears that everyone recognized him as an uneducated mountebank.

This pleasant interlude ended abruptly in May 1586, and the pair escaped fiery death only by a piece of good luck. The Papal Nuncio to Prague, outraged by the talk of angels in Dee's crystal ball, petitioned Rudolph to expel the two as heretics, and fortunately Rudolph complied, giving Dee and Kelly only one day in which to leave the country. They were already on the road when orders came from Rome to seize them, and the magicians eluded their pursuers to make their way to the border of Rudolph's dominions in the nick of time. They moved from Erfurt to Cassel and at last to Cracow, eking out a living by casting horoscopes for anyone who would give them so much as a scanty meal.

Kelly, still smarting from his treatment in Prague, gazed into the crystal and came up with the vengeful prediction that Rudolph would soon be assassinated and King Stephen of Poland would gain the crown and the imperial dominions. This delighted the king, and he supported them for a while, then grew bored.

Their next patron was Count Rosenberg, owner of an ancient castle at Trebona in Bohemia, and there they went to set up the laboratory once more. The location was perfect: only Bohemia would permit truth to copy Gothic fiction so precisely. The castle was a towered, turreted stone hulk dominating the wooded country around it. Dee and Kelly had returned to their customary murky atmosphere, exchanging the dankness of the house at Mortlake for the even more haunted environment of Trebona.

During their wanderings, Edward Kelly had become more and more unmanageable. He flew into violent rages during which he tormented and humiliated Dr. Dee without mercy. Nothing could stave off the skryer's anger, for its cause was beyond remedy. Wherever they went, Dee was respected as a scientist and scholar, while Kelly was detected for what he really was. The jealousy smoldering in Kelly flamed into spite, which he vented by punishing the helpless doctor, who was now utterly dependent, the slave of the divine voices only Kelly could hear.

MÉNAGE À QUATRE

After a short time in the gloom of Trebona Castle, the melodrama took a sexual turn. Kelly became enamored of Dee's young wife, and his strategy for possessing her was to hear a spirit voice speaking through the "great crystalline globe," a voice commanding Dee and Kelly to share and share alike, to hold all things in common, their wives included. Kelly's passion was probably more complex than simple lust for a pretty woman. From the beginning, envy of Dee gnawed on him. The doctor came from a background of the royal court; Kelly from an unknown pig-sty farm in Lancaster. The doctor was welcome anywhere, he was learned and courtly; Kelly, earless, physically repulsive, and ill-bred, met only suspicion and slights. For Edward Kelly the taking of Dee's wife would be a final triumph and the ultimate humiliation of his superior.

Dee became frantic when he heard the pronouncement from the crystal. The skryer, seeing the doctor's real agitation, played a sly game, professing horror at the dreadful command for immorality. Surely, he said, fiends and imps had invaded the glass. Surely he was in contact with hellhounds out to insure his damnation! Claiming he dared not continue in such abominable company, Kelly renounced his post as skryer and left the castle. No pleading by Dee could change his mind, no reminders of the old oath of fidelity unto death could move him.

The doctor, cut off from his world of dearly familiar spirits, fell into despondency. An attempt to make a skryer of his son, Arthur, failed, and Dee's subsequent anguish reminds one of an addict suddenly deprived of his drug supply. He was physically ill and utterly disconsolate. Then, in answer to the doctor's fervent prayers, Kelly returned! He received the Prodigal's welcome, and Dee was quite unaware that he had been deliberately given a lesson, a demonstration of the skryer's power to give happiness or withhold it.

Kelly gazed into the crystal, then repeated the divine order about wife-sharing. Although Dee yielded at once, the wives protested, and we can imagine the scenes enacted in the halls of Trebona Castle. At last the men prevailed, and all agreed to sign a strange four-way contract which the doctor, with startling honesty and naïveté, recorded in his diary. "I, John Dee, Edward Kelly, and our two wives covenanted with God . . . [for] all things between us to be common as God by sundry means willed us to do." Thus Kelly achieved his sexual object, but his triumph must have been marred by the fact that Dee did not realize the extent of his own humiliation. The doctor had bowed to necessity and had accepted a divine order. If he had pangs about who was sleeping with whom, he did not reveal them but returned blissfully to his occult work. Predictably, the wives were not so easily reconciled. Their jealousy erupted into violence; there were screams, slaps, and cloutings. Edward Kelly's beating both women failed to tame their tempers.

Gradually Dee realized that he was near the end of his days and there was little prospect for peace or comfort in Trebona Castle. Harried by his wife, ridiculed by his son, and suffering from the clamminess of his lodgings, he steeled himself to part with Kelly forever. Sick at heart, he set out for England with his family and servants.

Queen Elizabeth received him with a noticeable lack of enthusiasm for his experiments. The fortune he had garnered at Trebona was quickly dissipated on other hopeless endeavors and he was bilked by two swindling skryers, men who not only robbed him but could not even give him spiritual satisfaction. The doctor, despite all he had endured, often longed for Edward Kelly. Indigent, he won the petty position of Chancellor of St. Paul's Cathedral and later became warden of Manchester College until failing health forced his retirement to Mortlake, where he ended his days as a penurious fortuneteller.

If toward the last Dee's faith in the crystal ever faltered, he did not admit it. Yet he must have known that he was a failure, must have suspected that he had wasted his life pursuing a chimera. And, in this, Dee's case illustrates a human factor that endangers complete objectivity in psychical research. What man after years of study and investigation cares to admit that he is a specialist who knows everything about something nonexistent?

John Dee's last public act was a pathetic petition he submitted to James I on June 5, 1604, begging his sovereign's protection against dangerous slander circulated about him. Dee, who seems again in fear of the gibbet, denies he is a wizard or "an invocator of devils." Nor did he brew up storms, cause plagues, or engender demon-possession of children and livestock.

Death must have come as a relief in 1608. Few remembered that he was the author of scientific and historical works, a skilled translator, and one of the finest mathematicians of his times.

Dee, as we have said, serves as a consummate example of an affliction that could be called a compulsion to believe. This craving can distort and at last vanquish the judgment of even the most intelligent men. The obsession is nothing like ordinary credulity or gullibility; it is both a craving and a mental blind spot. One thinks of John Dee when one reads the saddening books privately printed by widows, unintentional revelations of how a bereft woman has been defrauded by tricksters. Skeptics have charged that such men as Sir William Crookes, Sir Oliver Lodge, and the late Bishop James Pike all suffered from the same compulsion that destroyed Dr. Dee. There may be some truth in this accusation, but Lodge, at least, was well aware of the danger and took precautions against it.

Dee's life was far more dramatic than the lives of countless men who appear in the history of the search into the unknown, yet it is typical of many of the most unfortunate. He was not the first man to lose everything in the quest for the occult grail, and his successors are still with us today, as they will be tomorrow.

Edward Kelly met the just deserts which always await the villain in a Gothic melodrama. If his life copied fiction, so did his death. After Dee left him, he unwisely returned to Prague, a blunder that could be made only by a monumental egotist. The first day he tried to peddle the elixir of life from Glastonbury, he was seized and imprisoned. Eventually regaining freedom, he attempted his usual swindles in Central Europe, but with little luck.

When he tried to ply his trade in Germany, the authorities jailed him on charges of heresy and sorcery. Life imprisonment was the best he could hope for, and Kelly made a bold bid to escape by scaling the slippery wall of the dungeon into which he had been cast. Within inches of success, he lost his hold and crashed to the stones below, where his bones were shattered. Thus, in February 1593, he "died in his sins, an unregenerate heretic and an Enemy of God."

Eusapia Palladino of Naples, Amazon of the occult. *(Brown Brothers)*

The hands of Eusapia. *(Brown Brothers)*

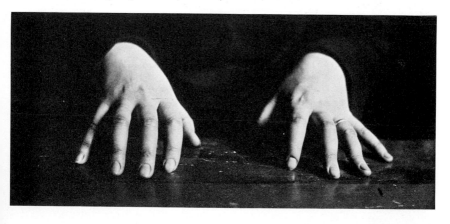

Katie King, "a gentle ghost who provided much consolation to the bereaved," at a nineteenth-century Philadelphia séance. *(Culver Pictures, Inc.)*

Mrs. Leonora Piper of Boston. Her case offers the most convincing evidence for ESP ever presented.

(Brown Brothers)

Fox cottage, the shrine of modern spiritualism, where Katie Fox first called to Mr. Splitfoot. *(Culver Pictures, Inc.)*

Arthur Ford, the world's best-known medium today. (*Pictorial Parade, Inc.*)

Daniel Dunglas Home. The Flying Scotsman was said to have floated through a window 7 feet from the ground. (*Culver Pictures, Inc.*)

A "light circle" at the Eddy homestead near Chittenden, Vermont, called "Spirit Capital of the Universe" in the late nineteenth century. (*Culver Pictures, Inc.*)

William Henry Eddy: in ordinary dress *(right)*, entranced *(below)*. *(Culver Pictures, Inc.)*

The ouija craze. MRS. BILTER *(to Aunt Jane, who is visiting her)*: "Shall we go to the movies, play cards or pass the evening with our deceased relatives?"

(Culver Pictures, Inc.)

John Dee (1527–1593), Elizabethan man and master of the necromantic arts. *(Brown Brothers)*

D.ʳ DEE *avoucheth his* Stone *is brought by Angelicall Ministry.*

Edgar Cayce, the best-publicized prophet of the twentieth century. *(Culver Pictures, Inc.)*

Peter Hurkos, occult consultant in the Boston Strangler case. *(Black Star)*

VII

A Host of Prophets

On March 1, 1881, a bomb exploded in St. Petersburg, and its impact was felt not only in Russia but throughout the world. The explosion was the work of a nihilist revolutionary, and it brought an abrupt end to the life of Czar Alexander II, a liberal reformer whose policies, had he lived, might have forestalled the Russian Revolution, or at least have tempered its character.

Alexander's death was especially shocking because previously he had enjoyed a charmed existence. Seven times assassins had tried to destroy him, but the lucky czar escaped death. A cat supposedly has nine lives, and it turned out that Alexander was blessed with only two fewer.

At the time of the murder thousands of believers in

the occult savored the satisfaction of saying, "We told you so." Years before, a clairvoyant had predicted in no uncertain terms that Alexander would survive seven attempts on his life but would fall victim to the eighth. The prophecy was common knowledge.

To come up with the exact number of attempts and to foretell the fatal one is a remarkable feat of fortunetelling—or an astounding coincidence. The faithful will declare that it is yet another convincing proof of second sight; skeptics will emphatically condemn such a view as preposterous and superstitious. In the matter of fortunetelling we discover a curious contradiction: it is by far the most popular and widespread of all occult practices, yet it remains the most thoroughly denounced, and is in most ways the hardest to accept. Even people who avoid walking under ladders and exercise the greatest care in handling mirrors will usually deny that the future can be foretold. . . . And then they will enjoy having their tea leaves read, although, of course, they don't *really* believe it.

Mediumship may have a greater immediate impact on spectators, but the gift of foretelling the future has always been the most sought after of all supernormal abilities. If it can be done, it offers the solution to everything. Even a tiny peephole into tomorrow is better than a tunnel into Fort Knox. The seer who can predict Tuesday's race-track and stock-exchange results on Monday will not long have to earn his bread by fortunetelling. (There has never been such a prophet. The common explanation is that the "gift" will not work for the prophet's own advantage, or that it is beneath him to pervert his sacred talent for personal gain. But many businessmen consult seers. J. P. Morgan received astrological readings from Evangeline Adams. Not a man to give away the secrets of success, he made no public comment about the advice she gave him. We do not know if he followed it. Miss Adams, the great popularizer of modern astrology in the United States, practiced in New York from 1899 until 1932. She gave forecasts for Enrico Caruso, Mary Pickford, England's King

Edward VII, and many prominent businessmen who wanted to know how stars affected stocks.)

On a nobler scale than money, correct forecasts could save nations from disaster, protect leaders from assassination, and avert all sorts of tragedies.

Or could the tragedies really be averted? Prophecy instantly opens a Pandora's Box of problems too complex and Hegelian to explore here. If the future is determined—as it must be if it can be foreseen—can we change it if we have advance warning? Does prophecy negate free will? If a soothsayer tells you that you will break your leg tomorrow, can you avoid injury by staying in bed all day? Or is it foreordained that the bed will collapse and cause the fracture despite your caution? In that case, the only value of the prophecy is that it might prompt you to check your insurance policy. But would that help? The state of one's insurance must be a predetermined matter, too.

This sort of speculation is endless, and we will make no attempt to solve the metaphysical riddle of whether the future is plastic or already set. However, the difficulty is major and remains a bar to believing in second sight. Most Western minds rebel at the idea of absolute predestination.

Many modern fortunetellers, like Hollywood's Carroll Righter, avoid the problem by predicting "tendencies," "threats," and "favorable signs." The notion is summed up in the line, "Man creates his own destiny. The stars influence, but do not control." This is the safe way to prophesy, since the seer can never be caught later in an outright error. The ancient Greek oracles learned the danger of being too specific and consequently became so vague that the word "Delphic" now means ambiguous. Such cloudiness satisfies only true believers, and if prophecy forecasts only tendencies and not events, then we must rule out the most striking predictions made in the past, for they were exact; a future situation was perfectly described well ahead of time.

We will dodge discussing the nature of the future and whether prophecies show trends or facts with the classic and not quite pertinent reply of many soothsayers: Some forecasts show probabilities, unknown forces at work. Others reveal unchangeable happenings, things absolutely unalterable. As the Washington seer Jeane Dixon says, "My visions are never wrong." Her visions come from God and show certainties. Other premonitions this famous lady receives are not visions, so they reveal only great likelihood. If a potential victim is warned in advance and takes precautions, the coming pitfall can be avoided.

Those who profess to foretell coming events can be divided into two classes: seers who have a psychic gift called *precognition;* and practitioners of certain sciences or arts called *divination.*

There is a certain overlap between the types in practice, but the basic difference is readily apparent. *Precognition* is a paranormal mental faculty, an innate talent that is purely psychic. It is often called second sight or clairvoyance, but clairvoyance is an awkward term because it becomes confused with ESP, and though all precognition is derived from ESP, most ESP is not precognition. Precognition is not "mind-reading." It is foretelling the future by psychic means. *Divination,* on the other hand, is any technique of predicting events to come by studying omens, signs, and auguries. Since all forms of divination are supposedly sciences or arts, anyone should be able to acquire the skill—at least to some degree.

Predictive astrology, now the most popular method of divining, offers a good example. Its followers call it a science, and admittedly it deals with a body of traditional knowledge. There are techniques and rules. In theory if several different astrologers are given a single set of facts—a birthdate, time, and location— they should independently arrive at the same or similar forecasts. In practice, alas, this is not always the case.

Near the end of 1969 one client obtained forecasts from three different professional astrologers, two by mail and one after a personal consultation. Astrologer X advised extreme caution and conservatism in business affairs during the year 1970. Astrologer Y, who was quite vague, failed to note that there were "malefic influences" at work. Astrologer Z produced a contradictory interpretation which urged the bewildered client to "seize all opportunities and expand activities in all fields of endeavor during the next year. . . ."

(Happily for the millions of believers in astrology, we can report the more favorable findings of Vernon Clark, formerly a clinical psychologist for the United States Veterans' Administration. Clark's tests, detailed by Allen Spraggett in his book *The Unexplained*, pitted a control group of laymen against twenty astrologers who were, among other tasks, to link the birth charts of ten individuals to the various occupations these persons pursued. The astrologers made a significantly higher score than the laymen. Clark concluded that although the results were not spectacular, they definitely favored astrology.)

The case of the conflicting interpretations of horoscopes—and such disagreements are common and notorious—is mentioned here to show that predictive astrology, like all techniques of divining, is highly dependent upon the skill or talent of the interpreter. It has been suggested that some outstandingly successful astrologers, such as Evangeline Adams, who scored hit after hit and even forecast her own death in 1932, have been aided by a talent for precognition. This view makes parapsychological sense, but raises howls from two sides. Skeptics point out that it involves acceptance of not just one but *two* occult beliefs, making it doubly damned; astrologers object that it demotes their science to an art form at best, a "gift" at worst.

Those who suspect that the psychic qualities of an astrologer can improve his forecasts would do well to avoid the "computerized" horoscopes now flooding the land. A computer can, of course, be programmed to turn out astrological readings. Time Pattern Research Institute, Inc., of Valley Stream, New York, offers ten-thousand-word horoscopes ground out by a computer at the rate of one every two minutes. Such readings recently cost fifteen dollars, but the price is expected to spiral, and there are rumors that other companies are hitching their computers to the stars. Presumably such machines have no psychic talent, and so it might be safer to rely on one's friendly neighborhood astrologer, who may have an extra gift of precognition.

Despite the discrepancy between theory and practice, supposedly all the divining arts can be learned. Anyone with enough diligence, interest, and a basic textbook can cast his own horoscope. But Santha Rama Rau, a well-known writer on Eastern subjects and the dramatizer of *A Passage to India*, gives a word of warning: "As my astrologer said, there are no secrets. It's easy. But for greater detail, or even month-to-month information, take my advice, go to a professional astrologer. It's quicker." This astrologer is not hard to find. At present there are an estimated twelve thousand professionals in the United States.

Since divination is not a psychic or spirit matter, we will not delve into it here. However, all forms of the occult are so in vogue that the reader should at least be armed for cocktail conversation and ought to know that although astrology and *palmistry (cheiromancy)* are the most common methods of divining, there are many others, and so we will glance briefly at the field.

Card reading rivals palm reading in number of practitioners and adherents. Any type of card may be used and there are innumerable methods, but the Tarot pack, with its romantic wands, scepters, cups, and swords, is traditional and has the most interesting possibilities. Usually the Tarot pack is shuffled and cut, and then the client makes a wish, asks a question, or both. The cards are dealt in any pattern selected by the diviner—perhaps the cross, the star, the pentagon, or another time-honored layout. Each card has a meaning, but the meanings may be altered by their positions in the pattern. How much influence does the Drowned Man have if he is two cards removed from the ace of swords? In answering such a question the diviner must use judgment, and at this point the Tarot pack becomes a springboard for precognition, ceases to be a science, and becomes an occult art.

Legend says that the Tarot cards were first used by gypsies. Certainly the pack is Oriental in origin and it was once rare, expensive, and overlaid with mystery. Now the cards can be obtained, complete with instructions, at novelty counters and through the mail.

Dream interpretation, the famed specialty of Joseph in Egypt, remains popular, and new "dream books" are published every year. All objects that appear in a dream are considered to have meaning for the future. But there is a code which must be deciphered. For example, to dream of cauliflower means that your friends will neglect you or, worse, you will become impoverished and no one will come to your aid. There is disagreement among authorities about what certain objects signify, but most editors go along with Shakespeare in saying that rosemary is for remembrance and pansies are for thoughts. One of the best-selling books of all time was *Mother Bridget's Dream Book and Oracle of Fate.* Issued annually, it held sway in both England and the United States from 1800 until after 1850. This invaluable work not only made plain the dream code, but predicted the results of certain occurrences if they occurred on certain days.

Dream interpretation should not be confused with the psychic dream which thousands upon thousands of people claim to have experienced in all generations. Such dreams are visions arriving during sleep, and there is seldom any need for interpretation—they give clear impressions and prophecies. Usually they do not come true, but a dream which scores a direct hit is never forgotten by the dreamer. There are countless recorded cases.

Haruspication is the somewhat messy technique of divining by the examination of the entrails of animals, birds, and reptiles. In the squeamish twentieth century haruspication has few followers in advanced societies. But it was the basis of the Roman system of divining, and it ranked with astrology in ancient Babylon.

The Babylonians could take instant readings by dropping a sheep's liver into a specially molded vessel whose holes and marked-off squares guided the priest in knowing where to look for spots and inflammations on the sheep's liver, marks indicating future events. Roman divination, vastly complex, involved not only haruspication but the observation of wild birds and the behavior of domestic fowl. Many Roman writers list the ominous signs that preceded particular calamities, and Suetonius is especially detailed. Entrail examining also developed into a complicated and gory art of divination among the ancient Mexicans. Haruspication seems a doubtful science, and the only defense for it is the one that Dr. C. G. Jung advanced for astrology, an argument that says, in effect, that since all things in the universe are interrelated, all are parts of a whole; therefore . . .

Crystal-gazing is a form of divination only insofar as the practitioner is obtaining information from the glass itself. Used as a trance-inducing object, the result is precognition. The same applies to *shell-hearing*.

Necromancy, calling up the dead to announce future events, is not really divination because it is not entirely do-it-yourself but depends upon contacting a cooperative ghost. The Babylonians were specialists in this art. Necromancy is highly repulsive because it usually involved forcing a corpse, not a spirit, to speak. For nearly a thousand years in almost every country a discovered necromancer was fortunate to be hanged—burning at the stake was considered fitter punishment. Several famous names, perhaps exaggeratedly, are associated with necromancy, among them Roger Bacon, Albertus Magnus, and Arnaud de Villeneuve. The ghoulish Edward Kelly is the villain of the best-known case.

Arithmancy, widely believed in by the ancient Greeks, involves the use of numbers and evaluating letters to predict events. It forms part of Cabalistic studies, and survives today, influencing the eternally popular *numerology.* Books and individual readings are readily obtainable by mail at bargain rates. Numerologists work more cheaply than either astrologers or palm readers.

Axinomancy is divining by ax heads. Not surprisingly it was popular among the ancient Teutons, a people who, like the Highland Scots, were believed to have second sight. Axinomancy has been practiced in various forms through the ages, and authorities disagree about which rites are orthodox and which are heretical. We know from Psalm 74 that the ancient Hebrews divined with axes, but no details are given. Centuries later, northern Europeans danced around an ax whose head was half buried in the ground. When it fell, jarred loose by the dancing, the handle supposedly pointed toward escaped or unknown thieves. Another ritual, quite complicated, employed a red-hot ax and a round agate to find hidden treasure.

Rhadomancy bases its forecasts on the falling of rods, wands, or branches and should not be confused with *rhapsodomancy*, which is opening a book, preferably poetry, at random and gleaning a prophetic message from the first line the eye, or finger, falls upon. A very common version of rhapsodomancy involves opening the Bible and, with eyes closed, dropping a finger on a verse which will then give guidance. This form doubtless has its own special name (scripturomancy?) which diligent research has failed to discover.

Belomancy is divining by arrows. The Koran forbids it.

Capnomancy is forecasting by the behavior of smoke, and in its developed form is an intricate science not recommended for the casual or Sunday diviner.

There are countless other methods, including the ever-present tea leaves and casting I Ching. I Ching, the Book of Changes, is currently popular and a warning should be sounded: the symbolism of I Ching is far beyond the understanding of the untutored Western layman. Even in the Orient, where its traditions are familiar, commentaries are written on I Ching commentaries. I Ching is the basis of much Vietnamese thought, a fact which explains some of the difficulty of communication Americans have encountered in Saigon.

We have glanced at a fraction of the techniques. If anyone

doubts how far these things go, let him consider the science of *omphalomancy*, which tells all by reading the human navel. In its purest form it involved predicting an infant's future by examining the knots in the umbilical cord. Apparently this science, in the hands of careless practitioners, has been debased to mere navel-reading at various times. Omphalomancy was common enough before 1850 to attract the notice of Charles Mackay, author of *Extraordinary Popular Delusions and the Madness of Crowds*. The study appears to have no organized followers at the moment, but no one—except perhaps omphalomancers—can be sure what tomorrow will bring. The science has certain corroborative evidence from the experience of early mesmerists, who often could not get through to a hypnotized subject when addressing questions to his ears but had no difficulty when they spoke to his navel. This phenomenon, of which there is ample record, is called seeing with the stomach. (Omphalomancy is not to be confused with omphaloskepsis, which is meditative gazing at the navel.)

We stress again that the foregoing list, which has doubtless exhausted the reader, has by no means exhausted the subject.

All the above-mentioned techniques are supposed to work regardless of who practices them (assuming adequate training), but the fact that their use is often accompanied by apparent ESP was not lost upon Sigmund Freud. The founder of psychoanalysis wrote three separate papers about paranormal matters during the years 1919–1921. His approach is that of a scientific materialist, and he felt wary of dealing with subjects he considered "occult." (He uses that word in a broad sense, seeming to give it the same wide-encompassing definition that is applied in this book.) Freud's writing, as always, is lucid and provocative, far less mystical than many of Jung's statements on similar subjects. We need not here go into the matter of how occult belief fits psychoanalytical framework. The pertinent point is how Freud became interested in material which he confessed inspired "reluctance" in him.

He observed that many of his patients had consulted fortune-tellers, diviners who used various techniques. Freud had not the least interest or faith in the truth or falsity of the predictions but was fascinated to discover that in many cases the fortune-teller told the client exactly what he wanted to hear, although there was no apparent way the client's secret desire could have become known. Professional diviners are inclined to give their clients "good news," such as the classic: "You will meet a beautiful stranger, go on a long journey, and the money-card is close to you." But what about unusual wishes? How can their fulfillment be promised if the diviner does not know they exist?

A young man undergoing psychoanalysis harbored a death wish against his sister's husband. An astrologer, given no clue to this, cast a horoscope completely to the client's satisfaction: the brother-in-law would die soon. In another case a palm reader foresaw children in the near future of a woman whose husband was sterile. A wrong prediction, it turned out, but an absolutely correct assessment of the woman's deep longing, although no information had been given. Freud, after investigating, suspected the working of ESP. Powerful wishes had communicated themselves to the mind of the forecaster.

Freud's feelings are shared by "Dr. Charles," a psychiatrist of Chicago, who in 1969 expressed in a letter to the author interesting conclusions based on twenty-three years of work with disturbed patients, many of whom had frequently visited different types of "readers." He wrote: "Very often a professional fortune teller seems to sense the wishes of the client and can answer nagging questions before they are even asked. Sometimes there are obvious clues given by the clients' attitudes and reactions, but this is not true in all cases. Three of my patients who had such experiences were very skillful at concealing their needs and anxieties. They felt they had given nothing away, and I am inclined to believe them." (Dr. Charles's name is masked because, like many scientists and professional men, he does not care to express his views on thought transference "at this time." The stigma remains—a feeling that he who touches the occult, however gingerly, touches pitch and will be defiled.)

Thus we see that although divination and precognition are on the surface separate things, they may be highly related. The card-reader who correctly says, "You prefer home life to travel," may be relying not on science or art but on unconscious ESP.

The Seer of Washington

Jeane Dixon, a Washington, D.C., real estate dealer and psychic forecaster, was well known even before Ruth Montgomery's book about her, *A Gift of Prophecy*, hit the best-seller lists and stayed there a profitably long time. When she speaks of the future, newspapers take notice. For a reader, Dixon-watching is an exciting game and one he cannot lose. If Mrs. Dixon is right, he has found a new marvel; if she is wrong, he can feel smug at her failure.

She is the most famous Washington prophet, but not at all the first. Traditionally, the capital city has been a gathering place for psychic readers and all types of diviners. Most of them, unlike Mrs. Dixon, have been professionals and, again unlike Mrs. Dixon, much of their fame has been underground. No senator would care to have the voters back home learn that he accepts advice from a card-reader or palmist.

A medium whose professional name was "Marcia" held sway in the District of Columbia for two decades or more between the First and Second World Wars, fading from prominence gradually. She was consulted by senators, representatives and, according to rumor, members of the Cabinet. Her actual political influence is debatable, but she certainly carried more weight than any twenty thousand voters. Many other psychics have had successful Washington careers, but the names of their more famous clients have always been well-guarded secrets.

Mrs. Dixon, outspoken and anything but underground, is an entirely different type. Since she is not earning money directly by private consultations and is herself rich, there is no onus attached to a Dixon "reading." A long list of celebrities have heard her predictions, the most famous being Franklin D. Roosevelt and the late Senator Everett M. Dirksen. Unfortunately, FDR was occupied with pressing World War II toward victory at the time, and he left no account of his reaction to the meeting.

On what, exactly, does Mrs. Dixon's reputation rest? Her friends and fans submit a catalogue of correct predictions, and some of the hits are impressive. They include forecasts of the assassination of John F. Kennedy, his brother Ted Kennedy's injury in an aviation accident; the Alaska earthquake of 1964; Russia's initiating the Space Age with Sputnik I; a series of correct Presidential election results; the death of Dag Hammarskjold; the election and subsequent death of Pope John. And there are many more. A far longer list can be found in Ruth Montgomery's book, and a current list will appear in whatever newspaper or magazine publishes an article about Mrs. Dixon in the next few months. (We have no hesitation in prophesying that such an article *will* appear.)

It is unpleasant to be a Devil's Advocate in the case of such a sincere person as Mrs. Dixon, but it must be faced that the extent of her "gift" is less well established than many people have supposed. The prophecies tumble out at odd moments, they are multitudinous, and future recalling relies all too often on the memories of a few close friends and associates. So far as we can determine, her Alaska earthquake warning was sounded to only one witness, a friend. The foretelling of John F. Kennedy's death was impressive, and there is no doubt that she said, "The President's going to be shot!" only a week before the event. But did she say it would happen on November 22? Again one witness—

and the same one as for the Alaska quake. Did she really announce in advance that the assassin's name would begin with the letters "o" and "s"? Again, one witness—but at least a different one. The only part of the prediction that can be substantiated by the strict standards applied to other psychics is the fact of the shooting, undated. Even this becomes less miraculous when we consider that countless people are frequently announcing the future death of well-known figures. When they are wrong their words are forgotten; when they are correct, their second sight is hailed.

We do not charge that people surrounding Mrs. Dixon are prone to fraud or exaggeration or the convenient forgetting of her mistakes, but the standards of good psychical research require more evidence. Critical readers of the Montgomery book will notice how limited and close the circle of observers is. The testimony supporting the mediumship of D. D. Home and Eusapia Palladino is much more extensive than the proof of many Dixon precognitions, yet modern parapsychologists look askance at both earlier figures. One hopes that in the future Jeane Dixon's utterances will be recorded more exactly.

Another unfortunate fact is that the predictions she publishes herself tend to be much less successful than those recalled by friends and employees. Five Dixon forecasts were published in early 1965 and all five were wrong. (It is especially regrettable that she was mistaken when she announced that the war in Vietnam would be over by the end of the year. We may console ourselves, however, that the West Coast of the United States escaped a vast natural disaster which Mrs. Dixon predicted.)

On the other hand there is no denying her uncanny foreknowledge (or amazing luck) when she announced to the press in 1956 that the next United States President would be "a Democrat, but he will be assassinated or die in office, although not necessarily in his first term." At the time, Eisenhower had just won landslide re-election, the fortunes of the Democrats were at a low ebb, and the odds against death in office were, historically, four and a half to one. (The "odds" are difficult to determine, and depend on whether one begins with George Washington or not. Twentieth-century chances of a Presidential death are greater, especially if two terms are involved. The mathematical odds that any next president will be a Democrat are exactly fifty-fifty.)

What are the probabilities of lucky guesses? No one knows for sure, but guessing the future seems to be enormously difficult. A small-scale experiment begun at the end of 1968 had interesting results. Three people who were not believers in precognition and who felt they had never had a genuine psychic experience were asked to make ten predictions for the year 1969 and to answer ten specific questions about the future. Some vagueness was permissible, but complete generalizations and the forecasting of obviously probable events were barred. Of the thirty resulting "prophecies" twenty-eight failed to come true. One correct hit, the death of a former United States President, should perhaps have been ruled out in advance, because Dwight D. Eisenhower's health was known to be precarious, Harry S. Truman was advanced in years, and Lyndon B. Johnson was known to have suffered a heart attack. The thirtieth prediction, although rather indefinite, was a near-hit. "A great tragedy such as an earthquake or avalanche in a mountainous region of Europe" did not take place in 1969, but calamitous Alpine snowslides occurred early in 1970. On the direct questions the guessers had an equally dismal score, although two of them outdid Mrs. Dixon by saying that the war in Vietnam would not end that year.

The Washington seer divides her prophecies into two classes: those derived from paranormal ESP, and those that are "visions" and come from God. The ESP forecasts come as strong premonitions, some people would describe them as sudden hunches. Coming events which announce themselves in this manner can be averted or mitigated by human action—free will remains, and forewarned is forearmed.

The visions, usually involving far more serious matters, depict unchangeable fate. A vision, being godly, is always true, says Mrs. Dixon. But she readily admits the possibility of her own human error in interpreting the symbols she sees. For example, when driving past the White House shortly before President Kennedy's assassination, she envisioned the building as "draped in black crepe." Naturally this meant death, but it could have meant that fate would strike down Mrs. Kennedy or one of the Kennedy children. In this case Mrs. Dixon had no doubt, because she received corroborative visions indicating that Kennedy himself was the victim, but at other times the symbols are not so clear. Pinpointing the date of a future happening is not always simple, because Mrs. Dixon's visions are not like being able to read next week's newspaper at leisure.

Thus there are two ways of accounting for a Dixon mistake: human action averting an ESP-predicted occurrence, and incorrect interpretation of a vision.

Although we have put a good deal of emphasis on Jeane Dixon's failures, it must be said that a prophet should be judged more on hits than on errors. While Mrs. Dixon's public prophecies are not consistently reliable enough for anyone to gamble his savings on them, she has chalked up a number of solid scores. Since it is difficult for the average person to make one good guess out of a hundred when it involves such unforeseeable events as natural disasters and assassinations, the lady is remarkable in one way or another.

Taking an over-all view of her record, three facts are plain. First, in print she is far more likely to be wrong than right, but the occasional hits are impressive. Second, if we accept the testimony of her friends, employees, and close associates at face value, Mrs. Dixon is astonishing. Third, the case has received woefully inadequate attention from impartial investigators and too much attention from sensation-seekers.

Edgar Cayce

Sigmund Freud approached the occult with "reluctance and ambivalence," and in that same spirit we take up the matter of Edgar Cayce, the best-publicized prophet of the twentieth century. Here one ventures into a murky landscape, mined with emotion, beclouded by faith, and on every side there are tangles of testimony both spoken and written that cannot be unknotted because they lie beyond reach.

On the off-chance that there is somewhere a reader completely unfamiliar with Cayce's career, we will give a brief summary. The healer and prophet was born in Christian County, Kentucky, in 1877. There was some tradition of occult practice in the family: his grandfather was a water dowser and is alleged to have had psychokinetic power over a broom—he could make it dance; Cayce's father had a peculiar attraction for snakes, causing them to follow him about. As a boy, Cayce showed certain signs of paranormal talent. Later on he worked as a book salesman, although he had dropped out of grammar school in childhood. Then, for a time, he supported himself as a photographer. Meanwhile, his ability to diagnose illness came to light when he himself was undergoing hypnotic therapy. On October 9, 1910, the *New York Times* ran a Sunday feature on Cayce headlined, "Illiterate Man Becomes a Doctor When Hypnotized—Strange Power Shown by Edgar Cayce Puzzles Physicians." (Although Cayce never mastered spelling very thoroughly, he was far from illiterate.)

As a psychic healer he achieved modest success which increased over the years. Eventually the Cayce Hospital and the Association for Research and Enlightenment (known as A.R.E.) were established at Virginia Beach, Virginia, where he practiced and gave readings via the mails for many years. He died on January 3, 1945.

The diagnoses, cures, and prophecies were all uttered while

Cayce lay in a hypnotic trance. Questions would be asked him, and a secretary would take down his replies. Throughout the later years all Cayce's trance statements were recorded in triplicate, and they are now treasured in a fireproof vault of the A.R.E., an organization that still persists a quarter of a century after its leader's death. A.R.E. sells copies of a small black book containing Cayce's medical advice (twenty-five dollars) and sponsors such activities as a course in presenting reincarnation to children. Hugh Lynn Cayce, a son of the prophet, has worked energetically to keep his father's work alive and in the public eye.

Psychic healing, Edgar Cayce's strong point, is beyond the scope of our inquiry. We quote Nora Ephron's perfect description of it, written for the *New York Times*, because it also applies in part to Cayce's prophecies: "A strange combination of medicine, folk medicine, and osteopathy, delivered in a convoluted, almost incomprehensible style of speech." It should be added that it seemed to work well for a great many people.

Our concern, Cayce's gift for precognition, is a different story. Although his earliest and best biographer, Thomas Sugrue, mentions prophecies, the emphasis of the work is on Cayce as a psychic healer. The Seer of Virginia Beach was not considered primarily a prognosticator until the book *Edgar Cayce—The Sleeping Prophet* by Jess Stearn had a spectacular sale of a hundred and twenty-three thousand hardcover copies in 1967, and then enjoyed reprint after reprint in cheaper editions. Perhaps some of its great success was due to the catchy title, which, according to the author, was suggested by Cayce's ghost to a New York medium with the unlikely name Bathsheba Askowith.

We are not sure how many books have been written about Edgar Cayce—the number increases annually. But, having forged through five of them and scanned the collected cures as well, we conclude that author Stearn would have done better, except financially, if he had let a sleeping prophet lie. Although physicians may dismiss Cayce's psychic healing, it is supported by extensive testimony. His ESP, less well substantiated, remains interesting and worth further investigation. But in the field of precognition Cayce's record is a catastrophe, and one stands in awe of Stearn's achievement: seldom has a man been able to make so much out of so little. To verify the rambling, vaguely stated forecasts is to make bricks without straw and the results are the same—the prophecies hold up when glanced at, crumble when touched.

A few examples reveal Cayce's ability and Stearn's technique. One prophecy forecasts drastic physical alterations in the earth during an era extending from 1958 until 1998: "The early portion will see a change in the physical aspect of the west coast of America." Stearn points out that Alaska became a state in 1959 and in 1964 a major earthquake altered the Alaskan topography. But Cayce thought of cataclysms on a panoramic scale—for instance, the total demolition of San Francisco, Los Angeles, and New York, a city rather far from the West Coast. It can be objected that the quake, for all its force, did not make very drastic alterations on the Pacific Coast of the United States. Pre-1964 maps remain quite accurate. Stearn, anticipating this argument, meets it head on by announcing that the quake's impact was "even greater perhaps than Cayce had considered." Nonsense. Besides, if this is the extent of the change Cayce had in mind, then his prophecy was pointless. All coasts, especially those rimmed by young mountain ranges, undergo constant alteration. Even the British Isles, untroubled by volcanos and earthquakes, have shifting seaboards, and an English engineer writes, "The configuration of the coastline of Great Britain is not the same for two consecutive days." British maps and surveys show a number of towns "washed away" or "lost to the sea." If the Alaska quake was the fulfillment of a Cayce prediction, one concludes that the prophecy was banal. We do not need seers to tell us what is already obvious.

Cayce was lauded for predicting the stock market crash of 1929 and the subsequent Depression. What he actually said was, "Better than (*sic*) a few points were missed here and there, even in a spectacular rise or fall than to be worrying where the end would be. Forget not the warning here." Like the prophecies of Nostradamus and the Apocalypse, this is open to a dozen inter-pretations—prediction at its most Delphic. Other Depression forecasts are equally nebulous and become clear only when read after the fact and with the eye of faith. But the eye of faith, like the eye that hunts the sensational, discerns what others do not.

Stearn hails Cayce for spotting the year 1936 as the "critical turn away from peace," and lists events to confirm the pro-nouncement. Had Cayce chosen 1933, the prediction would have been verified by Hitler's achieving mastery of the Reich; 1937 could be established by the Hossbach Papers, Hitler's actual plan of conquest; 1938 by the march into Austria—and so on. Cayce, according to Stearn, was the absolutely accurate prophet of both world wars. But then Stearn opens his second chapter with the startling information that "Edgar Cayce was as stunned as any-body else when the bombs dropped on Pearl Harbor." This is all neatly rationalized, of course, yet the glaring fact remains that Cayce's purported meanings are much clearer after an event than before it.

One of Cayce's real howlers is the prophecy made in 1943 that in the next twenty-five years China would move toward Chris-tianity. And democracy. The Seer was quite emphatic about this, and since the time limit has expired one would think that such a major gaff might well be an embarrassment to Mr. Stearn, a man who says that Cayce's batting average was "close to one hundred percent." But not at all. Stearn starts with the slight understatement that "this would hardly seem likely," and then dodges artfully by letting an anonymous group of Cayce stu-dents and devotees point out that in one sense China is more democratic than before (although this is not at all what Cayce had in mind), that Formosa has enjoyed a new birth of freedom, and there exists a Christian underground on the mainland. But no amount of squirming will get the Seer off the hook, and when Stearn tries to distract attention by pointing out two modifying phrases in the forecast, he makes matters worse, for one of the modifiers says that the rise of Christianity and democracy "will be more in the last five years than in the first ten." It is all very unfortunate—and very typical.

It would be a tedious waste of time to go through more of the prophecies and their purported fulfillment. Edgar Cayce, unlike most seers, delivered messages almost daily. There are so many predictions and most of them are of such a general nature that one can be found—or stretched—to fit almost any event.

Cayce traveled backward in time as well as forward, and one of his favorite topics was the fabled "lost continent of Atlantis." Since Atlantis is perennially popular, much has been made of Cayce's discourses on it and an entire book devoted to the subject was produced by one of his sons and edited by the other. Cayce "discovered" that a great continent had once stood above the waters of the Atlantic. It was as large as Europe plus "Asia in Europe," and before its destruction and inundation, which happened about 10,000 B.C., the technologists of this marvelous land had developed television, death rays, atomic energy, and laser beams. These were only a few of their achievements.

The Cayce excursions to Atlantis are very much like Helene Smith's visits to Mars. And they are equally probable. Despite all attempts to bolster the Seer's position, his version of Atlantis is flatly contradicted by geology, history, and archaeology. Edgar Evans Cayce and Thomas Sugrue, in their respective books about the prophet, show at least a little caution. Mr. Stearn, of course, plays with all stops out, and brings forth a dazzling array of unrelated facts and the eye-catching distractions of modern volcanic eruptions. None of this elaborate case-making helps. All attempts to confirm the Seer's version of the lost continent are embarrassments, desperate flounderings in waters murkier than those which, in legend, swept over Atlantis.

Thomas Sugrue, in the preface to the first Cayce biography, states that Cayce was "an ideal subject for scientific study. But scientists shunned him. He and his friends regretted this; it might have been more evidential if they, not I, had made this report." Sugrue hit the nail on the head: it would have been much more "evidential." A difficulty in making any evaluation of Cayce springs from the fact that every study of the man has been produced by his worshipers or by sensation-mongers. The copious archives of the A.R.E. offer little help, since they were created and maintained by those highly interested in furthering the Cayce legend. Thomas Sugrue, obviously sincere, was telling a wondrous story—a gospel in effect—and he had no hesitation in putting down supposedly word for word conversations that had taken place half a century before he wrote, and of which there existed no record except the memories of Edgar Cayce and his wife. The result is a lively fictionalized biography, but dubious investigation. All accounts of Cayce's early life follow the facts in the same way that Irving Stone's biographical novels follow history. Long scenes are invented or inferred—a valid technique in a novel, an impossible method for factual biography.

At the beginning of Sugrue's account we encounter an old acquaintance, Professor Hugo Münsterberg of Harvard, who, it will be recalled, was a bane of Eusapia Palladino's career. (He planted an assistant under her séance table.) The words Sugrue puts into Münsterberg's mouth make him a caricature but are in keeping with what we know about the crusty professor—up to a point. However, when Münsterberg leaves the scene, after a cursory investigation of the young Cayce, we are given the impression that the Harvard savant, a specialist in exposing frauds, was baffled and even deeply impressed. Yet Sugrue gives no report from the professor himself, and the omission is serious. At that time the American Psychic Society was considering a study of Cayce, and since this study was never conducted we are led toward the suspicion that Münsterberg's opinion was negative. (The professor was a member of the Psychic Society, but we are never told whether his quick inspection of Cayce was in an official or private capacity.) Sugrue has Edgar Cayce remark wistfully to his wife, "We never heard a word from that professor. Not even a thank you note." And that sums up the whole problem of evaluating Cayce—one never hears a word from anybody except his disciples. The nearest thing to an investigation was a fiasco engineered by the Hearst newspapers in 1911. The prophet was gawked at in Chicago, interviewed, and invited to do psychic tricks. Cayce thought it a tawdry affair, and indeed it was.

Thus we have a major gap in the annals of parapsychology and psychical research. Undoubtedly the Virginia Beach seer was looked upon as just another quack faith-healer who prescribed such outlandish remedies as applying a dead rabbit to the body to cure cancer. (He did this once—"with the fur side *out*." Jess Stearn reports it without batting an eyelash.)

Apart from the healings, apart from the unfortunate excurisons forward and backward in time, there seems to be evidence of powerful ESP at work. It is possible that Cayce had talent of an unusual nature, for his entranced mind appeared to come up with information he could not have obtained in any conventional way: his subconscious searched the shelves of faraway drugstores and tracked down persons he had never heard of. We say "appeared" because the evidence is shrouded in fiction, faith, and exaggeration.

Cayce's public career, from 1910 through 1944, coincided with the ebb of psychical research in the United States. The men who gave it initial vigor, such as William James, had died or were elderly. Mediums, some sincere and some quacks, gained high office in the very organizations which should have been investigating them. Here and there researchers continued to work and made progress, but there was little money or trained manpower available. It would be comforting to think that science always advances, but in the matter of parapsychology this is true only in the sense that knowledge once gained is seldom lost. Had

Edgar Cayce lived twenty years earlier or later an examination of his psychic powers would have been almost inevitable. The study might be incomplete, but we would have at least some record of observations.

Despite the best efforts of certain individuals, the deplorable state of psychical affairs in the United States did not change much until well after World War II. By then, of course, it was too late for any first-hand examination of Cayce. The opportunity had gone and the omission can never be corrected.

Flashes of the Future

Even though men of all societies and all eras have had a certain belief in precognition, it remains a mysterious phenomenon, unexplored and hotly contested. Its firmest believers are at a loss to explain how it works. Yet precognition's unknown nature has not forestalled attempts to teach it. Harold Sherman, author of *How to Make ESP Work for You*, devotes a chapter to self-improvement in foretelling the future. Mostly he relates his own experiences, detailing how his paranormal mental ability allowed him to break the time barrier. The result, in one instance, was his obtaining permission from the estate of Mark Twain to dramatize the great writer's life. Sherman saw himself, in a sudden "precognitive flash," winning what he calls "one of the most coveted assignments in playwriting history." Suffering perhaps from a temporary malfunctioning of the ESP, he sold *Mark Twain* to producer Harry Moses, who died before the play could be brought to Broadway. However, Warner Brothers filmed the script as *The Adventures of Mark Twain*. Sherman attributes many other personal victories to his "extended faculties of mind." (An incidental benefit was his how-to-do-it ESP book, which went through at least eight printings.) Mr. Sherman's practical advice more or less boils down to having faith, keeping an open mind, and trusting one's hunches. It is all presented in a vigorous, optimistic manner. Mr. Sherman is the Dale Carnegie of the occult.

In history the most remarkable displays of apparent second sight seem not to have been the result of home-study courses. Precognition, except when a single experience is the only one in an individual's lifetime, appears to be a "gift," and nothing is so unpredictable as a talent for prediction. Usually the future is revealed in sudden flashes, glimpses, quick impressions very much like those Mrs. Dixon has described in detail.

The German medium known professionally as Madame de Ferriem had a sudden and horrifying premonition during a sitting in Berlin in 1896. She saw a mining disaster in brief but vivid detail and gave a full description. The vision became recurrent, more bits and pieces were added to the picture, and her forecast was published in 1899. Skeptics momentarily stopped jeering when the tragedy actually occurred at Dux, Bohemia, in 1900. Her prophecy tallied so closely with the details of actual events that observers said it seemed like an eyewitness account.

Also in 1899, the psychic lady predicted a major fire on the New York waterfront, and again her picture was detailed. The *New York Herald,* while not taking her utterances very seriously, published the prognostication in the issue of April 25, 1899. There was consternation the following year when on June 30, 1900, the docks blazed as if on cue. She was inexact in one matter: the conflagration, plainly visible from New York, actually flared in neighboring Hoboken. Even though it may be argued that one great fire is much like another, her details were again uncannily close to the reality.

Madame de Ferriem's achievements did not end with these accurate hits. An island in the West Indies, she said, would be blasted by volcanic eruption and earthquake in 1902. She was right; the island was Martinique. Lest it seem that the lady foresaw nothing but disasters, we add that she cheerfully and correctly predicted the year of Alfred Dreyfus's liberation at a time when his cause seemed hopeless.

A distinguishing quality of Madame de Ferriem's predictions is their clarity. She did not mince words when she said, "Captain Dreyfus will be freed next year." The same compliment cannot be paid to some other famous seers. Mother Shipton was the most famed of all prophets among the uneducated or ill-educated people of Tudor England. Her range of vision covered a wide time span, and she is credited with forecasting the suppression of monasteries by Henry VIII, the rise and fall of Anne Boleyn, and the execution of heretics in Smithfield. Going far beyond her own lifetime, she supposedly foresaw the beheading of Mary Queen of Scots, the accession of James I, and the London fire of 1666. Her accuracy, when all the symbols are carefully explained, seems astonishing.

But Mother Shipton, although she lived in an age noted for plain talk, spoke in riddles. Her words can be interpreted so many ways that at last they lose all meaning. Still, belief in her infallibility persisted for centuries, and as late as the Victorian era many of her utterances were being recast into contemporary rhyme, presumably so they would be easier to remember. The lady still has followers today.

The prophecies of the celebrated sixteenth-century French astrologer, Nostradamus, also rhymed, are as esoteric as Mother Shipton's. One finds what one looks for.

It was doubtless fortunate for Mother Shipton that she was in her grave long before the Great Fire of London took place. Another forecaster of the event, William Lilly, gave advance warning so unmistakably that when the flames broke out as previously announced, he was at once seized by the authorities on suspicion of arson. It was a great tribute to Lilly's ability, but probably one he did not appreciate. He was later exonerated.

Lilly is by no means the only example of a prognosticator's being too accurate for his own safety. An astrologer was so precise in his warnings of the murder of Prince Alessandro de' Medici that he was later held as an accomplice when the slaying took place exactly as he said it would. Actually, the prince was murdered in 1537 by his cousin, Lorenzino de' Medici. (Since Lorenzino was a believer in horoscopes, an interesting speculation arises: Could Lorenzino have studied his cousin's chart to determine an opportune time to strike? Meanwhile, the innocent stargazer would have been looking at the same horoscope and would have seen the same unfavorable signs for Alessandro. The murder would not have been caused by astrology, but its timing could certainly have been arranged by it.)

The fortuneteller in the de' Medici murder case must have been a foolhardy man. In almost every kingdom the prediction of the death of a sovereign has been a capital offense, and the law usually extended to all members of a royal family as well. Foretelling the accession of a new ruler, since this implies the death of a present one, was also banned. Although soothsayers are no longer officially believed, one can imagine what would happen to a psychic who wrote to President Nixon: "You will die a week from Friday." He would be in for some stern questioning, close surveillance, and no doubt temporary detention.

The belief that seers bring on the calamities they foretell has been universal, and no one knows how many men have been done to death because their grim premonitions proved accurate. In the fourteenth century a German soothsayer was burned alive because he was thought to have poisoned several wells. His real crime was correctly prophesying the arrival of the Black Death. This type of story has been enacted over and over in many centuries, many countries.

Absurd though this belief seems, it has a grain of parapsychological truth: a prophet wishes to be proved right, so he unconsciously longs for the predicted event to take place. The wish becomes father to the deed through the force of PK. This is the same conjecture we indulged in while examining the Bell Witch case.

This seems terrifyingly true with one class of prophecy: the foretelling of one's own death. It is well established that be-believers in voodoo and similar religions frequently die if they become convinced that an unbreakable curse has been called down upon them by a sorcerer, and the victim often announces the day and even the hour of his demise. This has been reported from not only the West Indies, but from Africa, Brazil, Mexico, and many other nations and islands. Nor is such foretelling confined to primitive minds—which brings us again to the founder of Methodism, John Wesley, whose fringe involvement with the occult was not confined to the haunting of Epworth Parsonage. Wesley's interest had been aroused by the writings of the famed Swedish mystic Emanuel Swedenborg, and he wrote to propose a meeting. Swedenborg declined politely, explaining that he could accept no engagements so far in the future because his death was scheduled for March 29, 1772. And die he did, aged eighty-four, on that very day—a natural death, not possibly suicide.

To a certain extent all these examples fall within the realm of conventional psychology and medicine. Physicians have long been aware that those who think they are doomed often "give up the ghost." But PK is involved to the degree that the mind is affecting matter, and there seems no doubt that believing in a prophecy can, in certain instances, make the forecasts come true.

However, the connection between precognition and PK is confined to a limited number of incidents. It seems unlikely that Arthur Ford, another prophet who foresaw the Kennedy assassination, was in psychic conspiracy with Jeane Dixon and at least three astrologers (who gave vaguer predictions) to bring about a tragedy. Nor did Madame de Ferriem, for all her talent, psychically engineer the holocaust at Martinique, the Hoboken Fire, the disaster in Bohemia.

Most accurate prophecies have foreseen a single event, not a series of related happenings. A doubter's explanation would be that it is obviously easier to make one lucky guess than several, and a soothsayer who utters too much will eventually err.

A notable exception is the remarkable group of predictions

known as the Black Prophecy of the peasant Matha, a mysterious figure who appeared in Serbia in the early nineteenth century and seems to have had a vague resemblance to Rasputin. At least he was a powerful enough personality to command attention when he prophesied.

The royal assassinations, depositions, and accessions in the Balkans are difficult enough to follow historically, let alone in advance. The uncertainties did not confuse the Serbian prophet. His visionary forecast covered a time span of sixty-five years. Prince Michael, although not the heir apparent, would attain the throne, said Matha. And the prince did in 1839. He would be deposed, then eventually regain power only to be assassinated— and so it came to pass.

The peasant also foresaw the rise to power of King Alexander, his morganatic marriage to Draga Mashin, a woman of scandalous reputation, and the ultimate outcome: the murder of Alexander and Draga, in 1903.

The Black Prophecies were made broadcast in Europe and believers in the occult eagerly awaited each new fulfillment. They had good reason to be smug. Matha's series of hits was astonishing. It is probable that the peasant gave many other forecasts which are now lost to us, and very likely the seer fell into error. But his record on the royal house of Serbia was unblemished.

THE PSYCHIC TRIGGER

Prophets are notoriously the bearers of ill tidings, and dark predictions outnumber happy ones by a tremendous majority. Neighborhood fortunetellers, the small operators who hang out a sign proclaiming themselves as "psychic," attempt to give their clients good news mixed with a few dramatic warnings. But seers of a higher level tend to be pessimists; they harp on wars, famines, floods, and earthquakes. An antique example is Mother Shipton, who seemed to report nothing but wrath to come. In modern times, the most famous prophecies of Arthur Ford and Jeane Dixon involve tragedy. (An exception is Daniel Logan's best-known hits, which lifted him to fame when he appeared on the David Susskind show to announce correctly the end of the Northeast water shortage—good news; coming racial riots in the summer of 1967—bad news; and an Academy Award for Elizabeth Taylor—good news for the actress, at least.)

There is a parapsychological reason for the usual gloom of seers. Psychic experience, whether it is simple ESP or apparent precognition, is more often than not triggered by some dramatic event, and the dramatic events in life are too often tragic. Dr. Louisa Rhine has gathered a voluminous file of reports from quite ordinary people who suddenly "knew something" or "received a message." They are housewives, merchants, business and professional men and women, not mediums. Over and over again the psychic communications they believed had come to them involved the death of a loved one or a serious accident. While not every message was grave, good news about winning a lottery or getting a promotion failed to arrive by ESP.

A case from the author's own collection is typical of thousands of others:

Mrs. Adams (a pseudonym) awoke in the night with "a terrible premonition" that her husband, who was on a business trip to another city, had suffered a fatal mishap. She was not sure if the apprehension had come to her as part of a dream or if it struck her mind just as she was awakening. Mrs. Adams was not a nervous type, not usually given to worry, and it seemed ridiculous for her to telephone the hotel where her husband was staying since it was almost midnight. Though strongly tempted to make such a call, she chided herself for being silly and eventually fell into a troubled sleep. When her bedside telephone rang about three a.m., she felt "absolutely certain of what the call would be about."

Her husband had finished his business much earlier than he had expected and decided to drive home instead of spending an extra night away. He had lost control of his car when it skidded on an icy stretch of pavement. The accident happened at about eleven-

278

thirty p.m., a few minutes before Mrs. Adams had her "warning" of it. Since the road was little traveled at that hour, the crumpled car, which had struck a tree, was not found by the state police until much later. Although Mr. Adams was seriously injured, his wife's worst fears were not confirmed. He eventually made a full recovery.

Mrs. Adams had never experienced anything that could be described as psychic before that night, and in the next ten years there was no recurrence. She would like to cross it off as a coincidence, but finds this impossible: "The feeling was just too strong."

There is no outside evidence to support this story. She was alone in the house, she did not make a phone call. It is possible that she later exaggerated a usual worry. But the lady is emphatic that the "warning" was positive and, to her, unique.

The Adams case does not involve precognition, of course. It is given here as a highly typical illustration of how closely psychic phenomena are bound up with violence, danger, and death. One of the earliest extensive investigations of the British Society for Psychical Research was to determine how frequently witnesses saw or thought they saw "apparitions" at a deathbed. The results astounded the investigators. After the careful questioning of more than seventeen thousand people, it became clear that observers of death either saw some manifestation or suffered such hallucinations thousands of times as frequently as in ordinary situations.

If "great events cast their shadows before them," is it possible that some of these shadows are psychic in nature—especially when the event is cataclysmic or charged with emotion? A host of prophets making thousands of correct predictions one after another would hardly convince some people that it is possible for a mind to travel forward into time. Their opposites are those who will seize upon any forecast, however ambiguous, and pronounce it verified if there is the least shred of plausibility connected with it.

There is no scientific proof of precognition—except that it sometimes seems to happen. It cannot be controlled, weighed, or measured—but the strange cases remain, and when enough of them have accumulated, one recalls the words of William James spoken about Eusapia—he deplored her trickery, knew there was exaggeration, but when all had been discounted, felt compelled to add, "There is still a residue of phenomena."

VIII

Occult Kaleidoscope

On the morning of August 1, 1856, Baron de Guldenstubbé sat in a dim room in his Paris residence, atingle with excitement although his bald head was bowed in prayer. The baron was deep in a mystical experience— a state not unfamiliar to him. Outwardly he looked anything but mystical. He was short and roly-poly, his plump face made broader by mutton-chop sideburns and its roundness accented by steel-rimmed spectacles. But Baron de Guldenstubbé was not at all the stolid, middle-class burgher he appeared to be. His noble family enjoyed high connections throughout Europe, and their comfort was assured by large holdings in eastern Prussia and in the Baltic provinces of the Russian empire. He took his nobility seriously, and preferred to fraternize with other titled gentlemen such as his friends the Comte d'Ourches and the Comte de Szapary. In recent years, however, his interest in new science and new religion had brought him into contact with social inferiors and even Americans.

That morning the baron meditated on the Book of Daniel, sure that he was on the verge of a magnificent discovery, a breakthrough that would revolutionize both faith and science and, better still, would silence the detestable mesmerists, men who had once doted on Guldenstubbé, yet now had the gall to impede his efforts and to call him an apostate.

As he mulled over the story of Belshazzar's feast and the astounding handwriting that had appeared on the palace wall, everything suddenly became clear to him. Only one childishly simple experiment was necessary! If it proved successful, the new revelation from the eternal would be forever established. The baron rose quickly and went to a small wooden chest. Inside it he put a blank sheet of paper and a pencil which he carefully sharpened, then locked the chest and slipped the key into his pocket. Now he had only to wait until the miraculous evidence arrived.

Somehow during the next days Guldenstubbé managed to keep quiet about his great project, a difficult task for a man so talkative and gregarious. Everything depended on what happened inside that wooden box—the entire future of science and religion!

Only a short time before, the baron's friend, the Comte d'Ourches, had initiated automatic writing and table-turning in France, but Guldenstubbé, inspired by the Rochester rappings of the Fox sisters, was the first impresario of spiritualism in the country. He had faced an uphill struggle, and the opposition, surprisingly, came not from churchmen or scientists but from the entrenched cult of mesmerism, whose members derided the marvelous knocks and thumps as "visionary folly." Not being gentlemen, they even stooped to writing sarcastic letters to editors.

Despite all the baron's fuming and fulminating it took him a full six months to organize a séance circle "on the American plan." It was not an easy chore. Baron de Guldenstubbé could not invite just *anybody* to join the circle, and the group had to be composed of exactly six men and six women so they could be seated with alternation of the sexes, thus "re-enforcing the fluids." Electric forces had to be considered, for while most women were negative and sensitive and most men were positive and magnetic, one sometimes encountered a sexual anomaly—a negative man or a positive woman who, obviously, could not be seated next to each other. The results of mis-seating would be akin to a short circuit, repelling to the spirits, perhaps dangerous for the sitters. Everything had to be arranged carefully.

At last the circle was assembled, although it was not entirely to the baron's liking. He had been forced to admit the Abbé Châtel, a rationalist given to asking unpleasantly plain questions; then there was Rousaan who, for all his zeal, had no title, not even a professional one. Rousaan, though simple, was sincere. A pity he had so little social background!

The group gathered and joined arms, and a medium they had engaged fell into a hypnotic trance in a chair which had been placed a little distant from the table. After a few practice sessions remarkable things happened. Everyone felt simultaneous electric shocks. The Comte d'Ourches, a highly spiritual man, could levitate the table—any table, it seems—without touching it, and the baron was even better: he could make the table skitter across the room and did not need the magnetic help of the circle to do it. Meanwhile, the strings of the parlor piano vibrated and sounded mysterious chords. It was all very satisfactory, indeed.

Next they turned to automatic writing and this activity, their greatest success, brought the loudest jeers from the mesmerists. Spirits? Rubbish! The pencils, pens, and pieces of chalk were grasped by the fingers of the spiritualists, who were obviously making all these hen-scratches themselves. This became Guldenstubbé's most vexatious problem—how to obtain the writing yet eliminate the human hands. The baron meditated. He thought of Daniel and the handwriting on the wall; he thought of Moses and the divinely written Ten Commandments. Then the answer came: he would put paper and pencil in a locked box, pray, and see what happened. Surely the Lord would confound the heathen!

Each day for twelve days Guldenstubbé, holding his breath, unlocked the chest and peered inside. And each inspection brought bitter disappointment. The spirits refused to cooperate. Then, on the thirteenth day, the miracle happened. "Astonishment! Mysterious characters traced on the papers!"

Like many another scientist at the peak of discovery, Guldenstubbé could hardly contain himself. He repeated the experiment ten times on that memorable day, August 13, 1856, and the results were invariably positive. More mysterious characters, more astonishment! The next morning he grew bolder. He left the chest open but kept a sharp eye on it, and suddenly letters and words appeared written "in the Esthonian language with no motion of the pencil." The spirits, he now knew, had their own invisible pencils and needed no help from man. He made twenty experiments, all, needless to say, successful.

Baron de Guldenstubbé was in a dither. He left blank sheets around the house, and messages promptly appeared. It was at last time to announce his discovery, to venture out into the world— and he did so. Accompanied by several friends, including the Comte de Szapary and the ever-present Comte d'Ourches, he led spiritualist sorties to the great public monuments and works of art in Paris. He left paper and, cautiously, pencils near statutes and on tombs. Expeditions were organized to descend on the Louvre, the Church of Saint Etienne du Mont, and once or twice on graveyards. Graves, however, made the baron uneasy. He had "no liking for cemeteries, while most saints prefer the localities where they lived on earth to those in which their mortal remains are laid to rest."

He did not need to visit cemeteries, for, elsewhere, spirit messages were pouring in from Plato, Cicero, and Juvenal. Saint Paul wrote. So did Mary Stuart, Edmund Spenser, Molière, Louis XIV, and Joan of Arc. There were communications in a dozen

languages including some indecipherable hieroglyphics that required an entranced medium to unscramble them.

The baron called his great discovery direct writing and he
wrote a book about it: *Practical Experimental Pneumatology; or,
the Reality of Spirits and the Marvellous Phenomena of Their
Direct Writing*. His work did not put to flight the mesmerists—
such people never seem to know when they are beaten—but it
did weaken their movement and the book brought many new
converts into the spiritualist fold. The baron had every reason to
be pleased—as, indeed, he was: "The Eternal, Whose mercy is
infinite, has abundantly answered my feeble prayer."

The amazing thing about the Baron de Guldenstubbé's career
is not that he did what he did but that he got away with it. His
book, handsomely printed and decorated with an engraved portrait of the author, caused quite a stir, and although many people
scoffed or dismissed the work as balderdash, Guldenstubbé gained
a certain fame. No one bothered to investigate.

Today parapsychologists would pounce in a second. The
fantastic nature of the baron's claims lead one to suspect that an
investigation would quickly center around one question: was
Guldenstubbé a liar or intermittently a madman? It seems likely
that at the beginning of the game, when he alone conducted the
experiments, he might have been so desperate for the writing to
appear that he wrote the messages himself in an unconscious
state. Later, others could have furthered the fraud. The baron is
a wretched reporter, heaping on details and sermons that are ir-
relevant, then omitting vital facts. We know that on one of his
sallies into the city a professional medium accompanied the group.
Was this medium always at hand when messages appeared? The
baron does not tell us. Professionals, however talented, were employees and hardly the sort of people a gentleman noted. Guldenstubbé, proud of his rank, takes for granted that a nobleman's
unsupported word is above question.

Modern investigators would soon dispose of latter-day Pauline epistles and get down to essentials. Despite the clouds of non-sense, was there any possibility that PK was at work, that the baron unconsciously *willed* the messages into being? This part of the case is a parapsychological problem. Guldenstubbé's mental condition would be a matter for traditional psychiatry.

The Guldenstubbé affair dramatically illustrates the advance of psychical research. Only a century ago the choice seemed to lie between believing in spirits or charging fraud. Today the possibilities are far wider, and if a seemingly paranormal matter receives much public attention, some sort of unbiased examination usually follows.

Often no investigation is necessary. The disturbed witches and warlocks of Los Angeles are enjoying—and reveling in—purely subjective experiences. They talk of "power" and of "the force of Satan," but they have demonstrated such force only in very physical ways. They are symptoms of an unsettled society, but the Los Angeles freak show is a subject for psychologists or sociologists, not for psychical researchers who are already pressed for time and money. When an actual manifestation occurs, such as the "miraculous image" which appeared on an American screen door a few years ago, a trained observer checks it out. (In that case the "image" was in the eyes of the beholders.)

Dr. Karlis Osis, a psychologist and the director of the American Society for Psychical Research, recently said, "Parapsychology is an infant, in its babyhood, but I believe it will ultimately tell us more about who and what we are." Unfortunately, such men as William James and Henry Sidgwick were saying the same thing in different terms eighty years ago. The study was an infant then and, despite advances, is an infant now.

In 1968 the American Society undertook the most ambitious and by far the most expensive project in its history. Fred H. Rindge, a business consultant, was sent globe-trotting to place rows of cards in far-flung places in order to determine the range of ESP under certain conditions. The cost, enormous to the Society and perhaps a financial landmark in psychical research, was fifteen thousand dollars—roughly the amount needed to furnish a modern high-school laboratory with the latest equipment.

This would be a piddling figure in electronics or medicine, a pittance in space exploration or nuclear physics. But to undernourished parapsychologists it is a tremendous sum of money. Parapsychology seeks to delve into the mysteries of the human mind. But although the proper study of mankind may be man himself, few people and no governments—except Hitler's in a horribly twisted way—have been willing to finance it. There have been rumors about the United States Navy's conducting experiments in ESP from the submarine *Nautilus;* no report has surfaced. The Russians have claimed research in the same field but give no information. If either government is doing anything, it seems not to be much. Some universities have ventured into the field of *psi*, but, encouraging though this is, the attitude of the administrators—not the researchers—has been cautious to the point of timidity. College presidents and deans are now gingerly putting a toe into the ocean of psychical research, and that is as far as most of them will go.

Mrs. Eileen Garrett, more than anyone else, was the mainstay of *psi* in the United States and perhaps in the world. The *grande dame* of the Unexplained, she died at seventy-seven in 1970. For more than half a century she had upheld the cause of parapsychology with sincerity, intelligence, and boundless energy. She had shown herself to be a talented editor, a capable woman with the strength for pioneering. She was also a medium—which made her anathema to some.

Mrs. Garrett at times had the rather disconcerting habit of greeting new acquaintances with instant prophecies or readings of their circumstances. Such a remark as, "You're going to have some unexpected news tonight or tomorrow morning. Good news!" was typical. Although by no means infallible, she had a high batting average with her quick predictions and insights. As a psychic medium, she patiently endured countless tests by scientists determined to prove her a fraud. They had no success.

Mrs. Garrett might not be invariably right, but her reputation, after every kind of checking, was unblemished. A lifetime of experience with practitioners of the occult enabled her to look upon them with an eye that was sharp, maybe slightly jaundiced, but not cynical. Unlike some of her fellow workers in the field, she had no hesitation about mentioning "cranks and liars and nuts." Mrs. Garrett knew very well that such quacks and fanatics hover on the fringes of parapsychology. Her bluntness was refreshing. Dedicated explorers of the paranormal have so often been beleaguered by skeptics that they have developed a tendency to be far too diplomatic. For instance, those studying precognition are ultra-careful (in print, at least) not to step on the toes of the reincarnationists or astrologers. Having endured much criticism, they are gentle in criticizing others. Not Mrs. Garrett. While she kept an open mind, her level of tolerance for nonsense or suspected fraud was blessedly low.

The United States Parapsychology Foundation, which Mrs. Garrett headed, is a fund-granting organization for the support of diverse projects related to *psi*. There have been some notable achievements, especially in the area of ESP, but money, always in short supply, remains a nagging problem.

There is irony in this. A dozen years ago a British confidence man named William Roy confessed to bilking bereaved clients of fifty thousand pounds sterling by posing as a medium. He used shills and confederates, and his tricks, mostly quite crude and unoriginal, seem so simple that they could have been detected even by so credulous a soul as Baron de Guldenstubbé. Yet Roy, like many other swindlers, had little difficulty in relieving the gullible of almost ten times the amount of money that the honest American Society for Psychical Research could spend for its "most costly project ever." The motto of the public seems to be: Millions for fraud, not one cent for experiment.

There is another side to the story. A widespread belief persists that parapsychology is a hoax and a dollar spent for its mythical advancement is a dollar down the drain. This view, now gradually giving way, remains dominant among scientists even though it has been successfully assailed by logic time and time again. Some of the strongest attacks on the know-nothing attitude have also been the wittiest. Charles Fort, author of three books and many articles, spent most of a lifetime compiling "a sanatorium of overworked coincidences," facts and happenings conveniently ignored by science, demonstrating again that the suspicion of the average man has always been right: there *are* some matters unexplained.

Precisely what has been established by parapsychology? Its accomplishments are small compared to the immensity of the problems unsolved, but the gains are by no means negligible:

The existence of ESP is now so clearly proven that only a scientific mossback or a completely uninformed layman will argue the fact. The public thinks of the Rhine experiments but, important though they were, they form only a fraction of the evidence. However, as proof keeps accumulating, so does exaggeration. The notion that the average man can somehow harness ESP and make it "work for him" is utterly without foundation at the present time. There are many explanations and theories of ESP, some interesting, others palpably absurd, but the plain fact remains that no one knows for sure how ESP operates. It seems to be capricious, freakish, and usually beyond human control.

A very few things about its nature are more or less established. Certain rare individuals have great talent as perceptors, an ability setting them far apart from most people. Mrs. Piper is a classic case; Peter Hurkos and Gerard Croiset provide notable modern examples. No one knows the origin of such a gift, but it is sometimes associated with an accident, an illness, or a traumatic experience. The power may improve over the years and then decline with old age and failing health, but it cannot be strengthened or cultivated by any known method. It simply exists.

Communication appears to be easier between people who are

closely associated—husbands and wives, good friends, members of a family. We stress *appears*. Close connection has meant nothing in the cases of great natural talents.

There is reason to believe that the receiver is aided by possession of some object handled previously by the sender. This sounds for all the world like voodoo or black magic, but evidence tends to show it is a fact. Touching an object frequently helped Mrs. Piper and other telepaths. In the American Society's around-the-world telepathy experiment the sixty receivers were provided with cards which the sender had carried on his person. How much assistance this gives the perceptor is wholly unknown, but those who have the most experience in dealing with ESP feel that it is a factor.

The bulk of evidence seems to show that in the life of an average man ESP is most likely to operate at a time of threat or danger. But this remains debatable. Possibly we remember only the dramatic situations and forget or discount ordinary "messages" because there is nothing to make them memorable or striking.

Communication is more accurate and frequent when the image being conveyed is decidedly visual. It is easier to "send" a design or picture than a word or number. Test scores indicate this strongly.

Recent studies are giving confirmation to the long-held belief that it is easier to receive ESP from a nearby source than from a far-away place. This does not apply to the few great "sensitives," whose perception has spanned oceans as easily as rooms.

These few facts, some of them debatable, very nearly sum up all that has been determined about the phenomenon. Researchers have come up with many additional probabilities, but hard proof is still lacking. More tests are needed; more will be made.

The dearth of knowledge about ESP's nature and operation is no argument against its existence. Modern experiments are not concerned with "whether" but with "how, when, and why."

PK, psychokinesis—or telekinesis or simply "mind over matter"—lacks the firm evidential backing which ESP has accumulated. Even if we admit its existence, the force is extremely difficult to test because it has seldom appeared under set laboratory conditions in modern times. It seems to be found, however, in a "free state." An investigator has to hear about a "haunting" and arrive on the scene in time to observe PK in operation. The force is utterly fickle, absolutely unpredictable. The studies of American parapsychologists W. E. Cox and J. G. Pratt of Duke University are convincing but quite limited. Much more investigation is needed, experiments and tests by a larger number of scientists.

J. B. Rhine and his followers observed extended trials of "talking to the dice." The result of the dice castings favored the presence of PK, showing patterns that were far above chance, but the test conditions are open to certain objections. Other attempts to isolate and prove PK in laboratories have been interesting but inconclusive. And the fact remains that the most striking instances of apparent PK have happened when an unconscious, rather than a conscious, mind was influencing matter. This presents a formidable obstacle to parapsychologists, but time is on their side. "Miraculous cases" will arise in the future as they have in the past and they will offer opportunities for trained observers.

The best argument for the existence of PK, aside from a very few well-documented cases and some limited laboratory testing, is that it explains so many occurrences which, without PK, defy reason. The recognition of such a force would give a needed rest to some of Charles Fort's heavily "over-worked coincidences," and would banish a huge number of ghosts.

Recently PK has received a boost by demonstrations involving the power of "prayer" to make plants grow. There has been a rush to publish, although the results are not fully known. Skeptical minds still rightly demand more confirmation.

If such confirmation comes—not only involving plants but objects—parapsychologists will be delighted, but some writers on the subject may find themselves in an embarrassing position.

Modern psychical researchers have been so eager to escape the stigma of gullibility that they have denounced the famous physical mediums of the past, brushing aside their performances as undetected trickery. If PK becomes established as a known fact, a second look will have to be given to some reported marvels. *All* the floating trumpets in séance rooms could not then be crossed off as "fraud because it can't be anything else." Eusapia and D. D. Home may cease to be "unpersons" or annoyances, and might enjoy at least a partial rehabilitation.

Precognition remains a battle-ground, the field of bitter, emotional struggles between doubters and believers. Prophecies, no matter how accurate, are always open to attack as lucky guesses, and there is little sign that this will change. The choice between remarkable coincidences and precognitive powers depends on the mentality of the individual who studies them. New evidence favoring precognition came recently as a result of the American Society's world-wide test of long-distance ESP. In some cases, the receivers seemed to know the order of laid-out cards before the cards were actually put into such a sequence. This is not the first time such a thing has happened, and if the occurrence repeats itself often and more dramatically in the future, it will become strong evidence. At the moment it can be described only as curious and surprising. But perhaps it is a beginning.

Modern parapsychology shies away from the acceptance of ghosts and from communication with the Other Side; spiritualism is now regarded more as a religious matter than as a question for science. An exception to this happens when psychical researchers undertake to expose gross frauds and hoaxes. The most notorious case of fraud in modern times came to light a decade ago when two researchers, the Reverend Tom O'Neill and Dr. Andrija Puharich, paid a visit to Camp Chesterfield, a summer gathering place for spiritualists in Indiana. The camp was established just after the turn of the century and at least a third of a million pilgrims have been welcomed there during its history. Attendance in a single summer runs over fifty thousand. O'Neill

Occult Kaleidoscope

and Puharich had no expectation of revealing a scandal when they attended a séance given by a famous medium, Edith Stillwell. The gentlemen intended to take infrared photographs in the darkness of the room, pictures to confirm the psychic's power. When, after two sessions, the photographs showed unmistakable deception by the medium and her confederates, O'Neill was in a state approaching shock. His report of the affair in the *Psychic Observer* is the writing of a bitterly disillusioned man.

This, sadly, is all too often the story, and parapsychologists seldom waste their time on the inspection of yet another gauze and wire ghost. Over the years, Mrs. Piper's "G.P." is probably the spirit with the best claim to independent existence outside the medium. At least he convinced the skeptical Hodgson and others. But it must be remembered that all the remarkable information "G.P." uttered was contained in the minds of living persons. William James thought that powerful ESP explained the matter. Here, again, the choice will depend on the emotional inclinations of the judge.

Examining the story of occult belief and psychical research is rather like gazing into a kaleidoscope: the least shift of time alters the pattern, changes the color and emphasis. Some elements remain constant, but each generation interprets the unknown in the light of its own faith and discovery—and its emotions. The Renaissance, which gave birth to modern science, sought its marvels in alchemy and astrology and projected its new materialism into very physical forms of magic. During the eighteenth-century Enlightenment, when sophisticated minds were rejecting religion, the wonder was mesmerism—a combining of the miraculous with the newly explored force of electricity. The more devout Victorian era saw the unknown in terms of spiritism and spiritualism, the return of the dead from presumably happier shores. In our own time, explanations involve the mysterious abilities of the human mind—a reflection of psychoanalysis and the individual's growing interest in his own psyche.

293

We have used the term "occult" to describe many things—
all that is "hidden from sight; obscure." But the occult, for all
its vastness, is shrinking. ESP, for example, is occult only in the
sense that its nature is still obscure to us, but it has moved into
the realm of known fact just as electricity and hypnotism did
in earlier times. Perhaps PK will soon follow this road, also.

Traditional scientists, when they venture into the unknown
world of *psi*, are still likely to exclaim, "Nonsense!" They might
do well to remember an unfortunate remark by Professor Münsterberg who, only sixty years ago, undoubtedly spoke for the
majority of the scientific establishment when (according to
Sugrue) he said, "The story of the subconscious mind can be
told in three words. There is none." Eusapia's ghost has the last
laugh. She may have been exposed as a trickster, but time has
exposed some of her critics as narrow-minded, utterly mistaken
reactionaries who would resist unto death anything that fell
beyond the scope of their simple materialism.

The new parapsychology is chipping away at the unexplained,
attempting to bring the unknown into the natural order of the
world. Its eventual success, which may require decades or even
centuries, will not diminish the wonder of thoughts that leap
from mind to mind, of objects that move though untouched, nor
change the uncanniness of ghosts that will walk in the future as
they have in the past. New generations, looking at present mysteries and at those of the past—as we have done—will express in
their own words the awe of Sacheverell Sitwell when he said,
"What, by all the powers of good and evil, are these sights and
sounds! No one can tell. It is still, and may ever be, a mystery."

Bibliography

Notes on Source Material

A researcher new to the field of occultism (and again we use that word in the broadest sense) might think at first that he faced an embarrassment of riches: literature on the subject is voluminous, ranging from the findings of scientific committees to Mrs. John Smith's personal glimpses of the Beyond.

Such an investigator will be quickly disabused. The vast majority of books about "mysterious powers of the mind" are unmitigated nonsense, pseudoscience, or wish fulfillments written by the gullible and for the gullible. Worse, many "studies" are cranked out by sensation mongers intent on bilking the public. Most of these books, whether sincere or cynical, are unredeemed by the least grace of style, warmth, or humor.

Bibliography

The best primary sources remain the annals of the Society for Psychical Research (both the British and American Societies, although the British reports are more complete and more consistently trustworthy). Duke University, through efforts of its parapsychological laboratory, has amassed an invaluable collection of records, many of them statistical. Such little-known papers as "Comparative Analysis of Some Poltergeist Cases" by Duke parapsychologist W. E. Cox are far more useful and certainly more interesting than the "mystic marvel" books that soar to best-seller lists. Stanford University, once a pioneer in psychical research, also has much original material. The author has relied heavily upon information first gathered by these four institutions, and grateful acknowledgement is rendered. Mention must also be made of the small but fascinating collection of nineteenth-century books made available by the Quebec Literary and Historical Society.

Periodicals devoted to serious psychical research or merely to occult oddities spring up from time to time and usually vanish as quickly as ectoplasm. *Tomorrow*, which was edited by the late Eileen J. Garrett, had a comparatively long life, reaching a circulation of more than ten thousand, and its demise is regrettable. There has been no satisfactory successor. Currently in the United States we have, among others, *Beyond, Exploring the Unknown, Fate, The Info Journal, Orion, Psychic*, and *Understanding Magazine*. Together they cover everything from sea serpents to poltergeists, from ESP to UFOs. It is noteworthy, although less than just, that the 1970 edition of *The Writer's Market*, a guide for free-lance authors, lumps all of them under the heading "Science Fiction and Fantasy." *Fate*, however, publishes interesting case histories, a few of which have been mentioned briefly in these pages. *Psychic*, a newcomer, seems well researched.

In recent years the best articles on parapsychology have appeared in magazines "outside the field," and the writer expresses his thanks to *Esquire, Harper's Bazaar, Life, Maclean's, McCall's, Newsweek, Time*, and *Yankee*. *McClure's Magazine*, long de-

296

funct, published numerous articles about mediumship and related matters early in this century.

The selected bibliography that follows attempts to give the reader a sampling of the field—both the good and bad—and an indication of the type of secondary sources used in this work. It is far from complete: there seems, for instance, little point in listing eight repetitious books about Edgar Cayce when three will tell most readers more than they care to know. Numerous privately printed memoirs are not included. Collectively such works testify to the desire for paranormal experience, but individually they are useless.

Also omitted are the many standard histories and biographies used in preparation of this book, but whose major subject matter is far afield. For examples, Elizabeth Longford's *Queen Victoria* offers a brief but colorful picture of early spiritualism with asides about D. D. Home; *Elizabeth and Leicester* by Elizabeth Jenkins provides an interesting glimpse of John Dee; histories by H. Trevor-Roper, William Shirer, Frederic Lilge, and Richard F. Gallagher provide insights into the dark mysticism of Nazi Germany. But, of course, none of these works is essentially about occultism, so they are not listed here.

Adams, Evangeline. *Astrology for Everyone.* New York: Dodd, Mead & Co., 1931. (A textbook by America's outstanding practitioner.)

Bell, Charles Bailey, M.D. *The Bell Witch. A Mysterious Spirit.* Nashville, Tenn.: 1934. (A rewriting and expansion of "Our Family Trouble," this appears to be the most reliable account of the Bell haunting.)

Carington, Whately. *Telepathy.* London: Methuen, 1945. (Reports of major experiments with ESP.)

Carrington, Hereward. *Eusapia Palladino and Her Phenomena.* New York: B. W. Dodge, 1909. (The remarkable lady presented by her greatest partisan.)

——, *Modern Psychical Phenomena.* New York: American Universities Publishing Co., 1920. (A blend of thorough investigation and peculiar pseudoscience. No longer "modern" but always lively.)

———, and Fodor, Nandor. *Haunted People.* New York: E. P. Dutton & Co., 1951. (An extensive bibliography of poltergeist cases and reports of other uncanny happenings.)

Coffee Table Book of Astrology, The. Edited by John Lynch. Revised edition. New York: The Viking Press, 1967. (A lavishly illustrated book covering all highlights of its subject.)

Fodor, Nandor. *The Haunted Mind.* New York: Helix Press, 1959.

———, *Mind over Space.* New York: Citadel Press, 1962. (Dr. Fodor is a psychoanalyst and he applies his science to occult studies with original results. Skeptics will consider him a mighty argument against all psychoanalysis.)

Ford, Arthur, with Margueritte Harmon Bro. *Nothing So Strange.* New York: Harper & Bros, 1958. (America's best-known male medium discusses his talents and career.)

Freud, Sigmund. "The Uncanny." (1919) "Psychology of Occult Phenomena." (1920) "Psychoanalysis and Telepathy." (1921). Included in *Complete Works.* New York: Macmillan, 1953. (Sharp, lucid essays that are foundation stones of modern parapsychology.)

Garrett, Eileen J. *Adventures in the Supernormal.* New York: Creative Age Press, 1949. (An intelligent woman gives a first-hand account of mediumship.)

Gurney, Edmund. *Phantasms of the Living; by Edmund Gurney, Frederic W. H. Myers and Frank Podmore.* London: Trübner, 1886. (A pioneer work by early giants of the psychical research movement.)

Heywood, Rosalind. *Beyond the Reach of Sense.* New York: E. P. Dutton & Co., 1961. Published in England under the title *The Sixth Sense.* (One of the few really excellent works on ESP.)

Hill, Douglas, and Williams, Pat. *The Supernatural.* London: Aldus Books, 1965. (A rational, well-balanced survey of a broad field by two fine reporters.)

I Ching or *The Book of Changes.* Translated by James Legge. New York: Dover, n.d. (The best version of the Chinese classic, thanks to a study guide by Dr. Ch'u Chai.)

James, William. *William James on Psychical Research.* Compiled and

edited by Gardner Murphy and Robert O. Ballou. New York: The
Viking Press, 1960. (A classic. Replete with clear thinking and
good sense.)

Jung, Carl G. *Memories, Dreams, Reflections.* New York: Pantheon
Books, 1963. (Considerably more mystical than Freud on similar
subjects.)

Lévi, Eliphas. *The History of Magic.* Reissued. London: Rider & Co.,
1969. (A strange and colorful world. A. E. Waite's translation and
corrections of Lévi's numerous errors make this the best edition
of the work ever published.)

Liljencrants, Baron Johan. *Spiritism and Religion.* New York: Devon-
Adair Co., 1918. (A Roman Catholic view, bearing the imprimatur
of the Archbishop of New York. The conclusions are predictable,
but the material is presented with a wealth of detail.)

Lodge, Sir Oliver. *Raymond; or Life after Death.* London: Methuen,
1916. (The best, most moving story of a survivor's attempt to
reach a dead loved one through spiritualism.)

Mackay, Charles, LL.D. *Extraordinary Popular Delusions and the
Madness of Crowds.* (Originally 1841 and 1852.) Reissued, New
York: L. C. Page & Co., 1932. (A landmark.)

Millard, Joseph. *Edgar Cayce.* Revised edition. Greenwich, Conn.:
Fawcett Gold Medal Books, 1967. (A drab portrait of the prophet
told as the Edgar Cayce Foundation, which holds the copyright,
wanted it told.)

Montgomery, Ruth. *A Gift of Prophecy.* New York: William Mor-
row & Co., 1965. (A wondering and uncritical examination of Jeane
Dixon.)

Myers, F. W. H. *Human Personality and Its Survival of Bodily Death.*
London: Longmans, Green & Co., 1903. (This created a sensation
at the time of its publication. The years have not treated it kindly,
but it remains a basic work on psychical research.)

Podmore, Frank. *The Naturalization of the Supernatural.* New York:
G. Putnam's Sons, 1908. (Podmore was a pioneer worker with a
skeptical turn of mind. His conclusions cannot always be trusted,
but his evidence can.)

———, *The Newer Spiritualism.* London: T. F. Unwin, 1910.

———, *Studies in Psychical Research.* London: K. Paul, Trench,
Trübner, 1897.

Price, Harry. *The Most Haunted House in England.* New York: Longmans, Green & Co., 1940. (The Borley story. Some of the evidence is questionable. The impact remains.)

————, *Poltergeist Over England.* (Ghost-hunting. Interesting, but involving dubious methods and snap conclusions.)

Price, Morton, M.D. *The Disassociation of Personality.* Reissued. New York: Meridian Books, 1957. (The classic study of multiple personality.)

Reichel, Willy. *An Occultist's Travels.* New York: R. F. Fenno & Co., 1908. (The carnival atmosphere of spiritism in America early in this century, as seen by the eye of perfect faith. Unintentionally hilarious.)

Rhine, Dr. J. B. *New Frontiers of the Mind.* London: Faber, 1938.

————, *The Reach of the Mind.* New York: William Sloane Associates, 1947. (The famous Rhine investigations and their meanings. Sound and cautious.)

Rhine, Dr. Louisa. *Hidden Channels of the Mind.* New York: William Sloane Associates, 1961. (A collector of ESP case histories, Dr. Louisa Rhine is virtually the Krafft-Ebing of parapsychology.)

Robbins, Anne Manning. *Both Sides of the Veil: a Personal Experience.* New York: Holt, 1921. (About Mrs. Piper, who deserves a better biographer.)

Rosher, Grace. *Beyond the Horizon.* London: James Clarke & Co., 1961. (Uncanny experiences in automatic writing.)

Sherman, Harold. *How to Make ESP Work for You.* Los Angeles: DeVorss & Co., 1964. (A perfect example of parapsychological quackery. Unsubstantiated, unscholarly, and unfortunately typical of hundreds of books in the field.)

Spence, Lewis. *An Encyclopaedia of Occultism.* Originally published, 1920. Reissued. New Hyde Park, N.Y.: University Books, 1960. (A monumental and fascinating work, invaluable to anyone interested in occultism.)

Spraggett, Allen. *The Unexplained.* New York: New American Library, 1967. (A collection of marvels and oddities. The author treats his subjects with kindliness and is inclined to faith. Nevertheless, it is a much better than average book of its genre.)

Stearn, Jess. *Edgar Cayce—The Sleeping Prophet.* New York: Doubleday & Co., 1967. (The worst of the dubious Cayce books.)

Sugrue, Thomas. *There Is a River*. New York: Holt, Rinehart and Winston, 1942. (The best of the dubious Cayce books.)

Trowbridge, W. R. H. *Cagliostro*. New York: Brentano's, 1910 (A biography correcting many errors which Thomas Carlyle made when writing about the magician.)

Worth, Patience. *The Sorry Tale*. New York: Henry Holt & Co., 1917. (A substantial novel by history's most celebrated "ghost writer.")

Index

Index

Balsamo, Joseph, 137-38
Balsamo, Peter, see Cagliostro, Count
Batts, Old Kate, 213
Beach, Mr., 178, 179, 185
Beattie, Mr., 152
Beauchamp, Christine L., 142-44
Beecher, Rev. Charles, 186
Bell, Allen, 220
Bell, Betsy, 211, 212, 214-23
Bell, Dr. Charles Bailey, 219, 220
Bell, Drewry, 211, 215, 219
Bell, Joel Thomas, 211, 216, 219, 220
Bell, John, 209, 210, 211, 213, 215-18, 220, 221
Bell, John, Jr., 211, 218, 219, 220
Bell, Mrs. John (Luce), 215-19
Bell, Richard Williams, 211, 216, 219-20
Bell Witch, 173, 209-23
Belomancy, 257
Bernadotte, Count, 21
Besant, Annie, 126
Bible, 32-33, 78, 193, 235, 257
Bingen (Germany), 172
Black, William, 159
Blackington, Alton, 123
Blavatsky, Madame Helena Petrovna, 122, 126, 127, 130-33, 240; *Isis Unveiled*, 132; see also Theosophy (Theosophical Society)
Book of Changes, see I Ching
Books, divining by, see Rhapsodomancy
Borley Rectory (England), 187-206, 240
Branches, divining by, see Rhadomancy
Brazil, 276
Breasted, James Henry, 9
Brisson, Madame, 59
Brofferio, Prof., 44
Brown, John, 17
Browne, Mr., 168
Browne, Charles G., 198
Browning, Elizabeth Barrett, 77, 108, 159

Browning, Robert, 107-108, 164
Buchman, Dr. Frank, 160
Buguet, 151
Bull, Rev. H. D. E., 190
Bull, Rev. Harry F. (and family), 190, 191, 192, 193, 195, 198, 200, 201, 202
Burdick, Gordon E., 159
Burke, Tom, 6
Butler, Samuel, 238
Byford, Mrs. E., 190

Cabalistic studies, 256
Caesarius, Saint, 172, 193
Cagliostro, Count (Peter Balsamo), 15-16, 138-39
Camp Chesterfield (Ind.), 292
Capnomancy, 257
Card reading, 254-55
Carlota, Empress, 14
Carlyle, Thomas, 15, 23
Carrara, Madame Paola, 40, 45
Carrington, Hereward, 53-67, 151, 174, 185, 186
Carson, Neke, 5-6
Cartwright, Fred, 191
Caruso, Enrico, 250
Cassandra, 31
Catherine de Médicis, 10
Catherine the Great, Empress, 141
Cayce, Edgar, 5, 34, 37, 180-81, 265-272
Cayce, Edgar Evans, 269
Cayce, Hugh Lynn, 266
Chaldea, 225
Châtel, Abbé, 283
Cheiromancy, 254
Children, and poltergeists, 173, 174, 185, 204
China, 225
Christian II, Elector, 243
Christian Science, 71
Christianity, 7-8, 9-10, 32-33, 70, 71, 78; exorcism, 172, 193-94; see also Bible; Clergy

304

Index

Himmler, Heinrich, 18, 20-22
Hitler, Adolf, 18, 20, 22, 23, 24, 34, 287
Hodgson, Dr. Richard, 49-52, 80-83, 85, 91-95, 293
Holland, Mrs. (Mrs. Fleming), 62, 63, 94, 114, 158-64
Home, Daniel Dunglas, 14-15, 18, 26, 31, 42, 68-69, 77, 79, 104-115, 117-123, 262, 292
Honto, 128, 129, 130
Horniman, Squadron-Leader, 199
Horoscopes, 253-54
Hortense, Queen, 14
Houdini, Harry, 67, 100
Houdini, Mrs. Harry (Beatrice), 100-101
Howard, James, 90-91
Howard, Mary, 90, 93
Hudson, Mr., 150, 152
Hugo, Victor, 77, 137, 159
Hurkos, Peter, 34-35, 289

I Ching (Book of Changes), 257
Imperator Band, 95, 136
India, 19, 114, 225
Indians, 225; as Controls, 78, 79-80, 130
Ingram, M. V., 220
Innocent VIII, Pope, 7-8
Institut Générale Psychologique, 53, 55

Jackson, Andrew, 71-72
Jackson, Shirley, 140-41
James I, King, 247
James, William, 67, 80-83, 92-95, 136, 271, 281, 286, 293
Japan, 114, 225
Joan of Arc, 284
John XXIII, Pope, 261
Johnson, Alice, 160, 161
Johnson, James, 211, 212
Jones, Enmore, 150
Jones, Dr. Louis C., 207
Joseph, 255

Juliana, Queen, 121
Jung, C. G., 256, 259
Justin Martyr, Saint, 193
Juvenal, 281

Kambakonan (India), 207
Kant, Immanuel, 223
Kasabian, Linda, 6
Kelly, Edward (Talbot), 236-48, 256
Kembden (Germany), 172
Kennedy, Edward, 261
Kennedy, John F., 261, 276
Keppler, Wilhelm, 22
Kerr-Pearse, Mark, 198
King, John, 40-43, 50, 95, 136
King, Katie, 41, 42, 50, 115, 116-17, 136
Kipling, Rudyard, 94, 161
Koons, Jonathan, 41-42, 77
Krosigk, Count Lutz Schwerin von, 23, 24

Lambert, G. W., 202, 203
Lang, Andrew, 225
Laski, Count Albert, 239-42
Latin America, 228
Leaf, Walter, 85
Leda Amun Ra, Princess, 6, 8
Lee, Mother Ann, 73
Lee, Robert James, 17
Leigh (England), 207
Leonard, Mrs., 137, 167, 168, 187
Lévi, Eliphas, 5, 237
Levingston, William, 181
Liljencrants, Baron Johan, 32, 107, 139, 161
Lilly, William, 274
Lily Dale Assembly Camp, 49, 101
Lindsay, Lord, 109, 110, 112-13, 114
Lodge, Lady, 167, 168
Lodge, Sir Oliver, 48-49, 50, 52, 66, 83-84, 85, 86, 95, 166-68, 247
Lodge, Raymond, 167, 168-69
Logan, Daniel, 277-78
Lombroso, Prof. Cesare, 43-44, 50, 52, 66

Index

Index

Palladino, Eusapia, 26, 31, 35-69, 94, 110, 111, 112, 155, 203, 214, 262, 270, 280, 292, 294

Palmistry, 254

Paracelsus, 10, 230-31, 238-39, 241-42

Park, Mr., 151

Pascal, Blaise, 14

Paul, Saint, 284

Pearson, Mary, 192, 202, 204, 206

Pelham, George (George Pellew; G.P.), 89-94, 97, 136, 293

Persia, 225

Peters, 111

Phelps, Prof. Austin, 176, 178

Phelps, Rev. Dr. Eliakim (and family), 176-87, 204-206, 222-23

Philosopher's stone, 241-42

Phinuit, Dr., 80, 82-86, 89-93, 97, 136

Phoenix, 238

Pickford, Mary, 250

Pike, Right Rev. James A., 29, 99, 247

Pike, Mrs. James A. (Diane Kennedy), 99

Pike, James, Jr., 29

Piper, Mrs. Leonora E., 31, 33, 35-38, 43, 68-70, 79-97, 136, 154, 159, 160, 162, 163, 164, 166, 168, 187, 289, 290, 293

PK, see Psychokinesis

Planchette, 77

Plato, 284

Pliny, 114

Podmore, Frank, 95, 110, 113, 114, 115, 121, 151, 173-74, 186, 204

Poetry, divining by, see Rhapsodomancy

Poltergeists, 171, 173, 204, 209; and children, 173, 174, 185, 204; and clergy, 171-73, 174, 176, 206-207; exorcism, 193-94

Polynesia, 225

Porter, William, 216

"Poughkeepsie Seer," see Davis, Andrew Jackson

Pratt, J. G., 203, 291

Precognition, 252, 272, 273

Price, Harry, 187-92, 195-96, 198-202, 204, 240

Prince, Dr. Morton, 142-44

Prince, Walter Franklin, 145

Psychokinesis (PK), 203-206, 290-91; see also Telekinesis

Puharich, Dr. Andrija, 292-93

Rama Rau, Santha, 254

Rasputin, Grigori, 18

Ravens, 238

Rayleigh, Lord, 87

Remnant of the True Church of God, 73

Reynolds, Mark, 208

Rhadomancy, 257

Rhapsodomancy, 257

Rhine, Dr. J. B., 25, 37, 205, 289, 291

Rhine, Dr. Louisa, 278

Richardton (Canada), 208

Richet, Prof., 44, 48, 50, 52

Righter, Carroll, 4-5, 37, 251

Rindge, Fred H., 287

Rods, divining by, see Rhadomancy

Roman Catholic Church: exorcism, 193, 194; Holy Inquisition, 8, 243

Roman Empire, 9-10, 225, 255, 256

Roosevelt, Franklin D., 261

Rosenberg, Count, 244

Rosher, Grace, 117, 159

Rosicrucians, 5

Rosna, Charles, 74

Rousaan, 283

Rousseau, Jean Jacques, 14

Roy, William, 288

Rudolf, Archduke, 13

Rudolph, Emperor, 242, 244

Ruskin, John: *Sesame . . . and Lilies . . .* , 164, 165

Santum, 130

Sardou, Victorien, 159

Satanism, 5-8

Saturday Evening Post, 214

Saul, King, 32-33, 34

Index